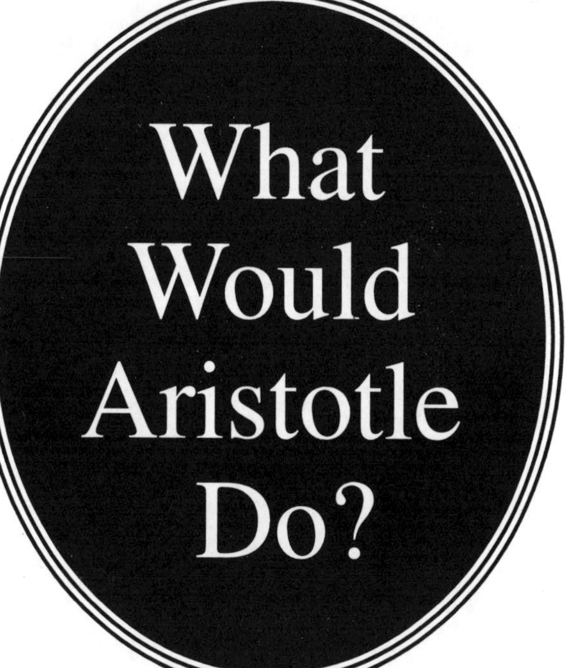
What
Would
Aristotle
Do?

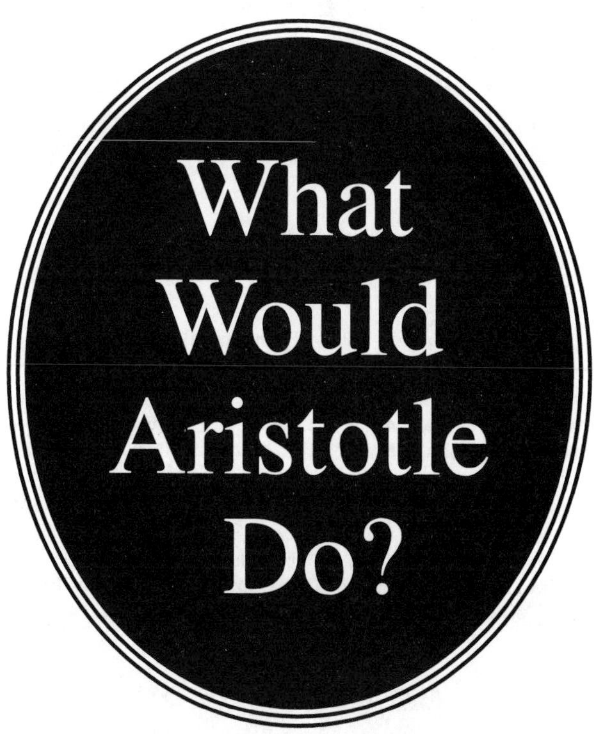

Self-Control through the Power of Reason

Elliot D. Cohen

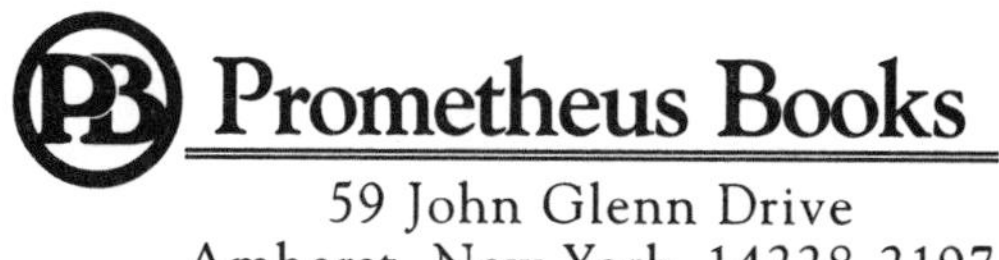
Prometheus Books
59 John Glenn Drive
Amherst, New York 14228-2197

Published 2003 by Prometheus Books

Inquiries should be addressed to
Prometheus Books, 59 John Glenn Drive, Amherst, New York 14228–2197
VOICE: 716–691–0133, ext. 207; FAX: 716–564–2711
WWW.PROMETHEUSBOOKS.COM

07 06 05 04 03   5 4 3 2 1

Library of Congress Cataloging-in-Publication Data

Cohen, Elliot D.
What would Aristotle do? : self-control through the power of reason / by Elliot D. Cohen
p. cm.
Includes bibliographical references and index.
ISBN 1–59102–070–0 (pbk. : alk. paper)
1. Philosophical counseling—Case studies. 2. Practical reason—Case studies. 3. Conduct of life—Case studies. 4. Self-control—Case studies. I. Title.

BJ1595.5.C64 2003
171'.2—dc21

2003001763

Printed in the United States of America on acid-free paper

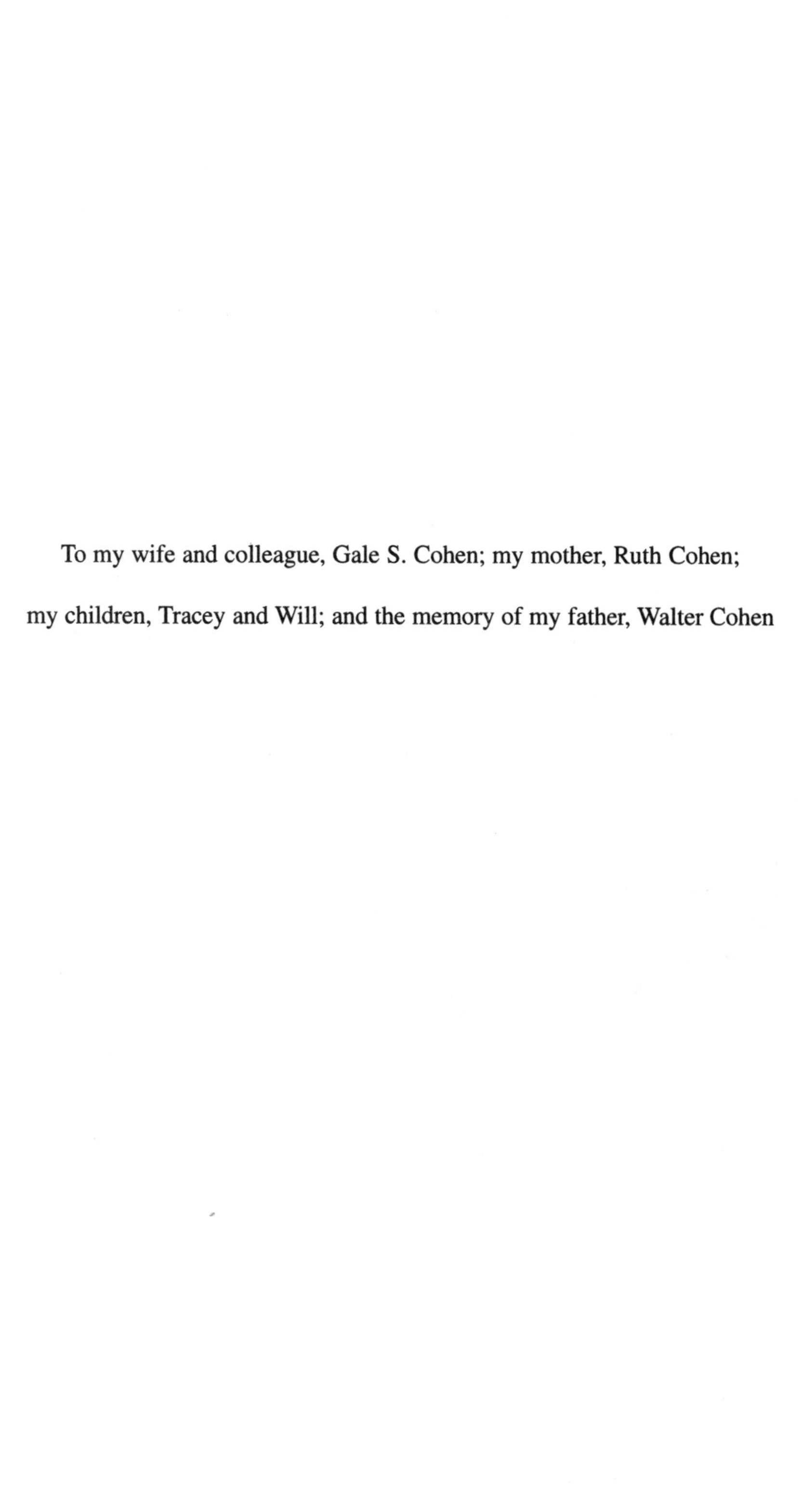

To my wife and colleague, Gale S. Cohen; my mother, Ruth Cohen;

my children, Tracey and Will; and the memory of my father, Walter Cohen

Contents

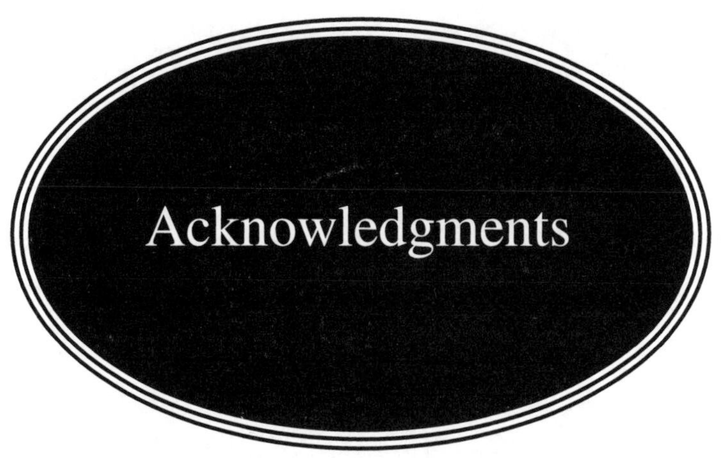

Acknowledgments

Those who have profoundly influenced the ideas expressed in this book have been many. First and foremost, this book would not have been possible without the trust and confidence reposed in me by my clients. Thanks also to my students who have provided useful feedback.

I am indebted to the esteemed psychologist, Albert Ellis, whose theory of Rational-Emotive Behavior Therapy has had considerable impact on my thinking. I first met him many years ago when I enlisted in one of his intensive workshops in Orlando, Florida. Since then he has supported and inspired my work, including taking time from his busy schedule to read and provide highly instructive commentary on several drafts of this book.

I am also grateful to my colleagues in the American Society for Philosophy, Counseling, and Psychotherapy who have over the years provided valuable feedback on my ideas. I especially wish to thank Kenneth F. T. Cust for his useful comments on an earlier draft of this book.

I owe a serious debt of gratitude to Steven L. Mitchell, editor in chief of Prometheus Books, for the time we spent profitably discussing the content and direction of this book. His adept insights have left an indelible imprint.

Finally, I wish to express deepest gratitude to Gale S. Cohen, Licensed Mental Health Counselor. Her invaluable, professional comments and criticisms of successive drafts of this book were coupled with loving support and tolerance during the many solitary hours it took me to write it. How much more could any author ask of a spouse, colleague, and best friend!

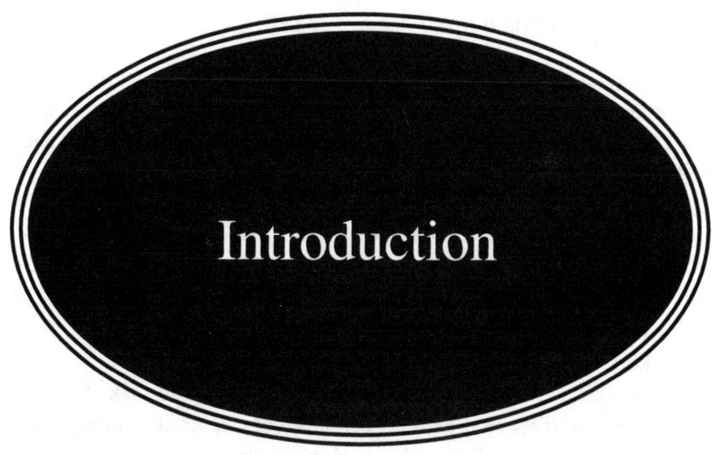

Introduction

Do you easily get angry or upset, even about small things? Do you feel down about the way things are going, about a divorce, about aging, about the loss of a job? Do you have a gnawing feeling about the futility of your life? Do you experience intense loneliness, grief, guilt, or shame? Do you have trouble getting along with others—spouse, lover, friend, family, coworker? Do you often act in ways you later regret? Do you feel overwhelmed with fear, worry, or anxiety? These and many other problems of living often have a pileup effect until you feel overwhelmed, lost in a maze of confusion, not really sure which side is up and which is down.

What Would Aristotle Do? Self-Control through the Power of Reason cleanses these common confusions of life with an ancient antiseptic from the revered sage Aristotle, who stressed reason in everyday life as an antidote to unhappiness. By taking control of your life through the power of your own native reason, you can overcome self-destructive, happiness-defeating ideas, emotions, and actions.

Reason Is Next to Godliness

What Would Aristotle Do? strikes a pious chord in prescribing reason for everyday life. As Aristotle himself astutely stated,

> he who exercises his reason and cultivates it seems to be both in the best state of mind and most dear to the gods. For if the gods have any care for human affairs, as they are thought to have, it would be reasonable both that they should delight in that which is best and most akin to them (that is, reason).[1]

In the thirteenth century, Thomas Aquinas, the celebrated scholar of Aristotle and Roman Catholic saint, reaffirmed this same message from a Christian perspective. "The light of natural reason," he said, "is nothing else than an imprint on us of the divine light."[2] And "the intellectual creature," he said, "is especially likened to God in that it is intellectual . . ."[3]

"But how can a human being be like God?" you may ask. "After all, we humans are *emotional* as well as intellectual creatures; and, unlike God, we are a far cry from being perfect." And this is right on the money! It's quite irrational for fallible earthlings to demand perfection. Nevertheless, as Aristotle stressed, it's quite *rational* for you to work on living *more* rationally, and on doing and feeling *better*.[4] So, if you would like a religious justification for asking, "*What would Aristotle do?*" then here's a highly regarded one. By placing reason at the helm of your life, you too can get more out of your life on earth, and, at the same time, get closer to God.

Philosophers Who Hang Out Their Shingles

This book grows out of a new wave in contemporary philosophy that goes by the name of *philosophical counseling* or *philosophical practice*. This is when a philosopher uses his training and skills in philosophy, especially logic and critical thinking, to help people cope with their emotional and behavioral problems. This innovative new field has seen steady growth throughout the world and in the United States in the past two decades, and this growth is likely to continue. If you are interested in learning more about this burgeoning movement and its practitioners, contact the American Society for Philosophy, Counseling, and Psychotherapy (ASPCP) on the Internet at www.aspcp.net.

Although the media has begun to give philosophical practice some welcome coverage, most books in the field have been written for professional philosophers and not laypersons. One recent exception is Louis Marinoff's *Plato, Not Prozac!* However, this book spends considerable time trying to show you *why* philosophy can be a viable alternative to psychotherapy and drug treatment; but it doesn't carefully show you *how* to cope with your life problems. Instead, it provides brief sketches of some major philosophical theories, refers you elsewhere for more complete accounts, provides brief case vignettes that are supposed to be related to these theories, and then tells you to "be your own philosophical counselor."

Unfortunately, if you are a novice in philosophy who is seriously seeking timely help, you are not likely to have the wherewithal to master and apply abstract philosophical theories on your own; and bits of wisdom of the ages may be more like *hemlock, not Prozac* for your soul.

By contrast, *What Would Aristotle Do?* gives you the tools of reasoning for *really* doing something about your problems. Written in plain English, it is up-front, self-help for the weary traveler of life who could use a reality shot. It carefully and methodically shows you how to harness your own *native* power of rational thinking to feel and do better.

Some *psychological* approaches to counseling also stress rational thinking, for example, Rational-Emotive Behavior Therapy (REBT) and Cognitive Behavior Therapy (CBT). I regard these approaches as cousins to philosophical counseling, and they can also be quite useful. But there is still a distinction that can be made between philosophical and psychological counseling. So what's the difference?

If you were seriously depressed and asked a psychiatrist to help you, she might be inclined to look for underlying repressed thoughts. If you asked an internist, then he might be inclined to prescribe an antidepressant such as Prozac. If you asked a social worker, he might be inclined to examine your family dynamics. If you asked a neurologist, she might be inclined to order a brain scan. The difference between these and other psychological (and medical) approaches is in *training*. As a result of the specialized training each receives, each kind of practitioner tends to see things differently.

Well, philosophical counselors are highly trained in logic and critical thinking. That's really their forte. Psychologists' and other psychotherapists' training does not normally stress logic and critical thinking to the extent and in the way that philosophers' training does. (Nor do philosophers normally study mental illness to the extent and in the way that psychologists do.) So here's the million-dollar question: What might a philosopher be inclined to do? You guessed it! Look at your logic. Examine your reasoning. Critical thinking, not head shrinking.

What to Expect from This Book

Can a philosophical approach provide a *cure* for your maladies? After reading this book, will you conquer anxiety, anger, depression, and guilt and cease to do self-defeating things? Much like undergoing surgery to remove a cancerous growth, can you cut out the infection, never to return?

I have both good and bad news for you. Here's the bad news first. There really isn't any way to completely eradicate these maladies because there really isn't any cure for being human. From one human to the other, do not expect to *never* get worked up over little things, to *never* have your bad days, and to *never* make stupid responses. This never-never-land might attain in heaven but it's futile whining here on earth. Remember, 'tis folly to demand perfection on this human front. Any book that promises you such a cure, or even a near-perfect cure, is selling you snake oil.

Now here's the good news. Many people can learn how to successfully control these maladies, and to feel better and do better, with a powerful medicine that is free and abundant, and for which you don't even need a prescription. This book is about learning how to put your innate reasoning power to work to live more happily. It is about helping you to distinguish between good strains of reasoning and bad ones. It is about helping you to use the good strains to fight off and control the bad (virulent) ones.

Unfortunately, it is the virulent strains that typically feed your emotional crises and regrettable actions. It is this kind that humans tend to play with carelessly, like children playing with fire. The probability that you will burn yourself is quite high indeed unless you have some sense of how to handle it.

Will this book work for *you*? It would also be disingenuous to make such a promise. You may be among a minority of people who need a medication that comes only by prescription from a trained medical practitioner. In some cases of depression and other mood disorders, there can be biochemical problems related to brain function that require such medication. But, even if you are among this minority, you may still benefit from what I have to say, because there are no pills that can think for you. Such medicine can make it possible or easier to think rationally, but you will still, ultimately, have to do your own reasoning. So, in any case, I would urge you to read on with this caveat in mind.

Is this book a substitute for professional counseling? No, professional counseling provides a structured environment for addressing your specific problems, while this book provides a self-help approach. But, even if you decide to seek professional counseling, you may still find this book useful in learning how to control irrational tendencies that may be blocking your happiness.

As you will see, there is more to achieving self-control than an intellectual grasp of how to reason properly. You should also be prepared to put forward the *effort* to make significant changes in the way you think, feel, and act. If you have developed some nasty thinking habits, then you will have to courageously defy the momentum of your old, well-worn ways of coping. Because this momentum is largely physiological in nature, it will be much easier to go with your old ways, the path of least resistance, and much harder to go against the grain. If you have an itch, say one due to an insect bite, then you are going to want to scratch it, even if you know that if you do, you will almost surely increase the irritation and pain. The case is similar with the bodily thrust imposed by intense emotions and behavioral tendencies. It often takes considerable effort to hold yourself back.

If you are used to throwing temper tantrums when you don't get something you want, falling to pieces at disappointing news, suffering anxiety attacks when you think something big is at stake, eating yourself up over perceived failures, or otherwise cooking your own goose, you are likely to find that stopping yourself is not so easy. It takes willpower. You will have to flex your willpower muscle. If your muscle is rather puny, as a result of disuse, then you will have to build it up through practice. Like a beginning body builder, you will have to be prepared to work up to the heavy lifting. As Aristotle long ago realized, self-control and strong character come with practice and the cultivation of good habits. So, to get in shape, what *would* Aristotle do? Get plenty of exercise! If you want a quick fix without putting in the effort, then this book is probably not for you.

Your willpower muscle comes into play when you need to stop an emotion or behavior that you realize is likely to get you into trouble. But this muscle is utterly useless unless you know when to flex it. This is where awareness of your own thinking comes in. Your emotions and actions are largely a function of reasoning, much of which is not fully conscious when you act or have emotions. As you will see, when fully spelled out, this reasoning consists of a *rule* that directs you to act or feel in a certain way, and a *report* that files your situation under the rule. When these two premises, or reasons, are joined in your mind, the conclusion of your reasoning is an action or emotion. When one or both of your premises are unrealistic or false, your action or emotion is likely to be self-destructive.

Finding such faulty reasoning is, in one respect, like finding a plumbing leak. You need, of course, to be able to find the leak first in order to fix it. Well, if the puddle of water is under the sink, then you have a pretty good idea where to start. For example, where do you look if you are having problems in your relationship with the opposite sex? The leak might be in a premise about your date—"He's after just one thing" or "She's a gold digger"—but that might be an oversimplification. Just as the water might be deflected from its source by running down a pipe, a source of your problem might lie higher up in the pipes—"Men are all bums" or "Women are all gold diggers." So you may have to troubleshoot in order to find the premises that are causing the disturbance.

How do you troubleshoot? By thinking. But the kind of thinking I have in mind is thinking about your *own* thinking. Indeed, all people think, but they do not ordinarily think about their own thinking. Rather, they think about what they are going to wear, what they are going to eat, where they are going to go on vacation, and so forth. The objects of their thinking are external—physical objects, people, and events past, present, and future. It is less often that the objects of thinking are *in*ternal, the thoughts themselves.

Here's the point. You can raise your level of awareness of your premises by thinking about your own reasoning. This is not the same as obsessing over your thoughts. What I am suggesting is that you can look before you logically leap by first inspecting your reasoning. Knowing what to look for and how to conduct your inspection are obviously important considerations. This book is largely devoted to giving you the tools for conducting this inspection.

Finding a hole in your reasoning is not enough. You also need to repair it. This is where finding an *antidote* comes in. An antidote corrects a flaw in your faulty thinking. It is the rational voice by which you speak sensibly to yourself. It is what diverts you from damning thoughts about others when you are angry, gives you new grounds for hope when you are wallowing in gloom and doom, reassesses the future when you are anxiously awaiting Armageddon, puts your misdeeds into perspective when you are drowning in guilt. It is the motive that directs you to a change of venue. It trivializes and denounces the irrational when placed alongside it. It combats your infected premises by giving higher ground for your emotions and actions. On its authority, you can, with the proper effort of will, gain the upper hand on nasty habits of thinking that may be obstructing your pathway to happiness.

Suppose you are down because your lover has left you for someone else. So you tell yourself that, because this is so terrible, horrible, and awful, you cannot stand to live anymore; that it was your fault in the first place because, had you tried harder this never would have happened; and that, therefore, you are nothing but a worthless failure. Just imagine how you would feel. Caught in such an emotional crisis, with no rational defenses, you are likely to stew in your misery, and to suffer considerable pain. An antidote does not distort the realities of your circumstances. Instead, it deflates the absolutistic rules you use to denounce yourself, and deposes the catastrophic and unfounded reports you file to bring your case under your self-defeating rules. "Change your 'I *can't* stand it' to 'I *won't* stand it,'" "What happened might be unfortunate but not really *horrific*," "What *could-a/would-a/should-a been* is just speculating," "A relationship that fails does not make you *a worthless failure*," "You have *freedom* to forge new, future relationships." In the midst of emotional turmoil, antidotes like these are likely to be your best medicine against faulty thinking, which, if untreated, will inevitably take its toll on your present and future happiness.

But an antidote is not a cure. Your irrational lines of reasoning can still gnaw at you even if you gain control of them. They can also reclaim their dynasty over you, even after it seems like they are gone forever. You can always lapse back into the same old routines of self-defeating thinking. A bad day on the job, disappointing news, unfair treatment by a friend, loss of something or someone of value, and sundry other inevitabilities of life can leave you vulnerable to your own damning thoughts, demands for perfection, catastrophic interpretations, absolutistic descriptions of reality, and hosts of other irrational baggage that you may still carry with you. Antidotes can help you to recover, to get you back on your feet, to get over your emotional and behavioral crises, and to keep you reasonably pain free. But an antidote cannot guarantee that you will never get sick again. This is why you need to keep up your rational defenses with daily doses of antidotal reasoning.

Aristotle's Aphrodisiac: Moderation Satisfies

Aristotle put his finger on a very important feature of self-destructive emotions and actions, namely that they involve extreme responses to situations. About such extremes he had this to say:

> For instance, both fear and confidence and appetite and anger and pity and in general pleasure and pain may be felt both too much and too little, and in both cases not well; but to feel them at the right times, with reference to the right objects, towards the right people, with the right motive, and in the right way, is what is both intermediate and best . . . Similarly, with regard to actions also there is excess, defect and intermediate.[5]

Sexual activity can be excessive when you are willing to risk your health, marriage, and reputation to have it; it can be deficient when you recoil from sexual activity entirely because you think that sex is dirty and depraved. Fear can be excessive when you are led to avoid dating or trying to advance professionally because you are afraid of rejection; it can be deficient when you knowingly put yourself in serious danger as part of a fraternity hazing. In such cases, it takes willpower backed by reason to overcome these dangerous responses. It takes rational thinking to expose the flaws in your thinking, to tell yourself whether you are overdoing or underdoing something, and to divine the "right" way to feel or act.

The idea that moderation satisfies is easily seen in the case of the treatment of your body. If you exercise too much or too little, you can do yourself harm; if you eat too much or too little, you can destroy your health. As Aristotle surmised, just how much exercise or food is intermediate between too much and too little—aka the "right" amount—is not arrived at mathematically. Instead, it depends on many variables, including preexisting health conditions, how old you are, and in the case of eating, how large you are. Similarly, whether your anger is justified will depend upon your circumstances. Becoming enraged at someone who cuts you off on the highway is excessive; yet letting someone sexually assault you without letting yourself feel anger is deficient under the circumstances.

Now here's the kicker. Behind extreme forms of emotion and conduct there is usually extreme or absolutistic thinking. Feeling guilty or depressed because you are telling yourself that you are a horrible person is to *under*rate yourself; while telling yourself that you are, or must be, perfect in every way is to *over*rate or demand too much of yourself. Being afraid to fly because you think that your plane will probably crash may be to *over*rate the probabilities of a plane crash; while thinking that "It will never happen to me," in pursuing a life of sexual promiscuity, is *under*rating the probabilities of contracting a sexually transmitted disease or AIDS. Being homophobic because you think that all gays are pedophiles, is to *over*generalize, while thinking that no one would ever molest your children is to *under*estimate the number of pedophiles there are on this planet.

It is such extreme or absolutistic thinking that comprises what I have called fallacies of emotion, actions, and reports. In this book, you will see just how virulent these strains of thinking can really be.

At one point, philosopher Ludwig Wittgenstein asked, "What is your aim in philosophy?" to which he immediately responded, "To show the fly the way out of the fly-bottle."[6] The philosophy cultivated in this book is precisely that. Like the proverbial fly in the fly-bottle, you may have unknowingly stifled your own freedom, and you may not know how to get out of the mess you have made for yourself. This book shows you how to expose and identify the faulty assumptions in your reasoning that have gotten you into trouble. And, then, by helping you to find rational antidotes to your self-destructive, unrealistic, freedom-curtailing thinking, it shows you the way out. This should leave you with a view of philosophy that is practical to the core.

Your Lesson Plan: A Brief Overview

Much of what I have to say in this book comes from many years of working with numerous clients and students, showing them how to illuminate, through the light of reason, the dark corridors of their psyche where unrealistic rules and distorted depictions of reality can undermine happiness. But what I have to say is not merely the result of observing others in their darkest moments. It comes from my own trials, the ups and downs of living a human existence. I have therefore chosen to share with you some of my intimate secrets about my inner challenges, emotional and behavioral, and how I have relied upon antidotes to get through them with considerably less pain. My goal is to help you too to find antidotes to the premises in your reasoning that may unwittingly be taking their toll on your own personal and interpersonal happiness.

In part 1, you will see how you can unknowingly deduce your own emotional and behavioral problems from defective rules and reports. And you will find out how to use antidotal reasoning to manage and control your self-defeating responses to such defective reasoning. Throughout this book, I have presented cases based on my clinical practice as well as on my personal life experiences to give you a clear, realistic picture of how antidotal reasoning works.

In part 2, you will be introduced to fallacies of emotions, actions, and reports. These forms of virulent thinking frequently infect the rules and reports that self-destructive human emotions and actions often rely on. For each fallacy, I have suggested rational antidotes that have proven useful against these virulent strains.

In part 3, you will find out how to read between the lines to fully formulate the reasoning behind your emotional and behavioral reasoning. You will then learn about useful techniques for refuting irrational premises, that is, how to expose fallacies in them. Finally, I will provide you with some useful tips for finding antidotes to fallacies, and I'll also summarize refutations and suggest antidotes for all fallacies covered in part 2.

In part 4, you will learn about the irrational rules and reports that are often behind common, self-destructive emotions—especially rage, intense anxiety, and depression. You will learn how fallacies can be combined to form dangerous fallacy syndromes, and how you can control these virulent combinations with antidotal reasoning.

Reason Is Drug-Free, Internal Medicine!

What I have to say in this book is informed by my experiences, both inside and outside the clinic, of ordinary folks wrestling with their own emotional and behavioral problems of living. These trials of living attest to the innumerable ways we humans have to upset ourselves and to destroy our own potential for achieving personal and interpersonal happiness. But these trials also attest to human resilience. Within you, as part of your native endowment, you also have a storehouse of very potent medicine, which can do a reasonably good job in fighting off self-imposed infections. And this nonprescription, drug-free medicine has no dangerous side effects. Fortunately, it can be habit forming. You are cordially invited to read on to learn more about this internal medicine, and about how it may be a potent antidote against your unhappiness.

Notes

1. Aristotle, *Nichomachean Ethics,* trans. W. D. Ross (New York: Oxford University Press, 1998), book 10, ch. 8. Hereafter referred to as *Ethics*.

2. St. Thomas Aquinas, *Summa Theologica*, in *Introduction to St. Thomas Aquinas*, ed. Anton C. Pegis (New York: Random House, 1948), quest. 91, art. 2.

3. Aquinas, *Summa Contra Gentiles,* in *Introduction to St. Thomas Aquinas*, ed. Anton C. Pegis (New York: Random House, 1948), ch. 25.

4. *Ethics*, book 10, ch. 6.

5. *Ethics*, book 2, ch. 6.

6. Ludwig Wittgenstein, *Philosophical Investigations,* trans. G. E. M. Anscombe (New York: Macmillan, 1968), p. 309.

Part 1

How You May Be Unknowingly Tormenting Yourself, and What You Can Do to Feel Better

Chapter 1

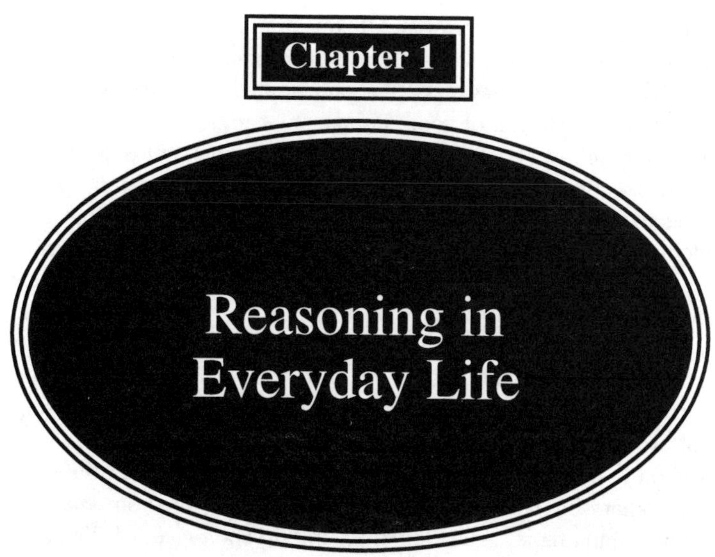

Reasoning in Everyday Life

> *That which is proper to each thing is by nature best and most pleasant for each thing; for man, therefore, the life according to reason is best and pleasantest, since reason more than anything else is man. This life, therefore, is also the happiest.*
>
> —Aristotle[1]

Conventional wisdom has it that, when you are suffering from a psychological problem, you should consult a psychologist or related mental health professional. Just as a medical doctor treats your ailing body and the clergy your wayward soul, the psychologist treats your troubled psyche.

Is There a Philosopher in the House?

It is less likely that you have been advised to consult a philosopher when you are having a psychological problem. "Philosophers!" you say with astonishment. "Don't they spend their time wondering about things like whether there is a sound when a tree falls in a forest and there's no one around? What good is that for someone who is depressed or suffering from panic attacks or obsessive-compulsive behavior?" The answer is that philosophy, its methods, and acquired wisdom can do a great deal of good. Philosophy can be good medicine.

There is presently a burgeoning band of professional philosophers, known as philosophical counselors or philosophical practitioners, who have dedicated themselves to trying to help ordinary folks reach lasting, philosophical solutions to problems of everyday living. While the first contemporary representative of this rare breed hung out his shingle in 1981, I began my work a few years later in 1985. In 1990, my colleague, Paul Sharkey, and I founded the American Society for Philosophy, Counseling, and Psychotherapy, whose primary mission has been to advance understanding of how philosophical wisdom and methodologies can be used to effect solutions to psychological problems arising in the course of ordinary living.

Early on in my work with clients, I became aware that the utility of philosophy for ordinary life was in the rigors of its rational, common sense approach. Philosophical thinking is logical thinking, and psycho*logical* problems are often rooted in the inability of people to think logically about problems of living.[2] The idea that logic has therapeutic value did not arise with the contemporary philosophical counseling movement. It is firmly embedded in ancient Greek philosophy, especially in the work of the venerable Aristotle, who was the first to present a detailed examination of practical reasoning. For Aristotle, life according to reason (*logos*) provided an effective antidote to mental pathology. Indeed, he spent his entire treatise on ethics showing how human happiness could be defined in terms of reason.

An unhappy person's passions such as anger and fear burn like brush fires out of control, igniting in fits of rage and panic, while a happy, healthy, well-adjusted person is even tempered and brave. A happy person avoids overindulgent behavior (gluttony, drunkenness, promiscuity, unbridled lust for power, fame, and wealth). An unhappy person is swept away by irrational impulses, desires, and fears and acts in self-defeating, regrettable ways.

In fact, for Aristotle, your rational self is really your *true self*. Thus spoke the philosopher:

> A man is said to have or not to have self-control according as his reason has or has not the control, on the assumption that this is the man himself; and the things men have done on a rational principle are thought more properly their own acts and voluntary acts.[3]

Translation: You're in your right mind only when your reason has control of your passions!

How You Deduce Your Actions from Premises

The plot now thickens! For Aristotle, there was also a sense in which what you do can follow, as a conclusion, from your reasoning. Suppose you are on a low-fat diet (due to dangerously high cholesterol) and you notice a deep, dark, rich, moist, plump, fudge brownie dripping with grams of delectable fat. You look at it and your mouth waters as you think to yourself, "How could I refuse the most delicious food on earth, and that fudge brownie is surely my absolute favorite." So you break down and reach for the brownie.[4]

For Aristotle, such lapses in willpower always resulted from being swayed by desire to act for the wrong reasons. So, in the throes of craving for the brownie, you neglect the rule, "It's bad for you to eat high-fat food" and instead think only about how wonderful it is to eat delicious foods. Like one in a drunken stupor, your guard is down, and you commit the regrettable act. Soon after, sobriety returns. "Oh, no," you protest. "I can't believe I ate the whole thing!"

So why *did* you eat it? In Aristotle's view, once you had the premises in your head, "I shouldn't refuse delicious foods" and "This brownie is a delicious food," and nothing prevented you, eating the brownie was inescapable. But notice that Aristotle was careful to say that the behavior—eating the brownie—was inescapable only when nothing prevented you from acting. So, your having eaten the brownie depended on other things too.

What other things? Well, someone else could have beaten you to the draw or you could have been struck by a disabling muscle impediment, or you could have also accepted other premises that pushed you in an opposite direction (this is called "cognitive dissonance," which I will discuss in chapter 4). There are countless things that could have conceivably prevented you from eating that sumptuous brownie.

Still, in the absence of any of these impediments, your action was inescapable. If you believed that "All humans are mortal," and "Socrates is human," could you avoid the conclusion that "Socrates is mortal"? Surely not! Once you accepted these premises, this conclusion would be inescapable. Yes, inescapable. It is a law of so-called "deductive logic." The conclusion can be deduced from these premises. And it is in a similar way that you deduced your act of eating that brownie from the thoughts (premises) that occupied your mind at the time.[5] This deduction from premises to action has profound practical importance. It gives you a good reason to look (at your premises) before you (deductively) leap into action.

The Tragic Case of Larry

Unfortunately, all of us—yes, all of us—sometimes leap without looking, or at least without looking carefully. A good example of this is the commonplace practice of Jumping on the Bandwagon (see page 98). Sound like a familiar phrase? Unfortunately, familiar, even obvious problems are often not addressed until it's too late. Not infrequently, we shake our heads *after* we jump, and chant those immortal words, "That was really dumb!" The sad truth, however, is that sometimes we don't get a second chance.

My boyhood friend, Larry, is a good example of the lethality of bad logic. A young man of eighteen with a speech impediment that often received the ridicule of others, Larry began to seek out the approval of a new crowd that made it a practice of drag racing through the winding back roads of Upper Saddle River, New Jersey. Concerned about his welfare, I entreated him to cultivate new interests, but Larry was determined to get in with this crowd. One dark night, Larry sat in the back of a car that went speeding out of control, striking a tree. The two boys in the front seat were killed instantly, but Larry was jettisoned through the back window and was hurled fifty feet. He remained in a coma for several months until he finally died in a nursing home.

Over the many years that have passed since this tragic event, as I have looked back and asked myself what really killed this kind-hearted boy, I have been driven to one unwavering conclusion. Larry's death was due to bad logic. Bad logic, you ask? Was that on his death certificate? Well, of course not. People rarely talk about the logic that produces tragic consequences. Yet what moves people to act in self-defeating ways is often bad logic, more exactly, deducing self-defeating actions from false or unrealistic premises. In Larry's case, I suspect that he was motivated by a *rule* that said something like "I should do whatever the in-crowd does." Since the young men, whom he perceived as "the in-crowd," were drag racing, he too was motivated to do the same. Putting this together, there was a rule and a report from which Larry deduced his action:

Rule: I should do whatever the in-crowd does.
Report: The in-crowd drag races.
Action: I go drag racing.

Rules, Reports, and Refutations

When you deduce an action, there will always be a rule and a report from which you deduce it. Rules are generalizations about what you *should* (or *shouldn't*) do, or how you should (or shouldn't) feel. Irrational rules often use the word *must* and many use strong language such as *damn, shitty, terrible, and terrific*. Reports state perceived facts. They say what you think *is*, in contrast to what you think *should* be. In filing a report, you file a perceived situation under a rule. For example, Larry filed his report (that the in-crowd drag races) under the rule that he should do whatever this group does. Unfortunately, nothing prevented Larry from acting on his premises. So, by filing his report, Larry deduced his tragic conclusion. You may not always be fully conscious of your own rules and reports when you act upon them, but they are there, driving you on.

Some rules are unrealistic. In calling them unrealistic, I mean that they generally lead to irrational, self-defeating actions. Some reports are unfounded or false. Your reports are unfounded when you don't have sufficient evidence to *prove* them; and they're false when there is sufficient evidence to *dis*prove them. By acting on reports that are either unfounded or false, you are also likely to get into trouble.

This is where looking at your premises before leaping into action comes in. If you know they are there, and you know how to deal with them once you find them, then you are likely to be in much better shape. I will talk later about ways of finding unrealistic rules and unfounded reports. But once you know what they are, you can refute them. If the rule is really unrealistic, you should be able to think up cases that would refute the rule. For example, what if the in-crowd was jumping into a swamp infested with alligators? Should you jump in too? I will talk later about some useful ways to refute rules and reports.

Antidotes and Antidotal Reasoning

Well, if it isn't rational to do whatever the cool guys are doing, what really *is* rational? Answering this question will give you an antidote to this unrealistic rule. An antidote to a premise is another more reasonable premise that corrects it. There is always an antidote (often more than one) to an irrational rule or report.

Can you think of an antidote to Larry's irrational rule? Well, here's a very basic one: "Instead of blindly imitating others, you should carefully think things through first." In other words, you should make an educated assessment of the risks and benefits of an action before doing it, and then decide whether the benefits really outweigh the risks. If you are considering doing something that has a good chance of winding you up in a body bag, then the benefits should be mighty high, indeed. I doubt that Larry thought much, if at all, about the Bandwagon rule, from which he deduced his tragic act.

An antidote is not effective against your irrational thinking unless it prescribes something, that is, it tells you how or how not to respond more rationally to your situation. This is where antidotal reasoning comes it. *Antidotal reasoning* is the prescriptive form of an antidote. It is the reasoning that you go through when you prescribe an antidote to yourself. This is the kind of reasoning that you can use against an irrational line of reasoning. It is the good (rational) reasoning that you can use to head off the bad (irrational) type. Like its bogus relative, the bad reasoning, antidotal reasoning consists of a rule and a report. The report accurately files the facts of your situation under a rational rule that, in turn, prescribes a rational response to your situation. Let's suppose that you are batting your head against the wall because you think that your next-door neighbor doesn't like you—in fact, hates your guts—but you absolutely want, indeed expect, everyone to like you. Well, as you will see, this demand is quite unrealistic in this imperfect world of ours. So, you are doing antidotal reasoning when you tell yourself "I shouldn't dogmatically and absolutely demand perfection in this imperfect world," and "Demanding that everyone, and therefore my neighbor, like me is doing just that." Together, this rule and report prescribes some rational medicine: It tells you to stop batting your head against the wall!

Some antidotal reasoning is positive. It tells you what you *should* do. Some is negative and tells you what you *shouldn't* do. In the immortal words of Aristotle, "practical wisdom issues commands, since its end is what ought to be done or not to be done."[6] An antidotal *should* tells you to respond in some rational way to a perceived problem, while a *shouldn't* tells you to refrain or hold yourself back from responding in some irrational way.

Here's an important precaution to follow in swallowing antidotes. You should not dogmatically, absolutely, and inflexibly hold on to your antidotal *should*s and *shouldn't*s. As you will see, not even antidotes are beyond the possibility of refutation. So here's some antidotal reasoning about antidotal reasoning. You shouldn't assume that any rule is rational once and for all and in all cases. So don't even assume that the rule I just now stated in my last sentence is rational once and for all and in all cases. There are no absolutes, not even that there are no absolutes.

Being rational doesn't mean swallowing the same medicine every time you get sick. What may have worked well on one bug need not work on another one, even if the prescription is, in general, very effective medicine. Having a stock of antidotes in your mental medicine cabinet is a good idea, but use them with caution. In some cases, there may just be some contraindications.

Here's a bit of preventive medicine that might have worked in Larry's case:

Rule: I shouldn't put my life on the line just to be accepted by others.
Report: I am putting my life on the line by going drag racing just to be accepted by these guys.
Action: I don't go drag racing with these guys.

I lament the fact that Larry didn't use this antidotal reasoning to successfully fight off the irrational reasoning that directed him to jump on the bandwagon that tragic night he got into the backseat of that car. His tragic tale, nevertheless, is a reminder of how lethal bad reasoning can really be, and how an antidote to such reasoning can sometimes be as important to your survival as antibiotics are to a person with pneumonia.

Notes

1. *Ethics*, book 10, ch. 7.

2. See also my book, *Caution: Faulty Thinking Can Be Harmful to Your Happiness*, Self-Help Ed. (Ft. Pierce, Fla.: Trace-WilCo, Inc., 1992).

3. *Ethics*, book 9, ch. 8.

4. By a *premise* I mean any belief of yours that you use as a reason, or part of your reason, for thinking, feeling, or acting in a certain way. This further belief, emotion, or action is what I mean by your conclusion. So, in the present case, your premises would be "How could I refuse the most delicious food on earth," and "That fudge brownie is surely my absolute favorite"; and your conclusion would be your act of eating the brownie.

5. Logicians usually use the word "deduce" to refer to reasoning in which a *statement* necessarily follows from another statement or statements. For example, if the statements "All men are moral" and "Socrates is a man" are true, then the statement "Socrates is mortal" *must* also be true. Aristotle also applied the concept of deduction to practical reasoning where the conclusion was an action rather than a statement. In Aristotle's own example, "if 'everything sweet ought to be tasted', and 'this is sweet' . . . the man who can act and is not prevented *must* at the same time act accordingly." *Ethics*, book 7, ch. 3, my italics.

6. *Ethics*, book 6, ch. 10.

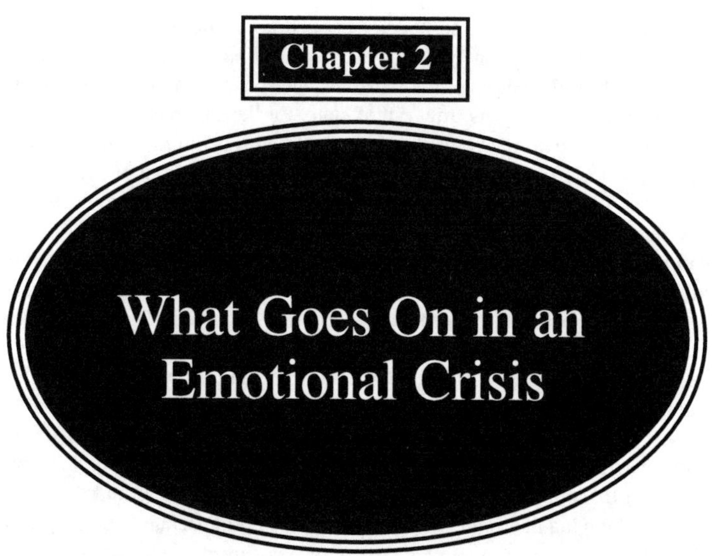

Chapter 2
What Goes On in an Emotional Crisis

[O]utbursts of anger and sexual appetites and some other such passions, it is evident, actually alter our bodily condition, and in some men even produce fits of madness. . . . It turns out that a man behaves incontinently [has such outbursts of emotion] under the influence (in a sense) of a rule and an opinion [report].

—Aristotle[1]

What I have said so far about deducing your actions from premises (rules and reports) is only the tip of the iceberg. Not only can human beings deduce their actions from premises, they can also deduce their emotions.[2] This is quite extraordinary. But, to see this you need to have a handle on what an emotion is.

Hiding Out in the Bedroom: The Case of Jason

Listen to the following first-person account of the emotional crisis of a former client of mine, Jason, a fifty-year-old research scientist, married thirty years to the same woman:

> I was flat on my back in the solitude of my bedroom, staring up at the sparkles in the ceiling, on a very lonely Friday evening. Just outside my closed bedroom door I could hear the voices of my wife, teenage son, and my wife's mother and father who were visiting us from out of state. Earlier that day, my teenage son (the same one who now sat outside my door while I was hiding in my room) had mocked and jeered at me, calling me insane and stupid in front of my wife and her parents. I had agreed to take my son on a father-son trip the next day, and I knew that my wife wanted very much for me to go; but, after hearing him degrade me, the thought of being confined overnight in the same motel room with my son, who was prone to such mistreatment, made me cringe. So, in the privacy of our bedroom, I informed my wife that I decided not to go. My wife became enraged, threw some bedding in my face, raised her voice in an angry tone, told me how ugly I looked, stood over me telling me how evil I was, how I had no right to go back on my promise, how it was my fault that our son was like this, and how much she despised me and hoped I would pay for this. I quietly listened to her words, which felt like darts. The more she spoke, the more I wanted her to stop. I could feel my heart pounding in my chest, and I started to feel dizzy. Leaving the room crying, she began to commiserate with her parents in front of our son, who now seemed amused. For most of the day, I stayed in the bedroom, while my son socialized with friends, and my wife and parents went visiting. And there I was when the family returned later that evening.
>
> At first I kept thinking about how my wife had degraded and humiliated me, and what a no-good rotten bitch she was for doing this to her own husband. I envisioned her, sitting in the car with her parents, telling them what a bad person I was, and telling them personal things about me. The more I thought about it, the angrier I got. I could feel the quivering, throbbing tightness in my chest, and I could even feel the muscles sag in my cheeks, like they were being pulled down by weights. I could feel surges and tingles racing around inside me until I felt like exploding from inside out. I kept feeling worse and worse as I continued to think about what had happened. Then I started to think that she was right about me all along, that I really was no good. After all, I was the one who broke my promise to take our son on the trip. Everything seemed so futile and I started to hope that the ceiling would collapse and crush me. I felt as though all the energy had been sucked out of my body, like a car with a dead battery. My arms and legs felt limp. The thought of coming out was chilling. I could imagine them sitting around together, staring me down. I knew I could not walk out there like nothing had happened. On the other hand, I felt like a wimp—a term my wife had used earlier to describe me. I couldn't stand that I was so afraid of them, and the more I thought about it, the more disgusting it seemed.

Jason's emotion is unique only in terms of the details of his circumstances, but I don't doubt that you too have had similar emotions of anger, grief, and anxiety as you faced your own life problems, trials, and issues. For sure, to be human is to have emotions, some constructive and others misguided. So what goes on when you, like Jason, experience an emotion?

The Objects of Your Emotions

In general, when you get upset, you get upset *about* something or other. You are afraid *of* something, anxious *about* something, depressed *over* something, and so on. You typically do not just get upset.[3]

"Not so," some clever interlocutor might rebound. "Didn't you ever experience free-floating anxiety? Isn't that a case in which you are not anxious about anything in particular?" Oh, but the words "in particular" are quite revealing. Yes, you may be anxious without being anxious over anything in particular, because you might be anxious about *everything*, even about wiping up a small, almost imperceptible dirty spot on your clean white wall.

The objects of emotion can be events, states of affairs, physical objects, persons, and even other emotions. They can be actual, possible, or imaginary. In the present case, there were several emotional objects, each associated with one or more emotions. Take a look at this partial list of some of Jason's emotional objects and their respective emotions:

- His son calling him insane and stupid in front of his wife and in-laws (resentment);
- Being confined overnight in the same motel room with his son (anxiety);
- His refusal to take his son on the father-son trip (his wife's rage);
- His wife's episode of name-calling and accusations (anger, depression, and guilt);
- His wife's saying negative/personal things about him to her parents (humiliation);
- The voices he heard outside his bedroom (fear);
- Being "stared down" by his wife and parents (anxiety);
- His fear of coming out of his room (inwardly directed anger).

Notice the wide array of objects. In the last case, the emotional object is itself an emotion. Emotional objects like these may be stored in your memory and recalled, periodically, allowing you to continue your emotion. Often, as in the present case, it is the recollection, the constant rehashing, that permits your emotional experience to continue over time. Your brain works somewhat like a VCR. You can rewind, replay, and even fast forward. Objects can appear as mental images of previously perceived objects or, like virtual ghosts, they may not correspond to anything real at all. So, when Jason mentally pictured his wife sitting in a car with her parents, degrading him and disclosing secrets, his emotional object was a phantom. This event never actually happened; it was purely imaginary, existing only in his mind.[4] Nevertheless, Jason still *felt* humiliated over this emotional object, real or not.

YOUR BODILY FEELINGS

Recall that Jason described his emotional experiences in terms of pounding heart; quivering, throbbing, tightness in chest; cheek muscles sagging; surges and tingles racing around inside and feeling like darts. As a fellow human, it is safe to say that you are no stranger to such feelings. You have experienced them first-hand, from the inside. Right? Such internal perceptions are associated with bodily changes in your heart, lungs, gut, skin, skeletal muscles, endocrine glands (such as pituitary and adrenals), changes in brain chemistry (such as release of peptide modulators into the bloodstream), dilation and contraction of blood vessels, and immune system modifications. These changes can be largely automatic responses to your environment, managed by a network of interconnected, internal wiring known as the autonomic nervous system. But, as you will see, you can also engage this system through your thinking.

This system consists of two subsystems, the sympathetic and parasympathetic nervous systems. The *sympathetic* nervous system is responsible for raising your level of bodily activity in response to perceived stressors in your environment. These bodily changes include increases in heart and lung rates, blood pressure, supply of blood to large muscles, secretion of adrenaline, and blood sugar. In these ways, the sympathetic nervous system can get you ready for fight or flight. The *parasympathetic* nervous system counteracts some of the effects of the sympathetic system to conserve energy and to return your body to a normal level of bodily activity. These changes include reduction in heart rate, respiration, and blood pressure. Together, these two systems provide a means of making energy available to your body in stressful situations and of conserving and restoring energy for use in times of stress.

During an emotional crisis, signals from internal organs (viscera) affected by the autonomic nervous system are transmitted via sensory neurons to certain parts of your brain (such as the hypothalamus, limbic system, and cerebral cortex). You receive these neural signals in the form of *bodily feelings*. These feelings provide you with an internal perception of your body's condition. They have a range of positive (pleasant) or negative (painful) feeling tones, depending upon your emotional state. Remember the last time you felt a lump in your throat or your pounding heart? These feelings are typically combined with the perception or image of an emotional object. So, when Jason's wife threw something at him and raised her voice, his sympathetic nervous system sprang into action. Increased flow of blood to his gross muscles required increased heart action, and this response he received in terms of the unpleasant sensation of a pounding heart combined with the perception of his wife's action and raised voice.

Such emotional responses, in many cases, have useful, self-protective functions. In the current instance, Jason's body was probably responding automatically to certain general features of his present environment signaling danger, such as his wife's loud angry voice, and her hostile action. He was on automatic pilot. Can you remember the last time you were driving when the car in front of you suddenly came to a stop, requiring you to slam on your brakes? The bursts of energy and the sensations you received from such bodily instigations may well have saved your life!

Replaying Your Bodily Feelings

The parts of your brain known as the prefrontal cortices have the amazing ability to replay previously run bodily feelings, which have been stored in memory. This was probably what happened when Jason thought about spending the night in a motel room with his son. The thought triggered a replay of a bodily feeling he experienced on another occasion when he was alone with his son, even though he was not then in the exact same situation. This seems also to have been the case when Jason imagined his wife and in-laws "staring him down." The thought triggered a "chilling" bodily feeling he had experienced before. According to neuroscientist Antonio Damasio, these feelings, unlike automatic ones (such as the response to loud noises), are acquired through past experience, and help us to make rational decisions about future outcomes.[5] So the unpleasant feeling Jason got when he thought about spending the night in a motel with his son inclined him away from taking this option. Unfortunately, while such internal cues may be useful in some cases in helping you to decide, the range of human circumstances are far too complex for such a simple calculus. Just look at what happened to Jason. Succumbing to such feelings, without careful reasoning, left him needlessly locked up behind closed doors. I bet you can find cases where you failed to go with your gut and came to regret it. But I suspect that it wouldn't be too hard for you to recall other times when going with your gut was not, after all, really such a good idea.

In his seminal book, *Emotional Intelligence,* Daniel Goleman drives the same point home with this tragic story:

> Fourteen-year-old Maltida Crabtree was just playing a practical joke on her father: she jumped out of a closet and yelled "Boo!" as her parents came home at one in the morning from visiting friends. But Bobby Crabtree and his wife thought Matilda was staying with friends that night. Hearing noises as he entered the house, Crabtree reached for his .357 caliber pistol, and went into Maltilda's bedroom to investigate. When his daughter jumped from the closet, Crabtree shot her in the neck. Matilda Crabtree died 12 hours later.[6]

Bringing your emotions under rational control is not merely a luxury. In Bobby Crabtree's case, it made the difference between life and death—his daughter's.

Emotional Reasoning

If emotions just involved automatically generated bodily feelings and virtual replays of bodily feelings, then it is likely that your emotions would come and go with these fleeting conditions. A loud noise would stop and your autonomic nervous system (parasympathetic nervous system) would restore your body to its normal operating condition. While this is probably a fair description of less complicated creatures, it is far from true with human beings, who spend a significant portion of their lives upset about things that have gone wrong.

In humans, emotional control largely depends upon the ability (and will) to think rationally. As Aristotle stressed, when your reason habitually directs your thoughts, actions, and emotions, you have a good shot at living happily; but when you routinely allow irrational bodily tendencies and feelings to swell up inside and take control of you, then you are likely to live quite unhappily.

So, this is where your ability to reason comes into play. The reasoning from which you deduce your emotions and actions is what I'll call "emotional reasoning." (If you want to call it behavioral and emotional reasoning, that's OK too, but that's kind of long-winded.) Jason's reasoning could properly be called emotional because he deduced emotions and actions from premises (rules and reports). The feelings that rose in his chest were a consequence of the bodily changes he deduced from his premises. These emotional responses, as when he became angry, included increased respiration, heart rate, and endocrine activity. These changes went on inside of Jason's body and were perceived by Jason alone.

On the other hand, the muscular changes in Jason's face like scowling and frowning (recall that Jason could feel his cheek muscles sag) were visible to other people. Such visible responses are controlled by a subsystem of the human nervous system known as the skeletal muscular nervous system. In contrast to the autonomic nervous system, this system controls muscles that are attached to bone. These muscles (such as those in your arms, legs, neck, and face) are largely under your conscious, voluntary control and account for your ability to move. So, when you deduce an action from premises, you engage your skeletal muscular system. When you deduce changes inside your body such as changes in heartbeat and respiration you engage your autonomic nervous system.[7] When you experience emotions, you usually engage both systems.

This does not mean that you are always in the position to control your emotions through your reasoning. Your heart skips a beat and you jump in response to a loud noise; you feel an unpleasant sensation in your toe and turn your head quickly in the direction of the man who just stepped on your toe. These are examples of automatic responses, compliments of your autonomic nervous system operating on automatic pilot. But these knee-jerk types of emotion are usually dead on arrival. In order to keep them going, you must take up some rules and file some reports under them. In order to sustain your anger against the man who stepped on your toe, you would have to think something like "That stupid idiot! Why didn't he watch where he was going!" To see more exactly how this works, let's take a closer look at Jason's emotional reasoning.

A Closer Look at Jason's Emotional Reasoning

The bodily feelings you experience when you are having an emotion not only arise from your reasoning. They can also sustain and influence your reasoning. For example, Jason's unpleasant bodily feeling of being in the same room with his son strongly influenced the premises of his emotional reasoning. Fully expressed, this reasoning went like this:

Rule: I shouldn't allow myself to be degraded by my son.
Report: Being in the same room with my son overnight will expose me to degradation by him.
Action: I inform my wife that I will not be going on the trip.

Imagine for a moment what it was like being inside this poor fellow. There he was, with this image of being in the same room with his son while the endearing words, "Fuck you, Dad!" rebounded in his head. Couple this with the intense feelings—the throbs and quivers of actually being in this situation, and it is a small wonder why he filed his above report under a rule that directed him to avoid this situation.

In the aftermath of his wife's tirade, Jason also ruminated about how his wife had degraded and humiliated him, and what a no-good rotten bitch she was for doing this to him. Here Jason deduced *anger* that intensified as he ruminated:

Rule: A wife who (ever) degrades and humiliates her own husband is a no-good, rotten bitch.
Report: My wife degraded and humiliated her own husband.
Emotion: Anger about my wife's degradation and humiliation of me (with the thought of my wife being a no-good rotten bitch.[8] My body is now in the fight or flight mode.)

Notice that Jason's report of having been humiliated by his wife was expressed in a passive voice. He described his humiliation as something his wife did to him, rather than acknowledging what he himself might have contributed to his own emotional state. But he was the one who imagined his wife saying disparaging and private things about him, despite having little evidence. After all, he was not in the car when such alleged words were spoken. Yet it was this unfounded report that provided fuel for his emotion. This is a good example of how unfounded reports can lead to a self-defeating emotion.

Notice also that Jason never explicitly stated his rule, "A wife who degrades and humiliates her husband is a no-good rotten bitch." Instead, he assumed it when he deduced his anger. That is, the anger followed only because he accepted this premise. It is not unusual for someone to assume, rather than explicitly state, a premise. In fact, most of the emotional reasoning people do is not fully spelled out. As you will see (in chapter 8), learning to check your reasoning for faulty rules and reports often requires expanding your reasoning so that all the premises are fully stated. This permits you to get all of your premises out on the table to see if any of them are bad. Often, it is the hidden premises that are unrealistic, unfounded, or false. For example, in the present case, the exposed rule devaluates an entire person based upon an inappropriate action. You can easily refute this rule just by imagining a good person who makes a mistake. Human beings are not perfect. But this does not make them no-good rotten bitches. As you will see, a useful antidote to this unrealistic rule is "Criticize the deed, and leave the doer alone."

Did you ever find yourself on an emotional roller coaster where one minute you're flaming angry at someone and the next minute you're feeling guilty and down? Well such fluctuations are not uncommon when your emotional reasoning is infected with irrational premises. To see this, just look at how Jason's emotion changed from anger to depression and guilt when his thought shifted away from negatively rating his wife to negatively rating himself. His next line of emotional reasoning went like this:

Rule: A husband who breaks a promise to his wife is no good.
Report: I broke a promise to my wife to take my son on a father-son trip.
Emotion: Guilt for having broken a promise to my wife (with a painful consciousness of my own worthlessness).

Here, Jason deduced his guilt by accepting an unrealistic rule that turned anyone who ever broke a promise (which includes most, if not all, of us!) into the equivalent of a worthless pile of excrement. Instead of sticking to rating his act, he went after his own jugular, making himself feel like a car with a dead battery, with arms and legs that felt limp coupled with an aching consciousness of just how worthless he was for having broken a promise to his wife. It is also likely that this painful experience included the unpleasant sensory images associated through past experience and upbringing with disapproval from others (especially parents) for similar misdeeds.

Jason's guilt also appears to have escalated to a deep, self-destructive depression along these lines:

Rule: If I'm no good, then the ceiling should collapse and crush me.
Report: I'm no good.
Emotion: Depression about my own worthlessness (with a death wish).

This conclusion shifted Jason's emotional object to his own worthlessness and advanced it to depression with a death wish. Once Jason accepted his total worthlessness, his progression to a depression with self-destructive thoughts was not surprising. This shows you how one self-defeating emotion can set the stage for another, and how accepting unrealistic rules and unfounded reports can lead to self-defeating acts, sometimes even to the ultimate one—suicide.

Jason's emotional tale shifted to fear as the voices of his alleged accusers turned ugly, and the thought of facing them seemed treacherous. Jason's fear then became an emotional object from which he deduced further anger and frustration. With sensory images of a chilling stare playing ominously in his head, Justin deduced his fear of coming out of the room:

Rule: I couldn't stand it if my wife and in-laws stared me down.
Report: If I come out of the room, then they will stare me down.
Emotion: Fear of coming out of my room (with the painful thought of how unbearable being stared down would be).

Once again Jason's rule was unrealistic and easily disprovable. What if Jason's wife and in-laws did stare at him? Would he melt like an ice cube at room temperature, or, more realistically, would he still be left standing? Have you ever survived an unpleasant experience? No doubt you have, and will in the future.

At this point, something new and intriguing happened in Jason's emotional struggle. Jason's fear now became the emotional object of his disgust:

Rule: I mustn't be a wimp.
Report: Being afraid to come out of the room is being a wimp.
Emotion: Disgust over my own fear of coming out of the room (with the thought that he mustn't let himself become a wimp)

On the one hand, Jason was afraid to come out of the room. On the other, he was disgusted by his own fear (being afraid to come out of his room was being a wimp). So, he experienced an internal war between his fear and his disgust over that fear.

Jason finally did indeed emerge from the room with the expectation of doing battle with his adversaries. But much to his surprise, he was greeted by his parents-in-law with concern for his not having eaten diner. They seemed happy to see him and were anything but adversarial or judgmental. In addition, it was not long before his wife apologized to him for her earlier tirade and seemed eager to bring the episode to a close.

The ending to this story is instructive. It should remind you that the battles that you inwardly wage can be largely a product of irrational premises, ones for which you have not found an effective antidote.

The Emotion Loop

The saga of Jason should help you to understand the nature and complexity of your own emotions. This complex includes rules that tell you how to act or feel; emotional objects; reports that describe and file reality under rules;[9] internal bodily changes; feelings of these bodily changes, images, and actions. Psychologists and philosophers have disagreed about which of these elements are primary, but there is no question that they are all salient aspects of human emotional experience.[10]

This is not to deny that there are emotions that do not involve rules and reports, such as the automatic human response to a loud noise. Indeed, other animals with less highly developed nervous systems than ours seem to function rather well with little or no reasoning to pilot their emotions. My hunch is that this is why Fido will get angry at his master only for the moment, say if the master raises his arm in a threatening manner. Fido will automatically respond in the fight or flight mode (say by cowering or growling), only to quickly assume his usual affectionate demeanor when the master lowers his arm. Unlike its master, the dog does not continually evaluate and reevaluate its situation, thereby keeping its emotions going.

Human beings, on the other hand, are different. They tend to evaluate and reevaluate their situations—often to excess, and often relying upon unrealistic rules and unfounded or false reports. So your emotional life is considerably more complex than Fido's.

Usually, when you have an emotional experience, this experience embodies the interplay or back and forth between your thoughts, deeds, and feelings. This interplay between these elements of your emotion often has a looping effect, which can sustain and intensify it. First, your premises lead to internal bodily changes (autonomic effects), which lead to bodily feelings, and then to actions (muscular contractions), which back up your (original) premises.

So, you perceive your boss as having embarrassed you in front of your coworkers, and you think to yourself that anyone who does that deserves to rot in hell. These premises immediately engage your autonomic nervous system, releasing adrenaline into your bloodstream and increasing your blood pressure and heart rate. You feel your heart pound and a painful lump forms in your throat as you feel the blood rush to your arms and legs. All pumped up and ready for fight, your skeletal muscular system fires you into action. "You should rot in hell!" you shout, "You son of a bitch!" and your body moves closer to his, up close and personal, invading his personal space. The sound of "Rot in hell" resounds in your head, as the persuasiveness of your original premises mounts with the increased agitation of your body. As this circle continues to spin out of control, your responses intensify until your anger turns to violent rage. Like a wild beast, you attack your boss and wrestle him to the ground. After the police come and haul you off, you sit there in the corner of a small, empty cell, cooling down and sobering up.

Such vicious cycles of emotion are not uncommon in human existence. Often enough we humans do our sober thinking only after we screw ourselves. Some of us don't even do it then. Unrealistic rules and unfounded or false reports plot our self-defeating courses, often without a clue. Exposing such rules and reports, refuting them, and finding their antidotes can mean the difference between living in misery and despair and living happily and productively.

NOTES

1. *Ethics*, book 7, ch. 3.

2. As you can see from the above quotation, this also appears to be Aristotle's view.

3. This property that emotions and other states of consciousness have of being *about* something, has a name. Philosophers call it their "intentionality" and the object of an emotion is its "intentional object." But I will just call these objects *emotional objects*. Elizabeth L. Beardsley and Monroe C. Beardsley, *Invitation to Philosophical Thinking* (New York: Harcourt, 1972), p. 84.

4. When an emotional object does not really exist, this is sometimes called its "intentional inexistence." Roderick M. Chisholm, *Perceiving: A Philosophical Study* (Ithaca, N.Y.: Cornell University Press, 1969).

5. Antonio R. Damasio, *Descartes' Error: Emotion, Reason, and the Human Brain* (New York: Avon Books, 1994).

6. Daniel Goleman, *Emotional Intelligence* (New York: Bantam Books, 1997).

7. I am boldly saying that you deduce physiological changes, such as changes in heart rate, from your premises. This may not bode well with some who have a much stricter concept of deduction than I have used in this book. Perhaps these folks would feel more comfortable in calling such relations "causal" rather than logical or deductive. But if the brain works like a computer, then it may be that all deductive inferences that people make are translatable into digital brain circuitry (complex neurological networks of on/off switches). If that's the case—which I suspect it might be—then all deductive inferences are, in the end, causal anyway. See, for example, Herbert A. Simon, "Simulating Human Thinking," in *Philosophers at Work: Issues and Practice of Philosophy*, 2d ed., ed. Elliot D. Cohen (Fort Worth, Tex: Harcourt, 2000), pp. 494–517.

8. The thought that his wife is a no-good rotten bitch is also a deduction from his premises. If a wife who degrades and humiliates her husband is a no-good rotten bitch (rule) and his wife has done this to him (report), then it necessarily follows that his wife is a no-good rotten bitch. In general, when you deduce an emotion from premises, you also deduce thoughts.

9. As you will see in chapter 8, the report that you file under a rule is really a description of your emotional object.

10. See my discussion of this in "Philosophical Counseling: Some Roles of Critical Thinking," in *Essays on Philosophical Counseling*, ed. Ran Lahav and Maria Da Venza Tillmanns (New York: University Press of America, 1995), pp. 122–25. When I say that you deduce emotions from your premises, I mean that you deduce some or all of the listed elements from premises. You don't have to deduce all of them to have an emotion. For example, you can get angry without acting angry. You can be fuming on the inside but still be holding back the outward expression of your anger. Did you ever try not to act angry even though you really were?

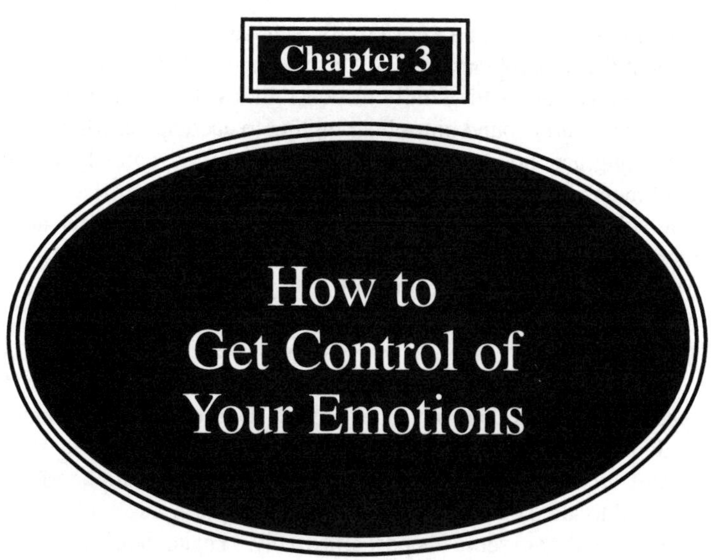

Chapter 3
How to
Get Control of
Your Emotions

[T]he incontinent man [person who doesn't control his emotions], knowing that what he does is bad, does it as a result of passion, while the continent man [person who controls his emotions], knowing that his appetites are bad, refuses on account of his rational principle to follow them.

—Aristotle[1]

All of us have, to a greater or lesser degree, tendencies to act and feel in ways that undermine our personal and interpersonal happiness. So if you thought that you were special, you should guess again. This is the bad news about being human. The good news is that you also have the capacity to control, and even abandon, your self-defeating behavior and emotions. The following example should illustrate my point.

A Trial of Nerves: The Case of Harry

Harry, a colleague of mine who chaired an academic department at a large state university, once came to see me about a problem he was having with one of his faculty members. Harry was a very prolific scholar who considered time to be one of his most valuable assets. Given his administrative, committee, and teaching duties as well as his family responsibilities (he was married with two young children), Harry found himself struggling to accomplish what was a challenging juggling act. So, when he found himself being routinely visited by a department member, Sam, who enjoyed stopping by Harry's office to chat (in a rather one-sided manner) about unimportant, often trivial events and issues (encounters with students and gossip about administrators), Harry was frustrated. These chats seemed to drone on interminably as Harry sat and listened, occasionally having time for a brief response or nod of recognition.

While Harry feigned listening, he was more aware of the swells of anxiety that seemed to rise up in his chest and grab him by the throat. Harry often felt like screaming, "Get the hell out of my office. Don't you know I have better things to do than to listen to this crap!" But Harry didn't say a word.

I asked Harry why he didn't politely ask Sam to leave, and he told me that he didn't want to alienate a department member because this could have repercussions on his ability to serve his post effectively. I began to reconstruct Harry's lines of reasoning, looking for his rules and reports, and found that there were actually two opposing lines of reasoning playing at once in his head, one short-circuiting the other and leaving him in a kind of suspended animation. The first went like this:

(A)
Rule: I must not waste valuable time when there's important work to do.
Report: My not telling Sam to leave is wasting my valuable time.
Action: I tell Sam to leave.

The second line went like this:

(B)
Rule: I must never do anything that could adversely affect my doing a good job as department chair.
Report: Alienating a department member could jeopardize my doing an efficient job as department chair, and telling him to leave would almost surely alienate him.
Action: I don't tell Sam to leave.

Look at the contradictory conclusions deduced by these two lines of reasoning. It's easy to see why Harry was in suspended animation. He could not both tell and not tell Sam to leave. Yet, the A premises were not entirely impotent, because his autonomic nervous system had kicked in and he could feel his frustration swelling up inside him, priming him to tell Sam to "Get the hell out of here!" Yet he still let him stay.

From the B premises, Harry deduced his conclusion of not telling Sam to leave, but the first premises still managed to stir up his bodily juices. So he felt like saying, "Get the hell out of here!" but still managed to control the outward expression of what he secretly felt like doing.

I did not know Sam, so I could not say that asking Sam even politely to leave would not alienate him. Nevertheless, I suggested to Harry that he might have been trying too hard. I suggested that his rule not to ever do anything that could adversely affect his doing a good job as chairman might have been shooting too high. This rule was easy to refute. Because it required that Harry never do anything that could, to any extent, jeopardize his efficiency as chair, this made him a virtual slave to his job. It meant that he could never weigh *anything*, not even life itself, above job effectiveness. Such an absolutistic demand was clearly unrealistic. So what was an effective antidote? To make a reasonable effort at doing a good job, but not to demand perfection. Harry agreed and vowed next time to politely tell Sam that he needed to tend to other matters.

I also directed Harry's attention to the A rule—"I must not waste valuable time when there's important work to do." As we talked, it became apparent that this rule was behind much of the anxiety in Harry's life. Even stopped at a traffic light, this rule seemed to orchestrate anxiety that reached concert pitch when he got behind an extra slow vehicle on his way to work.

Harry did not "flip off" slow drivers or get out of his car and threaten violence. But he often felt like it. His anxiety over his juggling of family and profession seemed largely due to this overly ambitious rule. It appeared that Harry downgraded most things that didn't amount to "important work" like writing books to more or less wastes of time. Like his other rule, this rule was absolutistic. It oversimplified reality by dividing it into just two types: important work and wastes of time. This was easy to refute, for Harry was quite willing to admit that it was important to spend quality time with his wife and children. Unfortunately, he had a hard time enjoying this time because of his unrealistic rule.

Harry's need for emotional control stemmed from his unrealistic workaholic rule, one that pervaded most aspects of his life. While the exercise of emotional control can be a healthy holding back of self-defeating behavior, it can also be a sign of unrealistic thinking, as in Harry's case. If Harry did not place such absolutistic demands on himself in the first place, he would not have been in the situation of having to constrain himself. And Harry is not a special case in this regard. If humans did not think in unrealistic ways, this mechanism might not have been part of our evolutionary heritage. I am not saying that emotional control does not make an important contribution to your life. Indeed, it can mean the difference between a productive life and one spent behind bars. What I am saying is that if you perceive a frequent need to control your emotions, even if you are doing a reasonably good job of controlling your outward behavior, then you may do well to check out your rules and reports for unrealistic thinking, as Harry needed to.

Of course, this is not always true; so don't assume that every time you control your emotions you have some underlying emotional problem to get at. There is a difference between living in a minefield and a cabbage patch. Controlling your contempt for someone who has molested your child or for a group of terrorists who have taken the life of a significant other does not count against your mental stability as it does against the child molester's or the terrorists'.

Emotional control refers to the power to direct your body's (inward and outward) responses to the objects of your emotions. One way you can exert such power is by controlling the internal changes that occur in your body in response to a stressful situation. Another way is to control how you act. It is probably true that the second way, as illustrated by Harry, is more easily accomplished than the first way. Still, you can also control internal bodily changes, even though you may not be conscious of your ability to control them. The therapeutic technique of biofeedback works off of the principle that human beings have the ability to change their autonomic nervous system responses by adjusting their thinking. Such techniques as thought stopping, systematic desensitization, and relaxation training are also examples of therapeutic means of managing your internal bodily changes.[2] Changing your negative perception of reality by seeing it in a more positive light, known as reframing, is still another.[3] I will say more about this later.

Using Antidotal Reasoning to Control Your Emotions

Techniques that effectively work on your autonomic system responses can help to calm you down, and make it easier to think more constructively before you do stupid things that you will later regret. But a more direct way to stop yourself from doing these things is to resist deducing conclusions from irrational rules and reports by exposing these premises, refuting them, and finding suitable antidotes. This means of emotional control does not guarantee that your potentially self-destructive behavior will be derailed. Its success largely depends upon your ability to exercise willpower.

Well, what's that? Willpower is a kind of internal muscle you can flex to overpower self-destructive bodily inclinations. This power is illustrated by Harry's ability to hold back from telling his colleague, "Get the hell out of my office." Indeed, Harry's bodily juices were up to concert pitch, his adrenaline pump was working overtime, and he was in fight-or-flight mode. Nevertheless, he was still able to overpower his bodily inclinations, and, through an effort of will, he managed to constrain himself.

Can you recall the last time you felt like doing something that you knew was wrong? You could almost taste the sweet relief of caving to the pressure of your bodily inclinations. But, like Ulysses, resisting the sweet allure of the Sirens, you still managed to keep yourself from succumbing. This is what I mean by willpower.

According to Albert Ellis and Russell Grieger, "only if we constantly work on and practice, in the present and future, thinking, feeling, and acting against our irrational beliefs are we likely to surrender them and make and keep ourselves less disturbed."[4] Practicing willpower over your irrational premises and the bodily inclinations and feelings that support them, you can eventually weaken the stronghold that these troublesome currents have on you. The exercise of willpower may often be a first step in making permanent change.

Imagine that you are on your way to work, traveling down a narrow two-lane highway framed on your right by an alligator-infested canal. (This is not unrealistic where I live!) Having left a few minutes late, you are somewhat uneasy about the possibility of being a little late, but you feel confident that you would not be terribly late, if at all. In fact, you are now moving along at a decent speed and even a little bit faster than usual, making up for lost time. Suddenly, an old, well-maintained, baby blue Cadillac pops out in front of you, and you come to a virtual stop to avoid a rear-end collision. Waiting impatiently for the driver to bring his Caddy up to speed, you soon learn that its top speed is 15 mph in a 55 mph zone. So you strain to see beyond this large vehicle for a clearing, but traffic is flowing consistently without a break. Moreover, the curvature of the road makes it virtually impossible to see what is coming on the other side of the road. "Do Not Pass," warns a yellow road sign.

What are you thinking and how do you feel? When placed in such a situation, many of us may find it difficult to maintain composure. Do you know why? Let's suppose you say to yourself, "Unless I pass that stupid idiot, I'll be so late that they'll fire me. He'll be responsible for my losing my job; and I'm definitely not going to let that happen!" So here's the logic:

Rule: I must not lose my job because of some stupid idiot.
Report: Unless I pass that stupid idiot, he'll make me so late that they'll fire me.
Action: I attempt to pass the guy in the vehicle in front of me.

So you feel your muscles tighten, as you clench the steering wheel with sweaty palms, the adrenaline circulates, and you prepare for the death-defying stunt. "Death defying?" Yes, you are about to put your life on the line, and perhaps the lives of others, so that you won't lose your job. Well, maybe you wouldn't lose your job anyway. Maybe you'll find a safe place to pass and get to work without being late, or very late. Your report is, after all, unfounded. Do you really have sufficient evidence to believe it?

Furthermore, while you may have reason to think that the driver in front of you is incompetent as a driver, that doesn't make him a stupid idiot. For all you know, he might have the IQ of Albert Einstein. And surely you have no evidence that this is a deliberate plot or conspiracy to make you late or that this is being done with malicious intent. But these are still not the only problems with your premises. Just look at this rule of yours. It effectively says that keeping your job is worth killing or mangling yourself or others. Is this really what you are willing to commit yourself to? Here's some preventive antidotal logic:

> *Rule*: I shouldn't pass when it would jeopardize my life or the lives of others.
> *Report*: Trying to pass this guy under the current circumstances is not safe and could jeopardize my life or the lives of others.
> *Action*: I wait instead of passing.

By taking the above reasoning as an antidote to your previous reasoning, you can effectively short-circuit the dangerous conclusion deducible from it. But you can do this only by flexing your willpower muscle, and forcing yourself into compliance with the antidote. Surely you feel like passing, because your body is saying "Right on!" to the rule that forbids you from letting a stupid idiot cause you to lose your job. Like the maddened crowd with lanterns lit on its way to slay Frankenstein's monster, you are likely to feel your agitated body's impulse to slay the evil monster that blocks your pathway to salvation. But despite this powerful inclination, you still can hold yourself back from attempting to pass the Cadillac. It is hard, even painful, but you can make yourself do it. Disputed and disarmed by the power of antidotal reasoning, you can flex your willpower muscle to defeat or disable the real monster.

Behaving Yourself

In addition to exercising your willpower to hold yourself back from doing unreasonable things, you can also exercise your willpower to push yourself to do things that are rational. When you are flexing your willpower muscle to do something rational that goes against the current of your body, your body will be strongly pushing back, and inclining you in some opposing, irrational direction. So it is understandable that your action will feel awkward, even painful at first. But, as you continue to keep it up, you can actually reverse or weaken your body's inclination to go in the irrational direction. You can reduce your body's resistance by changing your behavior. Here's an analogy that might help. If you tried to wear your watch on your other hand, it would feel rather awkward at first, but eventually you would get used to it. Your bodily feelings would actually reverse themselves, and it would eventually feel awkward wearing the watch on the hand you used to wear it on. So, after a while, the behavior that felt awkward can begin to feel in tune with your body.

Have you ever felt down about something and felt like moping and being by yourself? Probably all of us have felt like this, some of us more than others. Well, suppose that you feel like this but you know, rationally, that you should get yourself out of bed and go to work, school, the party you promised your best friend you would attend, or some other place to which you have committed yourself. So your rational side says, "You really should get up and go" while your irrational side says, "To hell with it all!" But, suppose also that you enlist your willpower on behalf of your antidotal reasoning and pull yourself out of bed, force yourself to groom and dress yourself, and push yourself out the door and to your destination. Well, let's say you arrive and there you are, surrounded by a bunch of people being their usual cheery selves. So, in an effort to adapt and cope rationally with your social circumstances, you also try to be cordial, even cheery, while your insides privately weep. But, keep up the charade long enough and guess what happens? That's right, you start to feel better inside. By behaving yourself, you succeed in fighting off those blues and relieve yourself of considerable pain.

Sound plausible? Next time you feel like hell, try it out. Find an antidote that gives you positive direction, put your willpower behind it, and push yourself to act on it. You are likely to find that your emotional loop is short-circuited by your reasonable action. Is your body and mind out of alignment? Put yourself back in line by behaving yourself.

Reframing Your Situation

Did you ever notice that, sometimes, when you look at things differently, you can also feel better, less stressed out? This way of controlling your emotions is known as *reframing your situation*. Instead of trying to fight off your unrealistic line of reasoning by first refuting it and then opposing it with another, more realistic line, you can simply change your perspective. In the face of adversity, when you are experiencing hard times, you can alleviate much of this stress by taking a different view of the same facts.

Let's face it. There are bad things that happen in this world, even to good folks. Your reasoning about these situations need not be unrealistic to be experiencing the pain of misfortune. Consider the survivors of family and close friends lost in the bombing of the World Trade Center on September 11, 2001. It would be folly to say that the grief experienced by these people was simply due to bad logic that needed refuting. As I'll discuss later, the process of grieving is typically a process of working through and refuting irrational rules and reports over time. Nevertheless, few, if any, of us would agree that there was no great evil or loss, and that there was not something real about which to grieve. Yet, many of us, including some of those who have been directly affected by the disaster, have found much consolation in the heroic efforts of valiant men and women who have risked their lives to save others; the resolve and selflessness of police officers and firefighters who have sacrificed or put their lives on the line; and the outpour of love, support and solidarity of the residents of New York City, the United States, and of the world community. Looking at the matter in this light, one need not refute a single premise to feel some consolation in the face of adversity.

The possibility of reframing a situation in this manner, in the face of adversity, was well understood by the philosopher Gottfried Willhelm von Leibniz, who sought to show how God managed to create the best possible world in spite of the existence of evil. "If you look at the very beautiful picture," he said, "having covered up the whole of it except a very small part, what will it present to your sight, however thoroughly you examine it . . . but a confused mass of colors, laid on without selection and without art? Yet if you remove the covering, and look at the whole picture from the right point of view, you will find that what appeared to have been carelessly daubed on the canvas was really done by the painter with very great art."[5] In a similar vein, philosopher John Hick, in attempting to reconcile evil with the existence of an almighty, all-good God, pointed to the impossibility of building virtuous souls in a universe devoid of pain and suffering.[6] How, indeed, could the police officers and firefighters of New York have shown courage in the face of great danger if there were no such thing as danger, tragedy, and the evil forces against which they mounted their courage? Friedrich Nietzsche, the same philosopher who once proclaimed that God is dead,[7] seems to have reached a similar conclusion, although from a secular perspective, when he proclaimed that, "Profound suffering makes noble: It separates."[8] He said, [w]hen a misfortune strikes us, we can overcome it either by removing its cause or else by changing the effect it has on our feelings, that is, by reinterpreting the misfortune as a good, whose benefit may only later become clear."[9]

Another poignant example of the power of the mind to reframe a tragic situation is given by the renowned psychologist, Viktor Frankl, who has eloquently described his experiences as a prisoner in a Nazi concentration camp. At one juncture, he relates an experience of marching in the dark to a worksite, traversing large puddles and stones, while being prodded on by shouting guards with the butts of their rifles.

> I looked at the sky, where the stars were fading and the pink light of the morning was beginning to spread behind a dark bank of clouds. But my mind clung to my wife's image, imagining it with an uncanny acuteness. I heard her answering me, saw her smile, her frank and encouraging look. Real or not, her look was then more luminous than the sun, which was beginning to rise.
>
> A thought transfixed me. For the first time in my life I saw the truth as it is set into song by so many poets, proclaimed as the final wisdom by so many thinkers. The truth—that love is the ultimate and the highest goal to which man can aspire. Then I grasped the meaning of the greatest secret that human poetry and human thought and belief have to impart: *The salvation of man is through love and in love*. I understood how a man who has nothing left in this world still may know bliss, be it only for a brief moment, in the contemplation of his beloved. In a position of utter desolation, when his only achievement may consist in enduring his suffering in the right way—an honorable way—in such a position man can, through loving contemplation of the image he carries of his beloved, achieve fulfillment. For the first time in my life I was able to under-

> stand the meaning of the words, "The angels are lost in perpetual contemplation of an infinite glory."[10]

Instead of belaboring the pessimistic premises toward which his tortured body and mind naturally inclined, Frankl simply looked elsewhere for a life-affirming rule, that the salvation of man is through love and in love—and that, therefore, there was still something left in this world to cling to, from which all else in the universe draws its meaning for human existence, the love of and for his wife. This new meaning directed his emotions and gave new purpose to his being alive, even if only temporarily. While not denying the reality of his suffering, there was achievement in enduring it, and, indeed, by seeing it as but a dark frame around a brightly illuminated reality more sanctimonious than the brutality and inhumanity of his imprisonment, whose luminous character stood out all the more against the darkness of his tragic condition.

This was bringing good out of evil, transforming suffering into human achievement and accomplishment. Such "tragic optimism," as Frankl called it, brought him to see a deeper meaning in life. The evil he perceived *in* the world, not *of* the world, accentuated the good fortune of having a wife whom he loved, and who loved him. The images he held in his mind's eye enlivened his premises and he could no doubt feel the blissful sensations associated with her presence. She was, in this way, there with him, smiling at him, encouraging him to go on.

You may be wondering how realistic or rational it was for Frankl to count his blessings when he was surrounded by death in a Nazi concentration camp. Was Frankl's reverie just a defense mechanism, a case of lying to himself to make himself feel better? Was he simply retreating from reality?

Frankl was surely doing what he could to cope with the bleakness of his circumstances. Yet he did not shrink from reality. He knew his situation to be one of utter desolation. His choice of how to view reality was not merely an automatic, psychological response; it was a philosophical choice, one that he consciously and freely made. He was exercising his free will in choosing a philosophical premise from which to view reality.

But, what if your philosophical position is just unrealistic or false? In personal correspondence with me regarding Frankl's case, Albert Ellis had this to say:

> Actually, Frankl's belief [that "the salvation of man is through love and in love"] in this respect is antifactual and unrealistic: since obviously, all humans do not achieve salvation through being loved and being in love. He has faith in this *un*realistic belief, and peculiarly enough it helps him weather his harsh incarnation. Having faith in *un*reality—such as the belief that the Devil is on your side and will always help you through your troubles—may at times help you in spite of its utter falseness. Your *belief* in this "fact" is what helps, not any factuality behind the belief. . . . Faith founded on *fact*—such as the belief that you can usually help yourself despite great adversity—is much safer and much

> more likely to not lead to ultimate disillusionment. But we'd better face the "reality" that blind and unrealistic faith, such as that had by Frankl, can sometimes be helpful.[11]

As I will later discuss, people value reality because it has practical merit. Being realistic about what can happen to you if you walk in front of a Mack truck traveling at 100 mph could save your life. So, even if Frankl's rule—"The salvation of man is through love and in love"—from which he drew some moments of consolation was unrealistic, it was unrealistic in a way that, under his *extraordinary* circumstances, worked like reality. As Ellis rightly sees, it would be very unrealistic to insist that you should *never*, not even under the most extreme circumstances, have "blind unrealistic faith" in something.

But being unrealistic in such extraordinary circumstances doesn't necessarily mean being blind. If you are optimistic about the world *as* a whole, this does not mean you are, or should be optimistic about each of its parts. What's true of the whole is not necessarily true of the part. There can still be evil in a basically good world. Frankl's optimism, no less than that of those who lost loved ones in the 9/11 tragedy, did not deny the existence of great evil. There was no unreality in seeing a light in the darkness. There was no denying the dark in seeing the light.

There was really no significant antidote for Frankl's circumstances, nothing to helpfully repair an unrealistic rule or unfounded report. In his moment of revelation he "understood how a man who has nothing left in this world still may know bliss, be it only for a brief moment." This was hardly to deny the harsh reality of his incarceration, the Nazis, the gas chambers, and the holocaust of millions of innocent lives. There was no antidote for the admission and bleak assessment of these realities. But there was still no contradiction in changing the subject, in looking with the mind's eye toward something more abstract, more poetic, and abundantly more pleasant than a preoccupation with what was far beyond external control. In this, you can see a distinction between simply reframing your situation and what I call finding an antidote. If you can find nothing in your premises to refute, and consequently no antidote to relieve your pain, and no further realistic recourse, then the only sane thing left may be to reframe.

Drug Therapy

Your native capacities to refute premises, find antidotes, flex your willpower muscle, and reframe your situation can be powerful resources for coping with stress and curbing self-defeating emotions. But are these always sufficient? Should you ever resort to that other kind of medicine? I mean prescription drugs.

The answer to this question is yes, when the emotion is due to a physiolog-

"It's a cool one, alright." I confirm and reflect how warm the days have been, even this deep into winter. With the early sunset and late sunrise, the sun doesn't have a chance to warm up the air significantly anymore, in particular when clear nights are cooling the air right down.

"Rob says that people are dumb," Paula states, focussing the group on the brief interchange we had whilst managing our salads. It rattles me out of my thoughts, and with that I find myself back on the sofa and in the group.

"I think it was more that you said it to me and that I confirmed, and we agreed on the job that you will raise the issue with the group, which you have done splendidly!" I counter.

A brief discussion follows, which is disrupted by Adam who has stood up during the discussions, moved to the bookshelf to pick out a very small and thin white booklet.

"I have to share this one with you," Adam says, holding up a small white booklet. "It is one of the most comprehensive books ever written about the human condition, and since it is so big, I most probably can quickly summarise it for you."

Laughter.

"It has been written by Carlo Cipolla in 1976, and is called 'the basic laws of human stupidity'. I can't agree more." Adam stands in the room, holds the book up, looks around the room with a serious demeanour, and gives any old-style lecturer a run for the money.

"The first law says that 'always and inevitably everyone underestimates the number of stupid individuals in circulation'. That's law number one."

"That certainly confirms a life-time of my experience," Brent pipes up and everyone laughs.

"What's the second law?" I ask.

"The probability that a certain person be stupid, is independent of any other characteristics of that person."

"Never mind whether you are rich or poor."

"Old or young."

"Male or female."

"Journalist or politician."

ical abnormality originating in the brain, for example, bipolar disorder (manic-depression), schizophrenia, and major depressive disorder. In these cases, chemical brain abnormalities can be treated with drugs such as lithium carbonate (for manic-depression) and Prozac (for major depression). Such drugs restore physiological conditions more favorable to rational thinking by regulating chemicals called neurotransmitters, which are responsible for neural conductivity in the brain. This does not necessarily mean that individuals who suffer from such disorders, and who go unmedicated, are incapable of rational thinking, but rather that there are physiological impediments that can, in some cases, make such thinking extremely difficult or unlikely. Under these conditions it may be advisable to medicate.

There is no litmus test for whether drug therapy is indicated and there is considerable disagreement among therapists about when drugs are indicated over other types of therapy, for example, behavior therapy instead of drugs for obsessive-compulsive disorder. Such an evaluation is often based upon the severity of the condition as well as the risk factor for suicide or other serious harm to self or others. It is also significant that drugs such as antidepressants may take several weeks or even months to begin to work. In this interim period, in the case of severe depression, some form of nonmedical therapy or intervention is still useful, especially in light of a high lethality factor.

Take the case of Dennis, who came to see me after seeing my name listed in the book, *Plato, Not Prozac!* Dennis had recently been separated from his wife. Ten years prior, he was psychiatrically treated for major depression; suffering from suicidal ideation, he was counseled and given drug therapy.

Inspired by the title of the aforementioned book, Dennis insisted on being given Plato, not Prozac. As we talked, he told me that the old feelings from ten years ago were now resurfacing, but that he was opposed to going back on medication. He also conveyed that, if he could not come to grips, philosophically, with his wife leaving him, he was prepared to kill himself. I told Dennis that I would see him only if he first submitted himself for psychiatric evaluation. When Dennis left my office, we both knew he would not be returning. Despite the fact that the book that brought him to my office clearly stated that some people with depression require medication, this finer print was no match for the bold print on the cover, which emphatically decreed, *Plato, Not Prozac!* This was all that stuck in his mind, perhaps because this was all that he really wanted to hear. I do not know what became of this poor fellow, but I am convinced that he would have significantly benefited from medication.

Nevertheless, no medicine exists that can do your rational thinking for you. The medicine simply removes obstacles to logical reasoning. It does not give you your premises. Unfortunately, some medical professionals refuse to make this distinction. For example, some physicians insist that they can successfully treat children with Attention Deficit Hyperactivity Disorder (ADHD) *just* by giving them the drug, Ritalin. Some even deny the utility of any other form of nonmedical therapy. Nevertheless, this view seems to be contradicted by the considerable number of patients who become listless and lethargic (or occasionally develop explosive rage) while on this drug. In these cases, the drug simply exchanges one emotional problem for another.

Some people have a manic condition without also having depression. Such a condition is characterized by persistent and abnormally excessive mood elevation. Symptoms may include overproduction of ideas, excessively rapid speech, delusions of grandeur, inability to concentrate, restlessness, irritability, and tendencies toward capricious, overly zealous, whimsical, or flighty behavior. Nevertheless, many of these people are discontented with the way they feel while on lithium. They actually enjoy their manic highs and don't feel like themselves on the medicine. In one instance, a young man with just such a condition came to see me to talk about his career goals. He disliked taking lithium, and told me that he was willing to choose his profession on the basis of whether he needed to take the medicine in order to do the work. So, he was willing to give up his goal of becoming a psychologist just to avoid taking the medicine. (He seemed to think that he could be a teacher without taking the medicine.) In any event, the medication itself raised a life crisis for this young man, which required his careful, rational consideration. How, indeed, could the drug, which was a major part of the problem, cure the problem?

I do not know where this young man is today or what job he ultimately decided on, but one thing is quite clear. If he decided to take the lithium as a condition of employment, then unless he rationally resolved his adjustment issues to taking the drug, it is unlikely that he would consistently remain on it. This could have negative consequences if, say, as a psychologist, he came to work high. Taking the drug could make it easier for him to think rationally about his issues, but it could not resolve them for him. He had to do this for himself. There is no escaping this fact. When it comes to doing your own thinking, there are no quick fixes.

You can, of course, seek out a mental health professional or philosophical counselor to help you resolve a specific issue with which you may be wrestling in your personal life. But, ultimately it is up to *you* to do the work, whether you wing it on your own or consult someone else to help you. In this book, I provide the basics of a logical approach to dealing with problems of living. While this book is not intended as a substitute for professional help, it is intended to give you some tools that you should find helpful. In general, it should help you to identify, refute, and find antidotes to your happiness-hampering premises.

Notes

1. *Ethics*, book 7, ch. 1.

2. Michael Spiegler and David C. Guevremont, *Contemporary Behavior Therapy*, 4th ed. (Belmont, Calif.: Wadsworth, 2003).

3. Albert Ellis, *Overcoming Destructive Beliefs, Feelings, and Behavior* (Amherst, N.Y.: Prometheus Books, 2001), p. 178.

4. Albert Ellis and Russell Grieger, *Handbook of Rational-Emotive Therapy*, vol. 2 (New York: Springer Publishing Co., 1986), p. 25.

5. Gottfried Wilhelm von Leibniz, "Essays in Theodicy," quoted in Samuel Enoch Stumpf, *Philosophy: History and Problems*, 4th ed. (New York: McGraw-Hill, 1989), p. 258.

6. John H. Hick, "The Problem of Evil: The Free Will and Soul-Building Arguments," in Cohen, *Philosophers at Work*, pp. 540–46.

7. Friedrich Nietzsche, *Thus Spake Zarathustra*, part 4, ch. 73.2.

8. Nietzsche, *Beyond Good and Evil*, no. 270 in *The Philosophy of Nietzsche* (New York: Random House, 1954).

9. Nietzsche, *Human, All Too Human*, no. 108 in *The Philosophy of Nietzsche*. See also James Scott Johnston and Carol Johnston, "Nietzsche and the Dilemma of Suffering," *International Journal of Applied Philosophy* 13, no. 2 (fall 1999): 187–92.

10. Viktor E. Frankl, *Man's Search for Meaning* (New York: Simon & Schuster, 1985), p. 57.

11. Albert Ellis, letter to author, 4 July 2001.

Chapter 4

How to Deal with Conflict between Emotion and Intellect

There seems to be [an] irrational element in the soul . . . naturally opposed to reason, which fights against and resists it, . . . but . . . in a sense shares in it, in so far as it listens to and obeys it.

—Aristotle[1]

Do you remember the last time you said to yourself that it was wrong to feel a certain way but continued to feel and act that way anyway? Human beings often stubbornly hang on to their emotional reasoning even when it is based on unreasonable rules and reports. In such cases, it is easy to say, "I just can't help the way I feel. There's really no point to even trying to feel (and act) any differently." But not being able to help something, and it being difficult are not the same, and it is all too easy to give up when you fail to distinguish the two.

An Emotionally Torn Mom: The Case of Myra

To see this, let's take a look at the case of Myra, mother of a seventeen-year-old son, Ronny. You have already met Ronny's father. Can you guess who Ronny's father is? *Hint*: He's the guy who locked himself away in his bedroom over a spat with his wife about their son.

Yes, that's right, he's Jason, whom we heard from in chapter 2. Let's now see how Myra's stubborn adherence to unrealistic rules contributed to a dysfunctional family environment rife with emotional turmoil.

Beginning at the age of twelve, Ronny began to act out at home, becoming easily angered at apparently minor things, refusing to obey his mother, and talking back. With each year, he became increasingly more aggressive, degrading and mocking his mother, using profanity (even in front of friends), making threats, refusing to comply with curfews and other requests, exploding into rage when his own requests for clothing and other material articles were not granted immediately. In earlier years, Ronny was more compliant with his dad, but gradually he too became a subject of Ronny's abusive behavior. Through all this, Myra maintained her usual posture as a loving mother, demonstrating concern and affection for him, making concessions to him, overlooking misdeeds, even after excessive brutality. At first, Jason participated in the confrontations, reprimanding his son, often shouting at him, but it gradually became apparent that this was not working. In fact, Ronny seemed to enjoy getting a rise out of his father; it gave Ronny an opportunity to denounce him as crazy and worthless.

After a while, the shouting matches between Jason and his son became less frequent (although not nonexistent) as Jason made an effort to avoid encounters with his son. Nevertheless, the abusive behavior continued and seemed to focus more on Myra with the lesser involvement of Jason. Myra began to blame herself as well as Jason for her son's conduct, refusing to hold Ronny squarely responsible for his own misdeeds. After all, she declared, "How could good parents have a child as disturbed as Ronny! We must have done something wrong." Jason's attempts at disciplining Ronny (by taking away such things as car and telephone privileges) for his disrespectful treatment became less aggressive as Myra began to dismiss such attempts as futile.

However, it became apparent to Myra that, when she did not express concern (did not ask him questions about his life), Ronny temporarily acted more respectful. But, as soon as she responded with affection (kind words, speaking in a sweet tone, hugs, agreeing to buy him special treats, etc.) or concern (where are you going, what time will you be home, etc.), the abusive treatment recurred. The abusive behavior seemed to form a repetitive cycle as Myra continued to become engaged and to suffer the consequences. It seemed that she could not be nice to her son without "paying for it." Jason urged Myra to maintain a consistent posture of nonengagement, but Myra had a problem keeping it up because she "loved him too much not to show it."

On the one hand, Myra came to believe that by catering to her son in spite of his disrespect, she was making it easier for her son to continue his reign of abuse. On one level, she seemed to accept the following line of reasoning about how to manage Ronny's abusive ways:

(A)
Rule: I shouldn't do anything that enables my son's abusive behavior.
Report: In acting concerned and showing affection for Ronny, I am enabling his abusive behavior.
Action: I avoid acting concerned and showing Ronny affection.

On the other hand, Myra appears to have *emotionally* accepted each of the following two lines of reasoning:

(B)
Rule: If I truly love my son, then I must show it (by my affection for him).
Report: I truly love my son
Action: I show Ronny affection.

And

(C)
Rule: If a child is troubled then it's the parents who are at fault and should be made to pay, not the child.
Report: Ronny is troubled.
Emotion: Guilt about having failed Ronny as parents (with the thought that we, not Ronny, should be held accountable and made to pay for our mistakes.)

Remember how resistant Myra was to Jason's attempts at punishing Ronny for his misdeeds? Egged on by the line of reasoning in C, this is not surprising. Her tirade against Jason, when he refused to take Ronny on the father-son trip, was largely directed at making Jason atone for his parental sins.

This position of blaming herself and her husband *felt* right to her. So, when she tried to feign indifference toward her son, she went against the tide of her feelings. She felt tense and uneasy about doing what betrayed these intense feelings. I suspect that the painful images conjured up by thoughts of withdrawing affection from her son were a product of her own upbringing. In chapter 11, I'll talk more about the role of upbringing or socialization in supporting such self-defeating emotions.

Cognitive Dissonance

You could say that Myra *emotionally accepted* the reasoning in B and C because they fitted in with the other ingredients of her emotion such as her bodily feelings and images. This made the conclusion in A—avoid acting concerned or showing Ronny affection—feel like a repugnant intruder in her emotional universe. This conclusion received a cold, flat nod as she came to see its practical value. But its power to direct her actions was thwarted by the other lines of reasoning that had her body on their side.

This tension Myra experienced between what she *emotionally accepted* and what she *intellectually accepted* is called "cognitive dissonance."[2] She had two opposing sets of premises, one backed by bodily feelings and images, the other not. When she tried to be less affectionate to Ronny, the premises backed by bodily feelings eventually regained control. The challenge for Myra was to reverse the emotional status of these dissonant lines of reasoning.

When you have cognitive dissonance, you are stuck with a kind of mismatch between knowledge and emotion. You know what you should do, but you don't *feel* like you should do it. This often leads you to act in ways that contradict what you know you should do.

Fighting Cognitive Dissonance with Your Strongest Antidote

Here's the upshot: When your knowledge and feelings don't seem to mix, you can try this: First, say what you *feel* like doing and back that up with a rule and a report. (In chapter 8, I'll give you some guidelines for finding these premises.) Second, try your best to refute the rule and/or the report backing up what you feel like doing. This should help you to see more clearly whether, and in what respects, it's unreasonable to persist in this line of thinking. Third, say what you think you *really* should (or shouldn't) be doing and back *that* up with a rule and a report. This line is supposed to be your antidotal reasoning, but sometimes what you think you know you don't really know. Your antidote could still be bogus. So, it can come in handy to look carefully at the premises of your antidotal reasoning to see if they can be refuted. If so, then try to find a stronger antidote. Finally, try like hell to *flex your willpower muscle* to act in line with your best antidote!

To apply this to Myra's case, take a look at her rule in B: If I truly love my child, then I must show it. Following this rule does not seem to be a problem in *most* contexts of parent-child relationships. If I demonstrate love (through my display of affection) for my child, then I am ordinarily justified in expecting the child to reciprocate. Unfortunately, this was not true in Ronny's case. The rule in question was not meant for exceptional situations where the giving of love worked in reverse to produce anger and hostility. It's much like saying that freedom of speech in the U.S. is a basic right, so I have a right to yell "Fire!" in an auditorium. Myra was trying to apply her rule to a situation it did not fit. Like trying to put a Cadillac muffler on a Honda, you just can't make it fit!

Myra's rule in line C is easy to refute: If a child is troubled then it's the parents who are at fault and should be made to pay, not the child. This is easy to refute because it assumes that the parents are *always* the culprits. This leaves out peer relationships, and all other sundry experiences and encounters, not to mention genetic endowments over which parents have no control. Second, by assuming that Ronny's misbehavior is a mere product of his upbringing, this rule seems to deny that Ronny has free will. It seems to assume that, like a preprogrammed computer, he has no responsibility for his actions. Instead of recognizing Ronny's freedom of action, this rule tells you to blame the programmer (the parent) but not the computer (the child). But when Ronny told his mother to "Shut the fuck up!" as he often did, was it not Ronny who acted, and was it not he who was responsible? Third, even if emotional problems were always traceable to poor parenting, this doesn't mean that the parents are blameworthy and should be made to pay. If, with knowledge and forethought, parents maliciously sought to harm their child, then this would be true. But one very obvious aspect of Myra's treatment of her son was her relentless love for him. Finally, the idea that the parents should pay and not the child sounds like Myra was seeking to assign blame for Ronny's problems, whereas her main concern was to help her child.

So, the lines of reasoning in B and C didn't have a solid logical leg to stand on. What about the line of reasoning in A? The rule here said, "I shouldn't do anything that enables my son's abusive behavior." Shouldn't do *anything*? This does, indeed, seem unreasonably demanding, doesn't it? It also means that Ronny's parents should never give him any form of affection since affection enables his abusive behavior.

An alternative antidote was to give Ronny affection sparingly to reinforce actual, significant accomplishments while maintaining a less affectionate position at other times. This was actually the antidote we finally tried. And guess what? It met with some measure of success. First, it was easier for Myra to consistently apply because it was less demanding, and second, it encouraged rather than undermined Ronny's sense of self-worth.

I also emphasized to Myra that this type of "tough love" approach did not require her to stop loving her son. Paradoxically, in this unusual context, such a posture seemed just what loving her son required. For Myra, this meant having the courage and perseverance to confront the premises, bodily feelings, images, and behavior that supported her self-defeating responses to Ronny's misbehavior. This meant consistently exercising the effort of will needed to overcome these internal impediments.

Flexing Your Willpower Muscle

Such an effort requires looking inside yourself. Turning your sight inward, you can actually *feel* a sort of power exerted over the direction of your outward behavior against the currents of your bodily inclinations. You know the feeling, don't you? This feeling is that of *willpower*. Like other bodily feelings, this feeling gives you a picture of the inner state of your body. You may feel yourself physically drawn in one direction rather than another, but you can also feel the power to resist this course of least resistance.

Philosopher C. A. Campbell says, "We are conscious of making an effort of will *only* when we choose [will] a course that is contrary to the course towards which we feel that our desiring nature most strongly inclines us."[3] This consciousness that Campbell has in mind feels like a kind of pushing from within. You can feel yourself pushing yourself from the inside to do what you think is right, against bodily inclination.

This internally perceived willpower or effort of will is an important part of the human emotional fabric. It is vital to emotional control. It's what defines us human beings as *free*. Without it, you would be a slave to your bodily impulses. You would always go with the flow of your bodily impulses.

By exerting your willpower you can change the way you act, think, and feel. You can stop doing self-defeating things, and you can start doing more reasonable things. By behaving yourself, you can, in turn, also improve the way you feel, as I discussed in chapter 3; and when you feel better, it is easier to think better too.

Your willpower can help you to fight off irrational thinking in two ways. If the antidotal reasoning you are using tells you that you *should not* do something, then you can flex your willpower muscle to hold yourself back from doing what you should not do. On the other hand, if your antidotal reasoning tells you what you *should* do, then you can flex your willpower muscle to push yourself to do what you should do. So, depending upon your antidotal reasoning, you can use your willpower to stop yourself from doing something irrational or to make yourself do something rational.

Philosopher Aristotelis Santas compares willpower to a muscle that needs to be cultivated through exercise and built up slowly in order for it to grow stronger. You need to grow accustomed to flexing it, working up to the harder tasks, doing easier ones first before you are ready for the harder ones.[4] Applying Santas's approach, I suggested to Myra that she try gradually decreasing the number of questions she asked Ronny about his life each week over a several week period until she had built up enough willpower to function at a level of involvement that didn't encourage her son's abusive responses.

It would be misleading to say that redirecting your emotions by flexing your willpower muscle and changing your behavior is easy when you are in a state of cognitive dissonance. In Myra's case, it was extremely difficult, but the last time I looked she was getting used to her new behavior, and had made some progress in reducing Ronny's abusive behavior.

I entreat you to work on your willpower muscle too. You can do this on a daily basis. The next time you reach for that extra chip, you can say, "I shouldn't overdo fatty foods, these chips are super fatty." Then put your willpower behind this antidotal *shouldn't* and hold yourself back. You can walk away, triumphant and proud of your inner muscle. Try it out when you feel like yelling at your child for playing the radio too loudly, or kicking the dog when he soils the rug. There is great dignity, a natural high, in being in control. It feels good!

Notes

1. *Ethics*, book 1, ch. 13.
2. Clifford T. Morgan and Richard A. King, *Introduction to Psychology* (New York: McGraw-Hill, 1971), pp. 513–14
3. C. A. Campbell, "The Psychology of Effort of Will," in *Free Will and Determinism*, ed. Bernard Berofsky (New York: Harper & Row, 1966), p. 346.
4. Aristotelis Santas, "Willpower," *International Journal of Applied Philosophy* 4, no. 2 (fall 1988): 9–16.

Part 2

Some Virulent Strains of Thinking

Chapter 5

Rules You May Be Using to Seriously Disturb Yourself

[O]ne ought to choose that which is intermediate, not the excess nor the defect, and that the intermediate is determined by the dictates of the right rule . . .

—Aristotle[1]

The ancient Greek philosopher Socrates believed that if you knew the good, then you would *do* it. Only ignorance, he thought, could lead us astray.[2] As our discussion in chapter 4 showed, the case is considerably more complex than Socrates suggested. Egged on by strong bodily urges, you could still be driven to do stupid things, even when you know better. But let's not throw the baby out with the bathwater. Socrates was on the right track. Beneath his idealism was the conviction that knowledge and personal happiness (doing what's really good for you) go together.

Here is an attenuated version of Socrates: If you know what's right, good, or true then you have much better prospects for achieving personal happiness than if you flounder around in ignorance. This is certainly a theme that is well represented in philosophical history. John Stuart Mill expressed his version by declaring, "It is better to be a human being dissatisfied than a pig satisfied; better to be Socrates dissatisfied than a fool satisfied."[3] A clan of American philosophers called Pragmatists, including Charles Peirce, William James, John Dewey, and C. I. Lewis expressed their version by proclaiming the "cash value" of knowledge and truth. Why do you fill your memory banks with truths rather than falsehoods? Their practical answer is clear: Because the truth promotes your satisfactory adjustment to the "blooming, buzzing universe," while falsehood, most often, eventually does you in. "'The true'," says James, "is only the expedient in the way of our thinking, just as 'the right' is only the expedient in the way of our behaving."[4] "The wise man," says Lewis, "is he who knows where good lies, and knows how to act so that it may be attained."[5] Aristotle himself captures this sense of the true under the banner of "practical wisdom," which he says is "a true or reasoned state of capacity to act with regard to the things that are good or bad for man."[6] I will run with this practical approach because everyday life is most concerned with the practical import of calling things true, realistic, right, and good, and of calling them false, unrealistic, wrong, and bad.

If your premises are true or realistic, then they fit in with other things that are true or realistic. On the other hand, if they are false or unrealistic, then they conflict with other things that are true or realistic. This is how truth satisfies. You can count on it. It satisfies your expectations. As James suggests, if you are lost in the woods and want to get out alive, the true belief about what path to take will bring you to safety. The false belief will take you deeper and deeper into the forest.[7] The veritable woods of life can be rather confusing without a store of true beliefs up your sleeves. Without such a stock, you are likely to perish.

Here, then, is a standard of truth and reality: If your premises can be counted on to "cash out" when you deduce your actions from them, then they are true or realistic. If the actions you get out of them are most likely to scuttle your goals and expectations, then they are false or unrealistic.

Fortunately, humankind's long, unsavory history of falling from grace into the hellfires of falsehood and unreality has not been a total fiasco. We have learned some things about how *not* to think! These timeworn fallacious modes of thinking have been recorded in the annals of logic to provide a useful checklist against which to test the veracity of your premises. As false or unrealistic reports and rules from which you deduce you actions, such *fallacies* can be seductive. But make no mistake about it. They have the power (if you give it to them) to undermine your happiness.

What's a Fallacy?

Fallacies are ways of thinking that have proven track records of frustrating personal and interpersonal happiness.[8] They typically infect your rules and reports. This infection then spreads, automatically, sometimes imperceptibly, to your actions and emotions, which you deduce from these infected premises. I implore you to watch out for these pathogens, and to find effective antidotes to them, for happiness' sake. They are intellectual blights upon humankind. Even when effectively treated, their emotional secondary infection (cognitive dissonance) can stubbornly hang on.

Fortunately, there is hope, even for the highly resistant strains. Don't expect to *totally* eradicate them, however. As you will see, to demand perfection in this imperfect universe of ours is among one of the most virulent of fallacies.

There are some fallacies that are common to rules and others that are commonly (although not exclusively) found in reports. Some fallacies of rules direct you to do irrational things. Let's call them *fallacies of action.* Other fallacies of rules direct you to *feel* in certain self-defeating ways. Let's call them *fallacies of emotion.* Finally, let's call fallacies that commonly infect reports *fallacies of reports.* If you know what fallacies to look for in your premises, where to look, and how to find them, then you will be in a much better position to fight off their infection.

Some Very Virulent Fallacies of Emotion

There are several kinds of fallacy by which human beings often seriously disturb themselves, and keep themselves upset. These are (1) Demanding Perfection, (2) Awfulizing, (3) Terrificizing, (4) I-Can't-Stand-It-Itis, (5) Damnation (of Self or Others), (6) I Just Can't Help This Feeling, and (7) Thou Shalt Upset Yourself. When you experience irrational, self-destructive emotions, it is likely that one or more of these fallacies has infected a rule in your emotional reasoning.

In Aristotle's terms, these rules go to extremes—from requiring that your life be perfect to condemning it as totally shitty. Rational antidotes to such self-destructive, absolutistic rules avoid the extremes and counter them with intermediate outlooks. For example, they realistically acknowledge the defects in the world without painting it all black. They are not overly pessimistic; nor are they pie-in-the-sky optimistic. They are realistic. These corrective rules recognize that shit really does sometimes happen, that you can and often do have responsibilities to confront your problems of living, and that not everything is within your power to control. On the other hand, they also recognize that things may not be nearly as bad as you make them out to be; that you don't have to devour your own prospects for happiness in order to live responsibly; and that you have a considerable amount of power over how you think, feel, and act. Let's take a look at each of these irrational rules and some rational responses to them.

Demanding Perfection

In its diverse forms, when you accept a rule of this nature, you tell yourself that the world absolutely, unconditionally *must* and cannot ever fail to conform to some state of ideality, perfection, or near perfection; that you cannot and must not ever have it any other way; and that shit (or a certain kind of it) must never happen—despite the fact that it does. In embracing a rule of this kind, you are likely to deduce intense feelings of outrage, anger, and dismay when the world fails to conform to your expectation or demand, which will inevitably be the case.

For example, you demand perfection when you think that the following things *must never* happen:

- Someone doesn't approve of you, or someone special doesn't approve of you.
- You make a mistake, or fail to perform perfectly.
- Things don't go your way, or exactly the way you want them to go.
- You are not treated fairly.
- Something bad happens to you or to a significant other.
- You can't control everything or something important to you.
- You can't get what you want.
- You do not succeed at something, or you are less successful than you want to be.
- You lose something of substantial value to you.

Indeed, things on the above list are bound to happen in your imperfect world. So it is clearly irrational to demand that they don't ever happen. Although most of us certainly *prefer* that these things not happen, this is not the same as demanding that they not happen. It is these absolutistic *must*s, *ought*s, and *should*s that, as rules in your emotional reasoning, direct intense, self-defeating emotional responses. You can easily see this by considering the emotional difference between accepting "I *must* get what I want" versus "I would *prefer* it." The first directs you to prepare for fight or flight if you don't get it; the second directs you to feel disappointment. Here then is an antidote to Demanding Perfection: Change your absolutistic *must*s, *ought*s, and *should*s to *preference*s, and save yourself some headaches.

Awfulizing

In accepting a rule that contains this fallacy, you tell yourself that when something bad or very bad happens, you must think of it as *totally* devastating, catastrophic, and the worst thing imaginable. In embracing such a rule of assessment, you are likely to deduce extreme anxiety or remorse when things happen or might happen that get in the way of your interests or values. For example, you are likely to feel intense anxiety if you think that the following things *will* or *might* happen in the future, and remorse, even depression, if they actually *do* happen:

- Your boyfriend/girlfriend breaks up with you or your spouse files for divorce.
- You lose your job, or don't get hired for a job you want
- You flunk an exam or a course.
- You find your best friend in bed with your wife/husband.
- Somebody steals your wallet.
- You get a traffic ticket.
- You get into a fender bender.
- You are late for work because a car in front of you that you can't pass is driving extra slowly.
- You have an argument with a significant other or close friend.
- You have to postpone a vacation or a purchase until you have the time or the money.

Such objects of emotion as losing a job that you covet or finding your beloved wife in bed with your trusted friend are not minor frustrations, and we can certainly empathize with someone who suffers such an ill fate. Nevertheless, if you think that these are the *worst* or nearly the worst things that could possibly happen to you, then you might try comparing them to macabre events such as being beheaded by a guillotine or being cooked slowly in an oven. Even these extremely bad things could be worsened, say by imagining that the blade of the guillotine is dull and does not completely sever your head, so that you linger in excruciating pain for hours, days, weeks, months, or even years.

Are you sufficiently repulsed by these thoughts? Can you now see how unrealistic it is to rank the loss of a job or even the unfaithfulness of your spouse as among the worst things that could possibly happen to you? On a relative scale of one to ten, are these really worth a ten? Definitely not! You may take consolation in knowing that, relatively speaking, things could have been much worse.

Accordingly, here is an antidote to Awfulizing: Keep yourself humble about your misfortunes. Here's how to implement this wisdom: Imagine something that is much, much worse and use it as a basis of comparison. Imagine what it could be like after that dull guillotine blade drops with a thud. Imagine it with its graphic, gory, pain wrenching, bloody, throbbing details. Then ask yourself if the speeding ticket you just got that will almost certainly cause your auto insurance to increase is really *that* bad.

Another useful antidote: Watch out for words like "terrible," "horrible," and "awful." These words tend to be used to exaggerate or overrate the badness of things. Is it really *horrible* that you missed your appointment with the hair stylist? In calling it "horrible," you tell yourself to respond accordingly. If it's horrible, then you must *feel* horrible. The *horrible horrifies*. If you don't want to horrify yourself, then you shouldn't call it horrible. Instead, try "unfortunate," "too bad," or "tough luck." Does it *feel* quite as bad now?

But aren't there *really* things in the world that are terrible, horrible, and awful? Don't people ever earn the right to apply these words to their misfortunes? Weren't the events of 9/11 really horrible? Wasn't the Holocaust truly horrible? Even if these events weren't the worst possible things that could have happened—even more innocent lives could have been lost—aren't they *bad enough* to be called terrible, horrible, and awful?

If you lost a loved one in some tragic event, then you may be telling yourself that it's so horrible that you *can't stand* to go on any longer. As a result, you may be keeping yourself in an emotional turmoil, fueling and refueling your horror. Working through the trauma of your loss would mean eventually putting the loss into perspective by seeing it against the background of a world that also has good things in it. It would mean assessing the relative badness of what happened by seeing it in the context of the sanctity and worth of your own life, and the lives of others whom you love and who are still among the living. It would mean seeing your loss in relation to the goals and values that still lie ahead for you in everyday living. It would mean seeing it in relation to the consolation and love you receive from others.

However, perceiving the world, or part of it, in terms of the terrible, horrible, and awful, can be like a loud, ominous noise that fills the air and makes all else inaudible. In hashing and rehashing the horror of your loss, you are likely to distract and prevent yourself from making a realistic comparative assessment of what's still left for you. Working through a great loss that understandably *feels* dreadfully terrible, horrible, and awful involves leaving these thoughts behind as you begin to get on with your life.

TERRIFICIZING

This is when you tell yourself that, if someone or something appears to have some desirable feature, then this person or thing must be absolutely and totally terrific, perfect, and the best of its kind in the entire universe, and that you should idolize and never expect anyone or anything else to measure up to it. If you embrace a rule of this nature, you are likely to set yourself up for disappointment, and to feel extremely down when the person or thing you idolized lets you down or is lost. Your use of such words as "terrific," "perfect," and "the best" is often a cue that you are exaggerating just how good something is.

Well, what about all the hype about positive thinking? Isn't it good to think positively? Yes, but only if the positive thinking is realistic. The problem with terrificizing is that it is *unrealistic* positive thinking. In fact, it can often be used to avoid confronting important realities. So you tell yourself that your husband is the best husband in the world because he gave you that precious diamond watch, and wined and dined you in that extravagant five-star restaurant. Oh, did you forget that last week he physically assaulted you, and gave you a black eye? "Well," you respond, "there must have been a very good reason for that. Too much stress at the office or maybe it was something I said. I'm so lucky to have him anyway." After all, he's god. Right? Wrong!

From the halo that forms around perfection you can even deduce depression. "My boyfriend, who just dumped me, was the nicest person. No one could *ever* measure up to him. *And now he's gone forever*!" Yes, he probably is gone forever. So, where does that leave you? Depressed.

"The grass is always greener on the other side." At least it might appear to be greener, if you don't look closely enough. In calling people or things perfect you often set yourself up for disappointment by not taking a careful look. Actually, few things in this imperfect world are truly perfect or the best, and when you return from never-never land to face reality, you are likely to find this out—hopefully not the hard way. Things are rarely if ever, terrific, perfect, and the best in the world; but neither are they apt to be awful, horrible, and terrible. As Aristotle would say, the answer generally lies somewhere in between these extremes. Learning to live with such realistic expectations is a useful antidote to unhappiness.

I-Can't-Stand-It-Itis

When you accept a rule of this kind, you tell yourself that, if you find something difficult or challenging to deal with, then it must be beyond your capacity to tolerate and you cannot and must not ever hope to succeed at it. In embracing this kind of rule, you are likely to deduce intense frustration upon encountering difficult or challenging circumstances. Your threshold of toleration is likely to be diminished to the point that you will fail to give yourself an adequate shot at things. This is known as "low frustration tolerance."[9] It prevents you from tolerating frustration in the short run in order to achieve a more lasting, future happiness. Quite obviously, many things in life worth having are things that you will need to work for. If you are unwilling to tolerate the measure of frustration that comes with trial and error, then you are not likely to succeed. This is what makes low frustration tolerance self-fulfilling. You really *won't* succeed.

Many things (such as the list of things mentioned under the discussion of Awfulizing) are difficult and frustrating, but this does not mean that you are *unable* to stand them. Human beings are quite resilient creatures and can often, eventually, get through tough situations even if it *feels* hopeless en route. While you can't literally stand up to a Mack truck coming at you at 100 mph, you really *can* eventually get through many situations that you find frustrating.

It is easy to miss this unrealistic *under*assessment of your powers of toleration partly because it is so common in Western society. Pop culture, including movies and songs, often trade on themes about the inability of people to stand things that they really can stand. It's common, for example, to hear songs and watch movies that deliver the message, "I can't stand to live without you, baby. Without you, I will just wilt and die." In reality, people who suffer great losses, including the loss of beloved family members, can usually stand to go on living.

This said, it is quite *understandable* how people who suffer serious losses such as the death of a loved one will even deduce depression by telling themselves how they can't stand to live with their losses. Empathy can go a long way in such cases, and those who suffer such losses can benefit from someone to express their grief to in these extreme circumstances. Expressing your grief by saying how you can't stand going on living is one powerful way of getting this unrealistic rule out on the table for inspection. Failure to grieve means failure to look at your premises, and this is likely to leave you deducing depression until you finally (if ever) do go through the grieving process.

A useful antidote to low frustration tolerance is to avoid language that disavows your ability to tolerate difficult or even crisis situations. The "I can't" in *I can't stand it*, should, more realistically, be replaced with "I won't" or "I choose not to" stand it. Reconceptualizing your situation in this way puts you in the driver's seat. It recognizes that you have the power to stand up to a frustrating situation, and to succeed. "I can't" is a language of disempowerment. It says that your emotional existence is beyond your control. "I won't" is an affirmation of your unwillingness to assert the power that is yours to assert. It portends your freedom.

DAMNATION

By accepting a rule of this nature, you tell yourself that, if there is something about yourself or about another person that you strongly dislike, then you or this other person is *totally* worthless. There are two forms of this rule. In the one, you damn yourself (Damnation of Self). In the other, you damn another person (Damnation of Others). In embracing a rule of the first kind, you are likely to deduce extreme guilt when you perceive yourself as having done something morally wrong; and you'll deduce depression when you perceive yourself as suffering from some deficiency, or as having failed at something significant. What is popularly called an "inferiority complex" is rooted in this form of rule. In embracing a rule of the second kind (Damnation of Others), you are likely to deduce anger, even rage.

As Aristotle suggested, it is irrational to underrate yourself just as it is irrational to overrate yourself. If you underrate yourself, he says, you are being "unduly humble." On the other hand, if you overrate yourself, you are being "vain."[10] The most extreme form of vanity is the "god complex"—telling yourself that you are perfect or near perfect, and that you rarely if ever do anything wrong. If this is what you are telling yourself, then there is a good chance you are accepting an absolutistic rule that says you must be perfect or near perfect in order to avoid being completely or almost completely worthless. So, to avoid damning yourself, you may be going to the other extreme of telling yourself you're god. This is a tough façade to keep up. Aristotle's antidote: Avoid *both* extremes. Give yourself permission to be an imperfect human being capable of making mistakes, but nevertheless capable of learning from them. It's a lot less stressful!

Have you ever told yourself that you were worthless, that you could never do anything right, that you were a complete waste? Many of us have, in our less profound moments, picked ourselves apart like this after we said or did something that we later perceived as being stupid. How do you *feel* when you say things like this? Low down and maybe even depressed, right?

There is a large difference between negatively rating the *deed* and negatively rating the *doer*. If you do something completely stupid, hurtful, or even very immoral, what you have done might well be completely worthless. But this does not mean that *you* are completely worthless! If you tell yourself that you are a worthless scumbag for having committed adultery with your best friend's spouse, you are likely to feel extreme, debilitating guilt. On the other hand, if you tell yourself that what you did was wrong, that you should not have done it, and that you can competently decide to try to act differently in the future, then your personal dignity is preserved. You will feel regretful and even guilty for having violated a moral principle to which you still subscribe, but you will not *feel* nearly so bad.

Have you ever said damning things of another person? Many, indeed most of us, have. "That piece of shit!" you exclaim. "That rotten, good-for-nothing bitch took my parking space, and she even saw I was waiting for it first!" How do you *feel* about the person whom you have just branded a piece of shit? Answer: *angry, very angry*. On the other hand, consider the look and feel of saying, "Taking that parking space was a pretty rotten thing to do, but human beings aren't perfect, and they sometimes act inconsiderately." Does this calm you down a bit?

I have sometimes been asked about how many misdeeds it takes before someone really does become a worthless person. Indeed, aren't some *single* acts—like murder and rape—bad enough to justify such a reduction to utter worthlessness?

The response I generally give to this query is this: There are different senses of worth or value. A person may be valuable in an *instrumental* sense because he or she provides a useful service. For example, a man who abuses his wife and children by evening, and, by day, picks up and hauls off trash, still performs a very valuable community service. I am aware of a pedophile who frequently also acted as a Good Samaritan when others were stranded on the roadside and in need of vehicle assistance. While I could understand why an associate of mine, who counseled some of the children whom he had sodomized, was happy to learn of his untimely death from natural causes, it would be false to say that he was *entirely* worthless.

A person can also be valuable in an *intrinsic* sense, if he or she is a subject of worthwhile experiences (such as rational insights, mental pleasures, and pleasures of the flesh). A person can also be considered to have value from a *religious* perspective, as a "child of God." A person can also have *moral* value (be morally good or bad). Commission of morally bad or wicked actions would then only tell against the person's moral worth, but would not make the person worthless in every other sense of the term. In the case of the child molester I just mentioned, his acts would seem to tell against his moral character, but not against his worth in every other sense. But even here, his Good Samaritanism may have saved him from complete *moral* devaluation.

So can a person ever be *entirely* morally worthless? If a person is said to be entirely morally worthless, this means that the person *never* does *anything* morally good. I doubt that there are very many people who fit this description. But never mind this. Surely there are, unfortunately, people who do more evil things than good, like the child molester I wrote of a moment ago. Can we not cut to the chase and brand them basically evil or no good?

I think that, even here, you would be speaking in shorthand about the specific things that these people do, which you deemed to be evil. Further, if you wish to speak clearly and precisely about what you disapprove of in such individuals, then you might as well just talk about these specific deeds. Global judgments about the person's worthlessness are vague and usually uninformative.

For Aristotle, to be a wicked or bad person, you had to be in a *habit* of voluntarily doing wicked acts.[11] For him, apart from such a persistent habit, the term was vacuous. But if this is what being wicked or bad means, then you need to *prove* that the person in question really does have such a persistent habit. In so doing, you are likely to find that there are only *some* specific deeds to which you object. In some cases, you may find that the deeds in question are not done voluntarily—but instead out of ignorance of certain facts. In other cases, you may find that these deeds are not even *a result* of habit. For example, suppose your child tells a lie. Does that mean that he's a liar? To be a *liar* means to be in a habit of telling lies. If telling a lie made a person a liar, then most, if not all of us, would be liars.

The point of serious moral criticism is usually to encourage constructive moral change either in doers of bad deeds or in those who may be influenced by their bad example. In either case, this requires that you condemn the actions, not the doers. In the case of doers of bad deeds, telling them that they are entirely worthless amounts to saying that they are incapable of doing anything good. So, you defeat the very point of moral criticism. On the other hand, if the point of the moral criticism is to instruct others in how to (or not to) *act*, then, once again, it is necessary to address the worthlessness of the deed, not of the doer.

Finally, global judgments about the worthlessness of human beings *dehumanize* those who are subject to them. In relegating persons to garbage, we give ourselves permission to trash them. It is well known that a soldier on the battlefield can much more easily kill the enemy if the latter is conceived as something less than human. This is a dangerous way to view other human beings in the arena of life, whatever its merits on the battlefield.

So, leave the doer alone, yourself and others, and stick to rating the deed. This is an extremely important antidote. Keep it handy as you inspect your own emotional reasoning.

Unfortunately, human beings have come up with a plethora of words for going after the jugular of personhood. Here's but a trifling: "weirdo," "jerk," "dork," "retard," "fat pig," "schmuck," "shithead," "nerd," "idiot," "scumbag," "motherfucker," "asshole," and "butthead." In their ordinary usage, such words frequently make no literal sense. Does a person ever really think with his butt? Is a person's head ever literally filled with excrement?

Some derogatory labels are gender specific. Here are some popular ones targeting women. Calling a woman a "bitch" classifies her under a rule that degrades her and directs you to feel and act disrespectfully toward her. Calling a woman a "whore," "ho," "slut," or "tramp," for some, pathologically classifies her as totally worthless garbage that can be raped or otherwise trashed. For others, this classification carries degradation short of such brutality but nevertheless still objectifies her entire person as a mere object of pleasure. On the other hand, calling her a "woman," a "person," or a "human being" militates against such hostility or degradation and keeps the door open for treating her as a self-determining rational being whose consent is always a condition of sexual engagement or other intimate relationships.

But, "Surely," you say, "aren't there really whores and sluts in the world? Aren't some women worthy of being called these things?" No! There certainly are prostitutes who get paid for sex. This is their profession. But some people call some women "whores" because they believe that these women are promiscuous, not necessarily because they think that they receive payment for sexual services. But never mind this. In calling someone a whore, you are doing more than simply pointing to indiscriminate sexual habits. You are berating the entire person, not merely assigning a profession to her or condemning her perceived sexual habits. You are directing contemptuous emotions and behavior against this person. This is doing more, much more, than attacking the deed.

This is also true of *racially* derogatory labels. Calling a person a "nigger" brings the *entire person*, and not just his or her skin color, under a damning rule directing discriminatory emotions and behavior. For some, calling a person this amounts to a pathological, *total* damnation and dehumanization, directing violent, abusive acts, even killing.

Derogatory labels of *sexual orientation* provide further examples. In calling a person a "homo" or a "dyke" you typically classify an entire person under a rule that directs ridicule, scorn, or other forms of unjust discrimination, and, occasionally, even killing.

People who mistreat or abuse other persons usually manage first to bad-mouth them. So classified, the defamed persons are subjected to oppressive, hostile, or otherwise abusive treatment. You have no doubt heard the cliché, "Sticks and stones can break your bones but names can never harm you." Like most clichés, this one is grossly oversimplified. Dirty names are typically the precursors of harmful treatment of others because they classify people under rules that direct such treatment. So, taking these damning labels lightly can be a serious mistake.

If you are on the receiving end of such verbal assaults, chances are that you are not *just* being called vacuous names. Instead, it is likely that you are being mistreated in other ways too. It is sometimes easy, over extended periods, to get used to being called dirty or unflattering names by people who play a significant role in your life. But the effects are not always apparent to those in this situation. To give you an example, I once had a twenty-one-year-old student whose father persisted in calling him dummy from the time he was a small child. As a consequence, this very intelligent young man came to regard himself as a stupid, unworthy person. He told me that it was not until he began college that he came to realize that he was not a dummy after all, and that he had impressive abilities in math and science.

If *you* are prone to berating others, then it is likely that your relationships with these individuals are suffering. In addition, you are probably needlessly causing yourself stress. How good could you possibly feel when you tell yourself that you are married to an "idiot," or that your son is a "reject," or that your best friend is a "schmuck"? Learning to avoid bad-mouthing others can save you as well as others a lot of unnecessary sweat.

When you have a gripe with yourself or with others, don't use derogatory labels to express your gripe. Don't say, "That *idiot* insulted me again." Say instead, "John said something again that I thought was insulting." Don't say, "What an *asshole* I was to trust her." Say, instead, "I erred in trusting her." Don't say, "That *two-timing whore* was having an affair all along." Say, instead, "Mary was having an affair all along." By avoiding self-defeating, derogatory, unrealistic, damning labels, and by rating the deed instead of the doer, you are less likely to get yourself into emotional and behavioral hot water.

I Just Can't Help This Feeling

In accepting a rule infected with this type of malady you tell yourself that, if you feel depressed, anxious, angry, guilty, or otherwise upset, then you might as well just accept and go with your feeling because it is really not in your control anyway. By embracing a rule of this nature, you, in effect, give yourself permission to continue your self-defeating and irrational lines of thinking, feeling, and acting. Through your acquiescence, you become an accomplice and sponsor of your own unhappiness.

You sustain your own misery by denying any responsibility for your emotions. You do this by blaming other people and external events. You tell yourself that it's not you but rather the things other people say or do, and the things that happen in the course of your life, that make you angry, piss you off, aggravate you, make you mad, sad, anxious, guilt-ridden, or depressed. You are the passive recipient of your feelings, along for the ride but not, yourself, in the driver's seat. You are exempt from responsibility for the way you feel. After all, why would you be so irrational as to inflict pain upon yourself? Right? Wrong!

Centuries after Plato and Aristotle, the stoic philosopher, Epictetus (60–117 C.E.) noted that it is not events in the world that upset us, but rather the ways in which we think about them. Following this lead, psychologist Albert Ellis advanced one of the most important and influential modalities of psychotherapy to date, known as Rational-Emotive Behavior Therapy (REBT). The keynote of this theory is that we feel what we think. Events and other people do not make us feel good or feel bad; we do it to ourselves, cognitively.[12] So, you are largely the culprit. When you get pissed off, you do a lot of the pissing yourself; *you* make *yourself* mad, sad, anxious, guilt-ridden, or depressed. You do these things by the thoughts you think.

"But how," you ask, "can I help what I feel if I can't even help what I think?" There is some truth to this, and here it is: You do not have *complete* control over your thoughts and your emotions. Associations with past experiences can conjure up thoughts that may seem to arise of their own volition. Autonomic nervous system functions that have evolved through a process can short-circuit thinking altogether in responding immediately to an environmental crisis. In cases of cognitive dissonance, you can have thoughts and feelings that, on an intellectual level, you know are unreasonable. In anxiety disorders such as obsessive-compulsive disorder, the thoughts you dread the most seem to control you.

In the case of obsessive-compulsive disorder, medicine may sometimes be needed to help you regain control over your own thoughts. But, even here, these thoughts usually do most of their dirty work because of what you are thinking about them. For example, by telling yourself that you "couldn't stand it" if you had that "horrible" thought again, you deduce your own fear of it, and *make yourself* into its passive victim, thus *giving* it power over you. On the other hand, by giving up your I-Can't-Stand-It-Itis, and Awfulizing, and instead saying, "Oh well, there's that unrealistic thought again. So what?" you can disarm the thought and thereby regain significant control over your own mind. Like Freddie Krueger, the phantoms of your own imagination can harm you only if *you* let them!

In cases of cognitive dissonance (where your feelings and knowledge disagree), you may have some irrational premises that still hold a grip on your emotions. Nevertheless, you are still free to find antidotes to them and to flex your willpower muscle to give them a voice. In cases of knee-jerk automatic responses to your environment, your emotions are short-lived and require your thinking to sustain them. And, by finding an antidote to your irrational premises, you can change your emotions. For example, instead of telling yourself that you must never make any mistakes on the job, you can more realistically give yourself permission to be imperfect. Just think of how much more relaxed you would feel. So, while you do not have *total* freedom to control your thoughts and emotions, you have a considerable amount of freedom. Do you agree? Think about what it would mean to disagree. It would mean that you are a walking, talking biological machine, albeit a complex one. As you will see in chapter 11, this is not a realistic hypothesis.

A useful antidote to I Just Can't Help This Feeling thinking is to admit your freedom and responsibility for your emotions. Refusing to do so leaves you passively in the throes of your emotions, letting your irrational thinking run wild, sustaining and permitting the looping and galloping of emotions. Admitting your freedom and responsibility in managing your emotions puts you in charge. It is a first and essential step in the process of taking control of your emotions.

Many freedom/responsibility-disavowing words exist in language. These include phrases that let you conceal your freedom/responsibility by falsely and unrealistically making you sound like a passive recipient of your emotions. Here are some examples: "aggravate me," "piss me off," "upset me," "depress me," "make me anxious or nervous," and "lay a guilt trip on me." In using words like these you divest yourself of any responsibility for producing and sustaining your own emotions, and thereby idly permit them to continue.

Do you believe in free will and responsibility? Are you more highly evolved than a simple organism that responds automatically and mechanically to external stimuli? Then try these instead: "aggravate myself," "upset myself," "piss myself off," "depress myself," "make myself anxious," and "make myself feel guilty."[13] If someone (or something) is aggravating you, then it is not your fault if you continue to be aggravated. After all, it's the other guy who needs to stop pressing your buttons. On the other hand, if *you* are doing the aggravating, then it's up to you to stop. The responsibility rests squarely on your shoulders. The ball is then in your court.

Thou Shalt Upset Yourself

With this rule as your credo, you tell yourself that if you encounter a problem in your life that you deem important, then you have a *moral duty*, yes, a moral duty, to ruminate over it, never stop thinking about it, make yourself miserable and upset over it, and demand that others, for whom you also deem it a problem, do the same. In embracing a rule of this nature you are likely to keep yourself in an unnecessary and prolonged state of irritability, anxiety, and malaise, and create a stressful emotional atmosphere for significant others who must deal with you.

"Well," you ask, "Isn't it the morally responsible thing to do to keep thinking about your problems until they are solved?" And I answer, "Not when your ruminating over a problem itself becomes a problem. While you may in most cases (but not necessarily all) have a moral duty not to covet your neighbor's wife, to honor your father or mother, not to kill others, not to steal, and so forth, there is no additional "eleventh commandment" to make yourself miserable when you have a problem. It is unrealistic to think that solutions to your problems must always be bought with personal grief. Rational approaches to problem solving involve clearly defining your problem, brainstorming about solutions, collecting evidence, reaching a conclusion, and implementing your decision in action.[14] No part of this approach says that you need to sweat bullets or that you need to work yourself up into a panic, or depress yourself or otherwise screw yourself over emotionally. This, in fact, is likely to adversely affect your ability to think straight. High levels of stress tend to have adverse effects on your ability to think clearly, to remember things, and to concentrate. By stressing yourself out, you may be defeating the very purpose of your worrying in the first place.

I had a client who worried almost incessantly about the health of her children. When one of her children needed a vaccination, she would spend hours and hours on the Internet researching studies about its possible adverse effects. This sounds reasonable so far, but once she had gathered her information, she would turn it over and over and over and over and over . . . weighing the benefits and potential risks, and then starting again for days and even weeks. In this period, she would rehash the same facts and raise the same questions during virtually all her contact hours with her husband. When her husband became annoyed and refused to discuss the matter further, she became angry with him and told him how he was an irresponsible parent. Eventually, she would reach a decision and go with it, but it was not without sweating bullets. This person was an extremely intelligent person, and she certainly gained a handle on her subject matter before she made a decision. Unfortunately, the rocky turf that had to be traversed in order to get to the final decision left her and her husband very stressed. And guess what? After she was finished executing this duty, she went on, in a matter of days, sometimes hours, to another crisis, which she *had to,* as a matter of moral necessity, slavishly pursue, dragging her husband along with her into the depths of this infinite, relentless black hole.

Behind my client's kind of relentless self-infliction of suffering was an unrealistic demand for absolute and ultimate certainty in the resolution of her problems. When she had a decision to make that could possibly have significant consequences for the lives of those whom she cherished, she sought to make *sure* that she made the correct choice. So not only did she dutifully and unrealistically upset herself, she also unrealistically vowed to keep it up until she achieved what she never really could achieve: absolute certainty!

Here's an antidote to this unreason. Don't demand absolute certainty about problems of living. Instead, content yourself with probability. Whether you like it or not, nothing in life is *ever* certain. OK, if you want to count death and taxes as certain, then go ahead, but even here these things are only *practically* certain, not theoretically certain. For all practical purposes you might as well count them as certain, but it is still conceivable that, someday we will manage to conquer death and do away with taxes. (Well, I admit that conquering death may be easier to imagine than getting rid of taxes!) *Nothing*, yes *nothing*, in this material world of ours is ever absolutely, *theoretically* certain. So you are being unrealistic if you try to get it!

Another antidote: You should be prepared to tolerate *ambiguity* in life decisions. Sometimes there just isn't a right answer; sometimes there's more than one; and most often, even a reasonable solution has its negative points. The latter is especially true in making moral choices.

In my work as a medical ethics consultant, I have seen many ethical dilemmas where no matter *what* choice was made, there was not likely to be a happy ending. In one tragic situation, a young, beautiful, bright seventeen-year-old girl had become comatose after her car went out of control and plunged into a canal. During her stay in the hospital, she developed an acute, systemic bacterial infection. While the hospital had the acute care facility for managing her infection, it did not have the facility for stimulating the brains of comatose patients. On the other hand, the other hospitals that specialized in treating these patients had no acute care facility for managing her infection. This girl's poor mother agonized over these two options and finally chose to transfer her daughter to a hospital that specialized in treating comatose patients. Unfortunately, the young woman died in this facility a few months later from the infection.

I often think about the agony this loving mother must have experienced in trying to do her best for her daughter. I believe that, in the end, she made a reasonable decision, but her decision might have been equally as rational had she decided to keep her daughter in the first hospital with acute care facility. In this inherently iffy world of ours, the best you may sometimes be able to do is to make reasonably informed judgments, and then hope (or pray) for the best.

Notes

1. *Ethics*, book 6, ch. 1.
2. "[N]o one, he [Socrates] said, when he judges acts against what he judges best—people act so only by reason of ignorance." *Ethics*, book 7, ch. 2.
3. John Stuart Mill, "Utilitarianism," in *The Utilitarians* (New York: Doubleday, 1973), p. 410.
4. William James, *Pragmatism* (New York: Meridian, 1980), p. 145.
5. C. I. Lewis, *An Analysis of Knowledge and Valuation* (LaSalle, Ill.: Open Court Publishing Co., 1971), p. 372.
6. *Ethics*, book 6, ch. 4.

7. James, *Pragmatism*, pp. 134–35.

8. Elliot D. Cohen, *Caution: Faulty Thinking Can Be Harmful to Your Happiness* (Ft. Pierce, Fla.: Trace-WilCo, Inc., 1992), p. 8.

9. Albert Ellis, *Overcoming Destructive Beliefs, Feelings, and Behavior* (Amherst, N.Y.: Prometheus Books, 2001).

10. *Ethics*, book 4, ch. 2.

11. *Ethics*, book 3, ch. 5.

12. Susan R. Walen, Raymond DiGiuseppe, and Windy Dryden, *A Practitioner's Guide to Rational-Emotive Therapy*, 2d ed. (New York: Oxford University Press, 1992), p. 16.

13. You should also avoid saying, "I am aggravated," "I am pissed," "I am depressed," "I am anxious," "I am feeling guilty." These expressions do not clearly recognize your free will and power over your own feelings. For example, you can say, "I am depressed and have no control over how I feel." But it is logically odd, if not inconsistent, to say, "I am depressing myself but have no control over the way I feel." Compare Ellis and Harper's use of what they call "E-prime," a form of English which eliminates the verb *to be*. Albert Ellis and Robert A. Harper, *A New Guide to Rational Living* (N. Hollywood, Calif.: Wilshire Books, 1975), pp. xiii–xiv. This linguistic approach to psychology is an application of principles first developed by Alfred Korzybski. See his *Science and Sanity* (Concord, Calif.: International Society of General Semantics, 1933/1990).

14. Elliot D. Cohen and Gale S. Cohen, *The Virtuous Therapist* (Belmont, Calif.: Wadsworth, 1999), pp. 35–47.

Chapter 6

Rules That May Be Impeding the Quality of Your Interpersonal Relations

In gatherings of men, in social life and in the interchange of words and deeds, some men are thought to be obsequious, namely those who to give pleasure, praise everything and never oppose, but think it their duty 'to give no pain to the people they meet'; while those who, on the contrary, oppose everything and care not a whit about giving pain are called churlish and contentious. . . . [T]he middle state is laudable—that in virtue of which a man will put up with, and will resent the right things and in the right way.

—Aristotle[1]

How are you relating to others and they to you? Are you getting along? Are your attempts at getting along or fitting in frequently getting you into hot water? Often, there are fallacies of action afoot when relations are rocky, unfulfilling, or getting you into trouble. If this sounds familiar, then chances are that you (and/or your significant others) are subscribing to one or more of these rules of action: (1) The-World-Revolves-

Around-Me Thinking, (2) Blackmailing, (3) Making a Stink, (4) Pity Mongering (5) Beating Around the Bush, (6) Poisoning the Well, (7) Getting Even, and (8) Jumping on the Bandwagon.

Let's take a look at each of these rules. Keep an open mind. At least some of them may ring a bell.

The-World-Revolves-Around-Me Thinking

When you accept this rule, you tell yourself that, whatever you prefer reveals the one true reality, and that, therefore, everybody else must also share your preferences. Reality must conform to your ideas rather than your ideas to reality. *You* are the center of the universe, the ultimate beacon of truth. So, if you like Swiss cheese, then Swiss cheese it is. If you think vegetarians are ridiculous, then let the steaks be served, medium rare, of course, if that's how you like them. If you dislike washing dishes and prefer that your partner do it, then it is right and good that your partner, not you, wash the dishes. If you are Christian, Jew, Muslim, Hindu, witch, atheist, capitalist, Communist, Democrat, Republican, liberal, or conservative, then the reality of God, Nature, Earth, humanity, state, nation, or Society is according to your personal fiat, and all else is but blasphemy or idolatry. Intolerant are those who disagree with you. Tolerance is thinking and doing as you do. Right? Wrong!

This is closer to the truth: There is often more than one reasonable way of slicing up reality. Many of the issues that people get embroiled over have alternative realities. Preferences for foods, movies, TV shows, religion, politics, travel, decorating, chores (cooking, cleaning, watching the kids), sports, and many other human interests are variable and always subject to disagreement. These disagreements cannot always be easily settled rationally by simply pointing out the facts. Rational argument can come to a screeching halt when you like spinach and your partner hates it. Reminding your partner that it's healthy need not settle the matter, and it may be pointless to belabor the point if your partner just doesn't care about how healthy it is. Insisting on the spinach is more likely to breed *unhealthy* resentment.

As a human being who sees things in terms of your own ideas, experiences, bodily influences, and so forth, you are not alone if you, to one extent or another, try to peddle your own view of reality to others. Most, if not all of us, do this to one extent or another, with respect to at least some of our preferences.

Most people have the unique human capacity to empathize with others. Do you recall how you felt the last time someone tried to force you to conform to *his* preferences? Of course you do. You can empathize, then, if you try to do the same thing. This does not mean that you have to agree with preferences that don't match your own. What it means is that you should not assume that someone else's reality must always accord with your standards, and that you have the right to force-feed your reality to others.

Here, then, is an antidote to this malady. If you find that the world revolves around you, try *empathizing*. Instead of picking the other guy apart according to your own view of reality, put yourself in his or her subjective shoes, and see what's right, good, and true from his or her perspective. Again, you don't have to agree in the end, but you don't have to share a perspective to *understand* it. Understanding breeds tolerance. Your goal should be understanding. In disputes over preferences it is often fruitful to agree to disagree!

This mutual respect and understanding can be given a practical voice through *compromise*. For example, when an interfaith couple doesn't see eye to eye about how to raise the children, both partners can agree to raise the children within the religious traditions and tenets of *both* faiths. If you like action thrillers, and your partner likes romantic comedies, then you can take turns choosing your movie or video. If neither you nor your partner like washing dishes, then you can take turns or get a dishwasher or use paper plates. If you try, you can usually find several mutually agreeable alternatives. So, here's to tolerance, mutual respect, empathy, understanding, and the willingness to compromise.

For Aristotle, right and wrong largely depended on people's circumstances. Six pounds of food, he said, might be "too little for Milo [a famous wrestler], too much for the beginner in athletic exercises."[2] The right amount of food—not too much and not too little—would be different for each.

An R-rated movie could be an excellent choice for you, given your level of maturity, but unsuitable for your ten-year-old child. Being a doctor might have been a good career choice for you, but a bad idea for your son who has different interests and aptitudes. A vacation in Tahiti might bode well for you and yours (if you happen to have plenty of money), but ill advised for friends struggling to make ends meet. Jogging a few miles daily might be healthful exercise for you, but dangerous for your partner who has a heart condition.

So here's another antidote: Before you judge what's good or bad for others, take a careful look at their (relevant) circumstances. Listen carefully to what they have to say about their own case. You may find that what's good for the goose, may not always be good for the gander (and vice versa).

Blackmailing

You know what it means to be blackmailed into doing something, right? Well the rule of blackmailing tells you to get what you want from others by withdrawing or threatening to withdraw something of value from them. This might be some material object such as financial support, but, in close interpersonal relations, it oftentimes is an emotion such as love or affection. It might also be sex or the refusal to honor a promise, or the threat to divorce or have an affair. So, instead of attempting to work out your differences, you resort to some form of force. For example, John tells Sally that unless she "puts out," he's going to break up with her. Samantha gives Art the "silent treatment" to get him to agree to spend their summer vacation visiting her parents.

Unfortunately, relations based on such coercive tactics are not usually worth maintaining, so conceding to the blackmailer's demands is as self-defeating as making them. By conceding, there is precedent for further blackmail in the future, so the problem usually doesn't end with the single instance but instead continues into perpetuity.

So, if John makes sex a condition of dating Sally, even though she is averse to this, then it is probably time for Sally to say "adiós." If she concedes now, she will end up conceding later too, and the relationship will continue in this vicious cycle of exploitation.

It is much better to base your relationship on mutual trust and respect than to base it on coercion and threats. If you are on the receiving end of a blackmail attempt, a useful antidote is usually to refuse to comply with the demands of the blackmailer, so long as this is a reasonable possibility.

This is true of close intimate relationships and it is also true of relationships in the workplace, school, and in the community. Doing sexual favors in the workplace in order to get ahead is not uncommon. But, while sleeping with the boss can land you a better job, you also need to consider the loss of dignity you suffer when the boss decides that he is finished using you. You are then reduced to an object that has been manipulated by another for his or her personal aggrandizement. The ending is not usually a happy one, even if it sometimes provides a monetary reward. You are worth more than this!

Most of us have resorted to blackmail of some form or other on occasion. But if this is your rule of action, then you too are putting yourself down. In effect, you are telling yourself that you, yourself, are not worthy of a respectful interpersonal relationship, and that the only way, yes the *only* way, you can get what you want is to blackmail others. This is a dark picture for you to paint of yourself. Better to save your personal dignity than to degrade your self-worth.

The great eighteenth-century German philosopher Immanuel Kant once said, "Act in such a way that you always treat humanity, whether in your own person or in the person of any other, never simply as a means, but always at the same time as an end."[3] Translation: "Treat yourself as well as other people, as rational, self-determining persons and not as objects manipulated." For Kant, this was a moral law. It is a useful rule to keep in mind in cultivating your interpersonal relationships. By giving those people, especially those closest to you, an opportunity to make their own free decisions without force or coercion, you are recognizing them as "ends," not as mere objects manipulated for self-aggrandizing purposes. Kant was onto something big here. A relationship founded upon mutual respect for one another has a good shot at being a happy, fulfilling, and enduring one.

Making a Stink

In accepting this rule, you tell yourself that you must kick, scream, yell, or other sundry manner of throwing a temper tantrum in order to be respected, understood, heard, or heeded. You make yourself sound deranged in the hope that you will appear a pillar of reason. Not very rational, is it? If your windows are open, the more likely result is that you will become well known throughout your neighborhood, not, however, for your philosophical wisdom, attainment of nirvana, or serenity. When you make a stink, the odor often remains for some time, creating an atmosphere of tension and disunity in the household.

An antidote? Well, you could close the windows and then sound off, but that might not shield the sound of your screaming voice well enough. For your significant others whom you may be blasting or your impressionable children, this may be the moral equivalent of the *Rocky Horror Picture Show*. Better not to sound off at all. But how do you accomplish that?

Many years of relating on this level can be a tough nut to crack, especially when both partners in a long-term relationship have grown accustomed to making jointly blended stinks. First step: Admit that you are subscribing to this nutty rule and accept its refutation. Second, think Kant's moral law, mentioned above, using it as an antidote to stonewall your bodily feelings, images, and stinky rule, when you feel the urge to expel.

Rule: I shouldn't treat myself, or my significant others, like mere objects incapable of rational self-control.
Report: Throwing a temper tantrum to get what I want makes such objects out of both of us.
Action: I refrain from my usual tantrum.

As I said, it may not be so easy to successfully deduce the above conclusion. You will have to flex your willpower muscle to back up this antidotal line; but, in the end, you will gain the sweet feeling of success, and that of increased self-respect. It really *is* an admirable feat! But, you should not give up if you falter when your urge to expel returns. There's likely to be more hard work ahead.

Pity Mongering

The Pity Mongering rule says that if you are in trouble or are having difficulties getting what you want, you should cry, sob, weep, pout, mope, whine, or otherwise make yourself look hurt, dejected, downtrodden, demoralized, dejected, rejected, crucified, or otherwise pitiful.

In embracing this rule, you attempt to get others to abandon relevant standards for settling disputed matters and to act on pity instead. While the human sentiment of pity is an important sentiment that is often well deserved, it also can sometimes be out of place. The classic case of this is the defendant in a murder case who brings his shabbily dressed, teary-eyed children to the trial in order to get the jury's sympathy vote. Of course, the issue is not whether the children will miss their father if he is locked up, but rather whether he did, indeed, commit murder.

Sometimes feeling sorry for someone is a big mistake. A young woman I know was dating a young man who wanted to marry her. The woman, however, found him to be boring and was not especially physically attracted to him. Nevertheless, when she tried to break off the relationship, he became very distraught, so she kept seeing him. Finally, she got up enough nerve to break it off. I believe she finally did the right thing. It was neither fair to her nor to the young man to continue a relationship that was destined to fail. So, she needed to resist being manipulated by the young man's Pity Mongering, and to base her decision on relevant standards. In this case, the most important standard was whether she wanted to marry him, and not whether she felt sorry for him!

I had a client, Eddy, who thought that his wife, Claire, paid more attention to his two adult children than to him. Indeed, Claire was very much involved in her children's lives, and would telephone them daily. She was regularly a part of their personal, day-to-day decisions, and she would discuss their problems with her husband routinely, over dinner and during much of their other time together. When Eddy tried on occasion to discuss his own issues with Claire, the discussion was generally short-lived and the topic would shift back to some concern about a child. Despite protests from Eddy, Claire kept up her continual vigil over her children's lives, and her children, especially one of them, came to expect and even demand this arrangement.

Feeling helpless, jealous, and unloved, Eddy stopped making overtures to his wife. When they were together, he acted withdrawn, stopped trying to share his intimate life issues with her, and was generally unresponsive to her occasional attempts at showing him affection. Yet, what Eddy really wanted was her consistent affections and care. He wanted her to treat their relationship as primary, and not as an addendum to their children. He figured that their children were now adults, and that it was now their time to focus on one another.

Neither Eddy nor Claire had any close friends with whom to share their intimate life issues. So, their free time away from work was usually spent together, isolated from any other personal contact. I believe that Claire attempted to fill this void to a large extent through her involvement with her children. As for Eddy, he had no close friends with whom to share his issues, so he found counseling to be his only outlet for their expression. I encouraged Eddy to try to share his concerns with Claire, who was adverse to the idea of participating in counseling. But, unfortunately, while Claire agreed to pay more attention to their relationship, little actually changed. So Eddy became a Pity Mongerer in an attempt to rescue his relationship. Did it work? No! Here's why.

Claire did not even perceive Eddy's attempt at securing her affections as deserving of pity. She perceived him as self-centered, and was often offended by his lack of responsiveness to her overtures. So, the relationship just got worse as a result of Eddy's attempt at Pity Mongering.

An antidote? It is, of course, easy to say, "Give up your Pity Mongering. It's not working!" but this hardly provided a useful antidote to the problem at hand. Nor was it sufficient to advise Eddy to discuss his problem with his wife, because he had already tried this. So what to do?

Eddy's hunger for Claire's affections and his jealousy of his children were probably partly due to Eddy's lack of any other personal outlet. Here's an analogy that might help. When you do not have a balanced diet, trying to eat more of the same food group is not likely to make you healthier. So, if you don't have enough protein in your diet, it won't do to eat extra helpings of spaghetti. Eddy lacked one of his essential social outlet groups—friends—so he tried very hard to fill this void by getting "extra helpings" of Claire. I think Claire, who also did not have any personal friends, was trying to do the same with her children. So the antidote was to attain a more balanced social diet by trying to make friends with whom they could share their lives. Pity Mongering as a way of attaining intimacy can be a sign of a poor social diet. Finding the dietary deficiency and taking remedial measures to correct it can be a constructive antidote in such cases.

Beating Around the Bush

When you accept this rule you tell yourself that when you perceive someone as having made an unreasonable or wrongful request of you, but you feel intimidated to say no, then you should save face by verbally consenting while nonverbally dropping hints of your disapproval. You know the scene. Someone, say your boss, puts you on the spot. You want to say no, but you feel intimidated about refusing, so you say OK—your words say, "OK" but your tone of voice says, "Take this job and shove it!" And when asked if you're sure, you flash a Woody Allen smile and nod consent jerkily like a preprogrammed robot.

Behind your words of approval, you cry out, "What gall! Why don't you take a flying leap! I would rather cut off my arm than do this for you. Get my drift?" Unfortunately, people often perceive only what they want to perceive, and your drift might fall on deaf ears, drifting aimlessly out into space while you end up agreeing to something for which you really have strong feelings against.

Years back, when I was starting out as a postdoctoral fellow, I was asked by my program director to attend a conference at Purdue University in Indiana. There had been a very large blizzard that had caused most flights out West to be cancelled, but my flight was still on. My program director really wanted me to go, but my pregnant wife pleaded with me not to go. I felt a responsibility to her not to go, but when my boss coldly said to me, "You really don't have to go if you don't want to," really meaning "If you don't go, then you're a horse's ass!" I responded, "No, it's OK. I'll go," really meaning, "You know damn well I don't want to go, and take these risks with a baby on the way!" Well, I ended up going, but not without regretting it to this day. The flight was uneventful and I returned safely, but I had failed to stand up for what I thought was right. It was a useful lesson. I have since tried to be more vigilant about not letting myself be intimidated into doing something I believe to be wrong. I have since tried to be more open and direct in responding to requests.

In your working and personal relationships, it is inevitable that you will be asked to do things that you, for good reasons, don't want to do. The best antidote is not to beat around the bush but, instead, to decline and state your reasons. Usually, the truth is the best excuse, but there are often diplomatic ways of turning down requests you don't want to honor. It is not uncommon for those of us who say "Yes" to virtually all requests in the workplace to be branded "Yes Persons" and to be called upon regularly. The more you consent, the more you are likely to be asked!

What's the antidote here? Again, learn to say "no," to things you have good reason not to do, and state your reasons for declining. You can practice, too. So, what do you say the next time the boss asks you to fetch him a cup of coffee? You, whose job description never included being a servant, should *resist* saying, "OK," with a hint of "Why don't you get it yourself!" Instead, assert your willpower, and say, "Sorry. This is really not my job." The more you say NO the easier it's likely to get. Then you won't have to add "Fetching my boss's coffee every morning" to the list of skills on your resume. People will generally respect you when you provide a rational basis for your refusal, and for your discreetness in accepting assignments. This is more likely to earn you respect from others than Beating Around the Bush.

Poisoning the Well

This rule says that, if you don't want someone to do or believe something, then you should use strong, negative language to intimidate and dissuade this person from doing or believing this thing. When you publicly put poison in the well, few are likely to drink from it.

So you tell me that I would be an asshole if I listened to that crazy bastard. In this case, if I take the bait, then I will buy the following line of reasoning:

Rule: Anyone who believes that crazy bastard must be an asshole.
Report: I'm no asshole.
Action: I don't believe it.

But, as you can say, the rule in question is a damning one. It condemns entire persons rather than sticking to actions. So I would be buying an unrealistic rule if I took this bait. This is generally how Poisoning the Well works. You are baited to buy an unrealistic rule and then you save yourself from its implications by denying that it applies to you. You proudly proclaim, "I'm no asshole." True enough, you may have an anus without *being* one, but, in accepting this line of reasoning, you are making a mistake.

Is it a good idea to bait people like this? Not ordinarily. Here's why. When you relate to others by using such tactics, you are supporting irrational thinking. Preying off of their irrational tendencies and gullibility, you encourage people to commit fallacies. If you care about others, then this is a bad idea. You may be the first to complain if your significant other deduces self-defeating emotions from unrealistic premises. Would you like to live with someone who comes to the conclusion that *you* are an asshole? Well, by encouraging this type of thinking, you may shoot yourself in the foot!

An antidote? Here's one. If you want to persuade someone, then use rational argument instead of intimidation. In so doing, you set a standard that you are likely to want others to follow in treating you. As I have emphasized, successful, lasting relationships between people are usually forged by mutual respect. A practice of modeling and encouraging irrational thinking and intimidation is likely to backfire.

Getting Even

When you accept this rule you tell yourself that, if someone does something to you that you think is wrong, then you should do something equally wrong back so that you even the score. You have heard the saying, "Two wrongs don't make a right," right? Well, while it is a good idea not to blindly accept clichés, this one is quite true when properly understood. 1W + 1W = 2W. In mathematics, at least, this is correct. When you add up wrongs, you get wrongs, not rights.

"But isn't revenge sweet?" you may ask. "Doesn't it feel good to do something wrong to someone who has done something really wrong to you?" I answer: This very much depends upon what you mean by revenge. There can be a profound difference between "bringing someone to justice" and vengeance. Getting Even does not mean that you have been just. Fair and equitable retaliation to someone else's wrongs means that there is no wrong perpetuated on top of a wrong. In our criminal justice system, when a criminal is sentenced and punished for a crime, we normally do not say that we are doing something wrong to him. If we do say this, then we must also speak of a miscarriage of justice. In our justice system, wrongs are rectified, not by committing other wrongful acts, but by rightfully punishing the criminal. If someone attacked you and you responded by defending yourself, so long as you did not unnecessarily use force, you would be justified in your response. Killing another in self-defense, in our justice system, is generally regarded as justified homicide. So, the cases you might have thought illustrate that two wrongs sometimes make a right are not really such cases at all.

I had a married couple as clients who were inclined to do things back and forth to one another that, each later admitted, were wrongful acts done in the spirit of getting back at each other. When one said something perceived by the other as being nasty or condescending, the other said something back that was admittedly intended to be *even more* nasty and abusive. After all, Getting Even, in such situations, *really* means—sticking the knife in a little deeper for "good measure," and then some. So now there were two wrongs, instead of one. It didn't stop here, however. The other responded by completely ignoring the other for days, and then there was retaliation by the other in the form of name calling and threats of divorce. As the plot thickened and the wrongful conduct escalated, there was sometimes physical as well as emotional battery. When the dust settled, each realized that he or she had acted wrongly. Nevertheless, egged on by an unreasonable rule that demanded getting even, the process ended in self-defeating actions and low morale.

A useful antidote to this rule is *not* to "fight fire with fire" but, instead, to put out the brushfire with reason. So, instead of retaliatory strikes strategically intended to hurt the other, it is better to fight fire with sobering remarks like, "I don't appreciate being told I am stupid." This, at least, stops the crossfire, because in every "tit for tat" there must be a tat. Without returning a wrong for a wrong, there is no Getting Even. Get rational, not even!

JUMPING ON THE BANDWAGON

I have already referred to this rule (in chapter 1) in connection with the tragic case of my friend, Larry. In buying this rule, you tell yourself that you should—indeed, *must*—act, think, and feel exactly the way other people do, such as your friends, the popular or trendy folks, your schoolmates, the crowd, or average people. So, you downplay, even shun, individual differences that you may have with your favored group. Your life, from soup to nuts, is carved out for you by your subscription to this rule.

In your quest for conformity you therefore look unfavorably upon such values as individuality, authenticity, and creative living. Instead, you are a pack animal. When anybody who does not run with your pack tries to convince you that certain pack behavior is unacceptable, you discount this advice and often see those who offer it as defective, uncool, nerdy, or weird.

Have you ever done things because others were doing them? Of course you have. Human beings are great imitators. As children, we develop our own personality by imitating others whom we admire, especially our peers. As adolescents and adults, we continue this tendency by keeping up with the Joneses and by purchasing designer clothing. Let's suppose that, other things being equal (price, quality, and so forth, being the same), you had a choice between a shirt that said "Big K" in big bold letters on the front, and one that said "Polo." Which would *you* choose? Since I just asked you to assume that *everything else* is equal (the quality, price, and so forth), the only other thing left (short of liking the name better), is that Polo is trendy and Big K is not. So, if you preferred the Polo, this is probably why. If you are among the minority who would go with the Big K, then you might have done so because you think of yourself as a person of the people or just an average working class guy. If so, you would just be running with a different pack. (You could, of course, choose the Big K just to be outrageous, funny, or different.)

So, human beings do tend to travel in packs. But, if you accept the rule of Jumping on the Bandwagon, then you have erected a *mind-set* against anything, or virtually anything, short of conformity to your favored group. No questions asked, you go out of your way to conform. This is pathological conformity. It is pathological because it is *blind* conformity, and it is this failure to watch where you are going that is likely to get you into trouble.

Don't get me wrong. I am not saying that joining a pack of experts in a certain field is a fallacy. If nine out of ten competent physicians say to take brisk, half-hour walks several times a week for better health, then you would be justified in Jumping on this Bandwagon. The fallacy kicks in when you are blindly conforming to a group that itself has no special expertise in the behavior to which you are conforming. This amounts to double blindness. It is a case of the blind leading the blind.

To give you another example of how dangerous this type of blindness can be, consider this tale. Once upon a time, there was a popular craze for children (even for some bigger kids) to own Cabbage Patch Kids dolls. These dolls came with adoption papers, and some kids owned a whole family. Well, a major department store ran a sale on them. With only one doll remaining on the shelf, there was a mad dash for it. Unfortunately, in the pursuit, someone was trampled to death. The moral of this tale should be clear: People who mindlessly travel in packs tend to do self-defeating, regrettable things. Think about the great atrocities committed throughout history by mobs, and even nations of blind conformists.

Did you ever rebel as a teenager or even as a middle-aged adult? If you are old enough to remember what it was like in the sixties or seventies, you may recall a lot of rebellion going on. There was a sexual revolution afoot and many people were protesting. This may sound like everybody doing their thing, but if you looked a bit closer, you would have seen a lot of young people looking, acting, and talking alike. The "really groovy" dudes who got high on marijuana, had promiscuous sex, and tripped on acid were rather avid conformists. Mindlessly, they conformed, and mindlessly they lost their minds in a world of drugs and STDs. This was not a good scene if you happened to value individuality. The very value that fueled the rebellion was, paradoxically, transformed into mindless conformity. The drug culture today is no different. It's another pack of blind conformity, one with dangers galore.

So, if you find that you have a tendency to go along with the pack, no questions asked, here's a critical antidote for you: *Ask questions!* And try hard to get answers. If the answers you get just don't add up, then try even harder—flex that willpower muscle of yours—to keep yourself from blindly leaping off the proverbial cliff. It's not easy when your body is poised to leap. It's much easier to go with the flow, but *make yourself* look before you leap. You will feel yourself teetering at the edge of the cliff. Hold yourself back long enough to see what lies beneath. At the bottom of the abyss may be the corpses and bones of your fellow pack members!

NOTES

1. *Ethics*, book 4, ch. 5.
2. *Ethics*, book 2, ch. 6.
3. Immanuel Kant, *Groundwork of the Metaphysics of Morals*, trans. H. J. Paton (New York: Harper & Row, 1964), p. 96.

Chapter 7

Reports That May Be behind Your Self-Destructive Emotions and Actions

Practical reasoning is not only concerned with universals [rules]—it must also recognize the particulars [reports], for it is practical and practice is concerned with particulars.

—Aristotle[1]

If rules of emotion and rules of action were your only premises, then you would not be moved to feel or act on them. It is only when you perceive these rules as applying to you, in a particular situation, that they become active in your life. So, even if you accept the damning rule, "Anyone who inconsiderately does something that could seriously harm me is a stupid imbecile who deserves hell and eternal damnation," this rule would still not drive you to anger unless you also perceived someone as having actually done something inconsiderate that could harm you in some way.

If someone sneezed in your direction and you perceived this as an innocuous sign that this person may be coming down with a cold, then you may, if you want to be polite, wish the person good health. On the other hand, suppose, thinking that you might have felt the warm breeze conducted by the sneeze onto your face, you look at this person with daggers while thinking, "That stinking bastard probably has the flu." And you blurt out in a chilling tone, "You stupid moron, why don't you cover your damn mouth when you sneeze! You think I want to catch the plague from you!" That really would be rather much!

So, you need to do more than subscribe to a rule in order to deduce an emotion or action. You need also to *file a report*. By filing a report, I mean your act of interpreting the facts as falling under a rule. As in the above case, you would have interpreted the sneeze as an inconsiderate act having the potential (indeed, the probability) to seriously harm you (by giving you a dangerous disease). You can file such a report exclusively with yourself. This is sometimes called "self-talk"—you can register a perceived fact, under a particular rule, when you consciously think it to yourself. You can also file a report *with others*, as when you blurt something out or tell a close friend what happened. It is this act of filing your report (with yourself exclusively or with others also) that makes your rule *relevant* to your particular circumstances, and, thereby, allows you to deduce your response. As in the present case, if your report is unfounded (you are unable to provide evidence to prove it) or false, this can lead you to act and feel in self-defeating and regrettable ways. Come on now! Did you really know that the sneezing guy *probably* had the flu or some exotic disease?

Being on the lookout for fallacies in your reports can help you to abort some of your troublesome actions and emotions. These are some of the more virulent strains: (1) Overgeneralizing, (2) Black-or-White Thinking, (3) Magnifying Risks, (4) Wishful Thinking, (5) Concocting Explanations, (6) Could-a/Would-a/Should-a Thinking, and (7) Personifying.

Overgeneralizing

Reports filed with this infection often confuse "some" with "all" or "almost all." One virulent form of this is *stereotyping*. Try this one out for size: "All men are after just one thing." Is that a stereotype? Perhaps you are smiling and thinking, "No, it's really true!" But this would be Overgeneralizing. Some men are after *other* things too, even if most want sex. They also want companionship, friendship, security, children, and many other things. Remember, the statement was that, "All men are after *just* one thing." Further, the palpable fact that some men are irresponsible and indiscriminate in exercising their sexual desires is not sufficient to support a generalization about all or most men. So, before you judge all men (or any other group), take a more careful look at whom you are judging.

Do you know the origin of the word "stereotype"? It doesn't mean a type of stereophonic system such as Sony or Panasonic! It derives from a printer's stamp used to stamp out the same message over and over again. Like the stamp, stereotyping makes no allowance for individual differences between people in the stereotyped group, but instead treats them all the same. Whether your stereotype is positive—"All blacks have rhythm"—or negative—"All blondes are dumb"—these departures from reality lump all together.

Have *you* ever stereotyped anyone? If you said no, I suspect that you have not looked carefully into your own mental closet. Most of us have at least some skeletons. Whether your stereotype is of used-car salespersons, politicians, lawyers, blacks, whites, Christians, Muslims, Jews, southerners, New Yorkers, gays, blondes, teenagers, or hosts of other groups, you are likely to find at least some stereotypes lurking in the corridors of your mind.

The environment of human interpersonal encounters and interactions is very complex. On a daily basis, you may interact with many other people, some of whom you know little about and others whom you may not know at all. To deal with this complexity, some streamlining of reality is inevitable. According to Walter Lippmann (the fellow who coined the term "stereotyping"), "for the most part we do not first see, and then define, we define first and then see."[2] You first pick out what your culture has already defined for you, and then you perceive reality through these definitions.

In this way, stereotypes condense reality into more manageable packages, so that your "blooming, buzzing universe" becomes tidier. This may well be a part of the human evolutionary endowment for survival. If you did not pick out some aspects of reality and bring them under certain useful categories, you would be inefficient in responding to emergencies. On the other hand, this reliance on stereotypes can bias your perspectives and lead to self-defeating responses.

This is often the case when you use cultural stereotypes of different groups of people instead of your personal knowledge. You might define the black guy or the white guy first, and then see and respond to him in terms of this stereotype. But you shouldn't *assume* the black guy is lazy (or has rhythm or whatever), or that the white guy belongs to an exclusive country club or the Ku Klux Klan (or can't jump or whatever). Here is another place where good old willpower comes in handy. Even if your old familiar stereotype *feels* right, you can still hold yourself back, resisting this illusory allure, and give yourself a chance to get to know the guy first.

To give you an idea of how willpower can work against stereotypes, consider the case of Wilbur, a former client of mine who was in the market for a new automobile. Wilbur told me that car salesmen were "slimeballs." He said that each time one spoke to him, he expected a great lizard tongue to come slithering out to devour him. So each time Wilbur went out to buy a car, he would come back empty-handed, having had a quarrel with the salesperson.

I talked with Wilbur about the importance of avoiding stereotypes in interpersonal relationships, and I gave him a little homework assignment. The next time Wilbur went out to look for a car, he was to exercise his willpower muscle to keep himself from going with the flow of his stereotype. Instead, he was to fight it off with the antidotal reasoning that included the rule of not judging car salespersons without first getting to know them.

So, the next time Wilbur went out, he flexed away, and, instead of perceiving a lizard tongue, he struck up a polite conversation with the car salesman. You see, my client had dropped out of law school in his earlier days, and so had the salesman. They hit it off, and Wilbur ended up buying his dream car from this gentleman. Oh, how my client loved the smell of the fresh vinyl in his new Toyota!

In an effort to bring the world under a tidy description, people often jump to conclusions about all members of a group based upon just a few. So, your husband cheats on you and you straightaway conclude that all (or most) men cheat. A woman rear-ends you and you straightaway conclude that all (or most) women are bad drivers. Often, you already have a preconceived idea about the group in question, and you then use your limited experience to confirm what you already believe to be true. Suppose you were brought up to think that women were bad drivers. As a child you recall your dad yelling out from his car, "Woman driver!" when a woman did something questionable on the roadway. So, now, when Mary runs into you, you use this as an opportunity to reaffirm what you already "knew" about women drivers.

But sometimes, your mind is not already made up. Instead, a bad experience sours your taste for the entire group. The man you were dating molests your child, and now you think that all men are child molesters. You eat in a Chinese restaurant and get food poisoning, and now you refuse to ever eat in a Chinese restaurant again, even though you like Chinese food. Indeed, such experiences should remind you not to trust people whom you don't know very well with your children, and not to eat in establishments that have been cited for health violations. Of course, you can do these things and still have bad luck, but this is true no matter what you do. If you want to live in a riskfree universe, then you are destined to be disappointed, sooner or later.

By generalizing about all members of a group based upon just a few members, you are assuming that these few members are *representative* of the whole group. But are they really? Is the child molester you dated for the past few weeks representative of all men? Is that Chinese restaurant that leaves chickens unrefrigerated all day in a hot kitchen typical?

A sample of a group is representative of the whole group only when it is large and diverse enough to stand for the whole group. This is how you know that all men are mortal. Men of diverse demographic backgrounds—age, race, geographical region, and so forth—have eventually died. So, even though nobody has examined all men, we have enough hard evidence to conclude that all men are mortal.

Is there similar evidence to show that all—even most—men are child molesters? That all—or most—Chinese restaurants are havens for food poisoning? No. So, the next time you generalize about all—or most—members of a group on the basis of just a few individuals, ask yourself if your sample is really representative. It may be that you are unnecessarily allowing your unpleasant experience with a few unusual cases to sour your view about the entire group. While this is understandable, it may also restrict your freedom and autonomy in ways that undermine your future happiness. In such cases, it may not be easy to overcome your cognitive dissonance, and you may want to avoid dating other men or trying out other Chinese restaurants. But, by pushing yourself to act against your bodily feelings and inclinations, in defiance of these irrational shackles, you can reclaim your lost freedom and autonomy.

Another form of Overgeneralizing is *cliché thinking*. A cliché is a timeworn, absolutistic claim about reality. Unfortunately, life is rife with exceptions, and even if some of these gems of wisdom work for you sometimes, they are not likely to work for you all the time. So, you decide not to take on a partner in your business because you think that, "Two many cooks spoil the broth." The fly in the ointment, however, is that you forgot the saying that, "Two heads are better than one." In reality, sometimes two heads are better than one, and sometimes not. It depends on the heads that you are talking about, what you are considering doing, and a host of other things. Do you recall the sayings, "The early bird catches the worm" and "Haste makes waste"? Well, sometimes the quality of the worm you catch might be better by waiting, and sometimes not. And, while haste, when it is unreflective and capricious, does indeed tend to lead you into trouble, you may still often need to hustle if you are to get a tasty worm. Reliance on clichés instead of careful assessment of the situation can be self-defeating.

I once listened attentively to the lyrics of a country song that said, "All a woman needs is a gentle moment," and I wondered if this meant that women didn't need food or oxygen too. Is it true that, "All you need is love?" In their effort to emphasize an important value—love—the Beatles, unfortunately, *oversimplified* reality. Do you really *need* love? Love is certainly something most of us *want*. So, is it at least true that *all* we really *want* is love? What about education, money, fame, food, and a roof over our heads? Surely we want these too. The main problem with oversimplifying reality is that you are likely to overlook important details in the effort to make life more manageable.

Did you ever say anything like "S/he's *always* complaining" and "S/he *never* spends *any* time with me"? If you are human, you probably have. It's easy to damn someone for *always* complaining or for *never* spending *any* time. But a more reasonable reporting of the facts would be that you prefer *less* complaining and *more* time. By presenting the facts without Overgeneralizing them, it becomes easier to resolve interpersonal problems. So, what is it that you would like me to stop complaining about? What shall we do to increase the amount of quality time we might spend together?

An antidote to oversimplifying: Look out for absolutistic and unrealistic uses of words like "all," "none," "always," "never," "any," "ever," and "only." This does not mean that *every* time you say the word, *every* (or any of the others just mentioned) that you have committed a fallacy. If you couldn't say these words without filing a defective report, then you would be driven to dismiss many true statements as false. Try putting a "not" in front of *any* false statement that uses the word "every," as in, "Not every case of using the word 'every' is a fallacy." True enough, right? *All* humans are mammals. *Whatever* goes up must come down. For *every* action, there is an equal reaction. *No*body, so far, has survived the Ebola virus. These generalizations about the world, and many others, are surely realistic. But watch out for the imposters that confuse the "some" with the "all".

BLACK-OR-WHITE THINKING

Here's a reality check. Fill in the blanks:

1. If you don't win, then you ____________.
2. If you are not smart, then you are__________.
3. If something is not true, then it's __________.
4. If something is not good, then it's _____________.
5. If you're not happy, then you are _____________.
6. If you are not beautiful, then you are ___________.

Hint: The answers are *not*: (1) lose, (2) stupid, (3) false, (4) bad, (5) sad, and (6) ugly. In fact, if you gave any of these answers or their equivalents, then you were doing black or white thinking. This is when you forget about the shades of gray.

First, you do not necessarily win or lose. There are times when you don't play the game, when you have a draw, or when you are doing something that has no winners or losers, such as sleeping, listening to the radio, or expressing your feelings.

Second, you are not necessarily smart *or* stupid. You can be of average intellect. Indeed, making such global assessments of the person, instead of sticking to his or her individual capacities, is a sort of Damnation, which is a fallacy!

Third, some things are neither true nor false. Your preference for soup rather than salad is neither true nor false, and there is no fact that says others have to agree with it. If you thought otherwise then you would be doing The-World-Revolves-Around-Me Thinking, which, as you have seen, is another fallacy.

Fourth, some things are neither good nor bad, such as an average grade on an examination. Fifth, you may be neither happy nor sad, as when you are feeling "just OK." And, sixth, you may be neither beautiful nor ugly as when you are "average looking."

The world might be easier to manage if there weren't such shades of gray with which to contend, just black or white. But this would not be to live in the real world, which does exhibit great variety. I have known clients to whine and howl at the moon as a result of black-or-white tunnel vision. To give you one example, a client, George, divided his world into the winners and the losers. He often had intense disagreements with his wife about personal issues and problems of living. These differences of opinion might have provided an opportunity to mutually explore each other's belief systems and values, learn from each other, empathize, grow closer through mutual understanding, and even to agree to disagree at times.

Instead, he perceived reality as a conflict of opposites whose resolution could only end with one victor and one loser. In his eyes, his wife was usually the winner and he the loser. By keeping up this competitive, gamelike style of relating to his wife, he made himself feel like a sore loser, feeling anger at his inability to win, and guilt about getting sore over losing. What was it about the status of losing a disagreement with his wife that precipitated such hard feelings?

Well, George thought that his losing to his wife was a mark of his unmanliness, and that he must not ever let his wife show him up (a popular cultural stereotype of unmanliness). So, his desire for victory became a rigid demand or *must* from which he deduced anger. But, when his emotional object became the anger itself, he felt guilty.

"Why guilty?" you may ask. Well, since he thought that it was his fault for losing in the first place, he concluded that he *shouldn't have* felt anger toward his wife for winning, and that this merely made him a sore loser. Carried by the force of this misguided moral indictment, the guilt rolled in like an ominous, dark cloud.

Even worse, under the direction of a rule that said, "Loser be damned," George deduced depression. In his mind, his "defeat" meant more than that he was loser of this or that dispute. Instead, it meant that he was a *total* loser.

As you can see, George's turbulent emotions were a result of unrealistic rules of emotion combined with Black-or-White Thinking. If he did not perceive things in terms of winner and loser in the first place he would probably not have made himself feel so miserable.

I have noticed that dysfunctional relationships like George's are often grounded in black-or-white conceptions of intimacy. In fact, many of the most dysfunctional couples, including those with a history of serious abuse, accept an inequality of power where one person in the couple is dominant and powerful while the other is weak and submissive. These couples assume that there must always be leader and follower, oppressor and oppressed, master and slave. But, between these, is there anything else?

To live together cooperatively, you need some measure of authority. Yet, in the effort to conform to authority, you should not let your personal autonomy and freedom slip away. Total conformity and total anarchy are surely not the only options. In fact, they are not even functional ones. You and your significant other can, instead, be *partners* in a joint life venture. In this way, neither one of you needs to be *the* dominant or submissive one. Neither has to be the boss or, if you wish, you can *both* be bosses. While you might mutually agree upon a plausible division of labor—I'll do this and you'll do that—this need not and should not signify a sexist form of oppression, according to which the man (or the woman) is, as such, *the* boss. This strain of Black-or-White Thinking commonly makes for very unhappy campers!

MAGNIFYING RISKS

This is where you exaggerate the chances of something undesirable happening. In one of its virulent strains, it goes by the name of Murphy's Law, which boldly proclaims, "Whatever *can* go wrong *will* go wrong." This dismal prophesy is often cited with the authority of the Law of Gravity, but it is neither lawful nor rational. The problem is in automatically and absolutely turning the *can* into the *will*. True, "Shit happens," but the probability of something shitty happening cannot be assessed merely on the grounds that it *is* shitty. For this, you need evidence.

To give you an idea of the lethality of Murphy's recipe for misfortune, take the case of my former client, Hank. Hank and his wife came to see me for couples counseling. The two were contemplating having a child, but Hank was reluctant to try. Why? Because he subscribed to Murphy's Law. You see, this was his second wife. His first marriage came to an end after his wife had a miscarriage. Now he was afraid that the same thing would happen to his present wife. He stated, "If she can have a miscarriage, then she will."

Obviously, it was possible that his present wife would miscarry, but was it probable? The fact that his former wife miscarried was not evidence to boost the probabilities. Being the wife of Hank was clearly not itself a risk factor for having a miscarriage, yet his reasoning seemed to be, "If it happened to my former wife, then it can also happen to my present wife, and whatever can go wrong will."

In fact, Hank's present wife did not have any history of miscarriages, and she had no known health risks to complicate her pregnancy. So, actually, the probability was low that she would miscarry relative to this *evidence*. Of course, this was no guarantee, but it was all that anyone could *realistically* expect.

Hank finally came to appreciate the irrationality of Murphy's Law, at least on an intellectual level, but he still *felt* apprehensive about going up against it. I encouraged him to flex his willpower muscle to try to defeat his irrational impulses, and after a few months he managed to impregnate his wife. In the end, the two had a healthy baby girl, whom Hank loved dearly.

Another client suffered from an acute phobia of going into elevators. This client, Barbara, walked many a dark, smelly stairwell to avoid having to travel in an elevator. What was her reason? Well, she thought that she would, or probably would, get stuck in an elevator and that she would suffocate before anyone could find her. And, she argued that her reasons for avoiding elevator travel were quite rational because this really could happen.

"Yes, it could happen," I told her, "but the odds of it happening are low." Unfortunately, this was not good enough for her because, under her Murphy credo, *any risk was high risk*. In fact, it appeared to be higher risk to travel dark, uninhabited stairwells than to get into an elevator. Although Barbara made significant advances by occasionally forcing herself to travel in elevators when accompanied by a friend, she did not succeed in completely overcoming her fear of elevators.

Another virulent strain of Magnifying Risks goes by the name of Slippery Slope. Like the proverbial slippery slope, once you begin to fall, you fall faster and faster with no means of escape, until you find yourself at the bottom of oblivion. Have you ever had insomnia on the night before an important event? You lie awake, tossing and turning, thinking about the speech you must give the next morning. "What's gonna happen now? I'll be so tired that I'll forget everything I'm supposed to say. I'll just stand there looking into the faces of all those strangers with a blank look in my eyes. I'll make such a fool of myself and then I'll get fired. My career will be over, and I'll end up pushing a broom for the rest of my life!"

If you did not mind pushing a broom for the rest of your life, this would not be a big deal. But, by Magnifying Risks, you have unrealistically predicted the event that you most fear. You think, "How awful, I just couldn't stand to live like that." This is the old "one-two-three." First, you take a slide down the Slippery Slope. Second, you Awfulize. Third, you give yourself a dose of I-Can't-Stand-It-Itis. The last two steps are the rules of emotion that you add to deduce your anxiety.[3] Now you are caught in the loop. Around and around you go. The more you spin your wheels, the more your body becomes aroused, the more convinced you become of your demise, and the more intense becomes your anxiety. So sleep becomes less likely as the adrenaline pumps and the heart thumps!

What do you do when you find yourself anxiously sliding down a Slippery Slope and caught in a loop? Of course, it's easier to nip your anxiety in the bud before it begins to gallop. In any event, you can still swallow some reality pills, that is, do some realistic self-talk. "Look," you say to yourself, "even if I screw up, that doesn't mean I'll end up pushing a broom or even get fired. And there's a good chance I'll get through it OK. I do really know my stuff. And, what if I do lose my job? That's not like gas chambers and guillotines. Oh well, what the hell, what will be will be!" Now breathe easy, relax those muscles, clear your mind, and catch some Zs.

Another version of Magnifying Risks is Fatalistic Thinking. Sound familiar? You think that, whatever your past plight, you are doomed to repeat it in the future, and there's nothing you can do about it. So, caught in a rut in the past means that you must stay in it in the future. Yes, you *must*, because no matter what you do, your past must follow you for the rest of your life. There is a mystical force afoot here that binds you to your past, like cosmic glue. Your fate is sealed. Once the cement has cured, you are forever stuck.

So, let's say that you are into your late thirties, and you have not yet found that Mr. or Ms. Right. Dating has generally been a bust, and except for that failed engagement, you have been pretty much a washout. So, you think, "I'll never find the right one. I'm just one of those people who ends up living alone forever."

And, if this is what you tell yourself, then you are pretty much sealing *your own* fate. Yes, you are doing it yourself by your own Fatalistic Thinking. In your mind, probabilities have been replaced with cosmic necessity. Whatever you do is impotent against this cement, which permanently binds you to your past.

Here is the best, general antidote I have. What happens in the future depends upon what you do in the present, not upon some mystical, unexplainable cosmic force. If you continue doing just what you are doing and have always done, then, other things being equal, you are likely to seal your own fate. On the other hand, making changes now can affect the course of your future life. So, maybe you wear the same unflattering clothes, drive the same old, beat-up car, go to the same old singles dances, meet and hang out with the same old crowd, and the same old same old. By telling yourself that your fate is sealed it is likely that you will not try anything new, and you will likely fulfill your own prophesy. Trying new things that bring you into proximity with new possibilities can change your future life. What exactly these things are is likely to vary from individual to individual, but you would do well to tinker a bit. If you like intellectual pursuits, then taking classes might work. If you like country music and culture but don't know how to square dance, then take some lessons, and take in a hoedown. By pushing yourself to explore new options, you can overcome the inertia of your old, stagnant, fatalistic thinking, and thereby open up new possibilities for the future.

WISHFUL THINKING

While Magnifying Risks exaggerates probabilities of something happening in the future, reports that involve Wishful Thinking discount or ignore them. A popular slogan that epitomizes one version of this fallacy is, "Things will be different." This means that something that has consistently happened in the past—which you don't want to happen in the future—will, in fact, not happen again.

It is correctly said that history is likely to repeat itself if we ignore the past. Well, the ritualistic chant that "things will be different" does nothing to change the facts of the past or to set you on a different path in the future. If you want something to change, then you will need to take constructive actions to bring about the change. This problem is no more clearly evident than in cases of domestic violence.

I have listened to many accounts of women (and some men) who had been emotionally and physically degraded and beaten by their mates, and who clung in vain to the hope that things would be different in the future. Such abuse usually turns in a vicious cycle. After the abuse, many perpetrators bear gifts to their victims in an attempt to undo their mistreatment. In this "honeymoon period," victims often become hopeful that things will be different. However, this period is usually followed by a period of walking on eggshells where the pressure rebuilds only to explode in further abuse.

If you are caught in an abuse cycle, ignoring the past is likely to keep you spinning your wheels and suffering repeated mistreatment. If neither you nor your mate have made any relevant change (such as seeking professional help or working diligently to improve your thinking), then it is highly probable that the abuse will continue over and over again. Wishful Thinking will get you nowhere.

If you are the one perpetrating the abuse, then Wishful Thinking will not help you either. Things will not be different unless you do something about your vicious tendency to abuse someone you may deeply love. If you are in this situation, it is likely that you are also buying into some of the unrealistic rules of emotion I have discussed earlier, such as Demanding Perfection and Damnation. So, you tell yourself that you are going to be different next time around, but when the time arrives, you feel those same old bodily urges, feelings, images, inclinations, and unrealistic lines of reasoning from which you deduce physical assault, degrading tirade, or the same old stuff, only to feel guilty later. So, what to do?

By flexing your willpower muscle in line with a good antidote, you can curb your nasty behavioral and emotional tendencies. Do you have free will? Are you strong enough and courageous enough to take a good look at your nutty thinking and overcome it? This challenge takes work and perseverance, but you can find great pride and happiness in defeating this beast by which you hurt those who mean the most to you.

Guess what Wishful Thinking has in common with Fatalistic Thinking? You sit back and do little or nothing about your situation. So you tell yourself that you are going to get that promotion or find that special person, but you still cling to the same old habits that haven't worked in the past. What, then, do you expect? As long as you make no relevant changes in your life, you should not be disappointed if things do not pan out. True, sometimes if you persist long enough in ways that don't appear to be working, they can pay off in the end, but the probabilities may still be stacked against you. "Try, try again" can be useful advice only if you have a reasonable plan of attack to begin with. If you want to meet someone, then sitting around and waiting for the same old people to call you is not likely to work. If you want a promotion, then meekly remaining silent about your interest and qualifications is not likely to capture your boss's attention. Using the evidence of your past successes and failures as a guide to the future can help you plot out a reasonable attack and prevent history from repeating itself. Positive thinking is not likely to work if it is blind to the past. Things are not likely to turn out differently if you do not flex that willpower muscle of yours to overcome old, stagnant ways of thinking, feeling, and acting.

Aristotle's Golden Mean can help set you free. Avoid the extremes in reasoning about the past. Fatalistic Thinking overdoes the past while Wishful Thinking underdoes it. What is the right posture toward the past?

Answer: The past grounds the *probability* of future outcomes. This is neither fatalistic nor wishful. Probability is an index of how *reasonable* it is to expect an outcome. If you have done nothing to change what has happened before, then the evidence of the past can be a reasonable predictor that the future will be repeated. Like conditions produce like effects. But change the conditions and the probabilities for alternative outcomes can change. So, if it's constructive change you seek, wishfully telling yourself that things will be different won't work. Flex your willpower and *make* a difference!

Concocting Explanations

By "concoct" I mean to unrealistically make up or fabricate. If your car didn't start and the gas gauge was pointing to empty, what would be your explanation of these facts? Right: The car is out of gas. But it might not be; there might be something else wrong, such as a broken gas gauge, or the car might have a clogged fuel line. Still, the more likely explanation is that your car is out of gas. So it would be unreasonable for you to replace your gas gauge or attempt to repair the gas lines without checking to see if you have any gas left. Sound logical enough?

Well, unfortunately, people often find it difficult to apply this same logical model of explaining things to their emotional lives. So, when your significant other doesn't come home on time, you straightaway think that he or she has *probably* gotten into a terrible accident. If you do not get hired for that job for which you recently interviewed, then it is *probably* a conspiracy against you instead of the hiring committee having found someone more qualified, or someone it liked better. If your boss is not especially friendly to you today, then he is *probably* getting ready to lay you off. If it rains again on your day off, then there *must be* some cosmic force that is plotting against you. If two of your officemates are talking to each other and occasionally glancing at you, then they are *probably* saying nasty things about you behind your back. If you develop a nagging cough, then you *probably* have lung cancer or some other chronic, fatal, or dangerous disease. If you have been forgetful lately, then it's *probably* the beginning stages of Alzheimer's disease. If there is a mistake on your phone bill, then it is *probably* a deliberate attempt to scam you out of money.

"But maybe these explanations are true," you might quip. And, indeed, they may be, but that doesn't mean that they're *probable* explanations. As long as there are other rationales that are at least as possible, then you are being unrealistic in settling on these. Sometimes people think the worst just because it *is* the worst. So you think lung cancer first instead of a common respiratory infection. But the fact that an explanation is undesirable has nothing to do with whether it is credible. For this, you need evidence. By convincing yourself that your symptoms are the result of some dangerous disease, or that your loved one is lying somewhere dead on the roadside, you are likely to seriously and unnecessarily disturb yourself. So is there an antidote to this nuttiness?

Be a scientist when you lodge explanations. Instead of panicking, do not file your report until you have completed your investigation. First, take a mental inventory of other credible explanations for the facts, as you know them. "Well, it could be something bad, but then again, the last time I had this symptom it was just a cough." Then go ahead and collect *more* facts. For example, get a medical opinion. The more you learn, the more likely you will disqualify some explanations and find others to fit the facts better. In the end, you are likely to find that the exotic explanation that you most feared is not, after all, the one that survives your scientific investigation. So be a scientist instead of a nervous wreck!

Could-a/Would-a/Should-a Thinking

A unique capacity that we humans have is our ability to speculate about what, contrary to fact, could-a, would-a, or should-a been. So, instead of sticking to what *actually* happened in the past, we are able to conjecture about a past that never even happened. If it were not for that traffic jam causing me to miss my plane, I would have died in that plane crash. If I had not noticed that car cutting into my lane, we would have collided. If we had left a day sooner, then we wouldn't have been caught in that blizzard. If I hadn't called ahead of time, then I wouldn't have found out that the meeting was cancelled. If my alarm hadn't gone off, then I would have been late for work. I should have stayed on the main highway instead of taking the scenic route; then I wouldn't have gotten lost.

The above statements can be reasonable as long as I am not making any unrealistic assumptions. For example, as long as it is not unreasonable to assume that the plane would have crashed whether or not I was on it, then my speculation that I would have been killed would also be rational. Unfortunately, it is common for people to make unreasonable assumptions in talking about what would-a or could-a or should-a happened. If I had taken vitamin C, then I wouldn't have come down with that bad cold. If I had gotten more sleep, then I would have been more alert and wouldn't have gotten into that traffic accident. If I had been a better wife/husband, then he/she wouldn't have left me for someone else. If I hadn't been so friendly to him or worn that sexy dress, then he wouldn't have raped me. I should also have tried harder to get away or fight back; then he wouldn't have been able to do that to me. If only I had gotten that part, I would be a famous movie star today. I could be a millionaire if only I had gone into business instead of teaching.

In these cases, can you be so confident? Not without making questionable assumptions. How do you know that popping vitamin C would have worked against that virulent bug you caught? Even if you had rolled out the red carpet for that spouse of yours, maybe he/she would have had roving eyes anyway. How do you know that that part in the movie would have been your big break or that your business would have been successful? The only reasonable response to these questions is "Well, *maybe*." But, on the other hand, "*Maybe not!*" This puts things into a realistic perspective.

Filing reports that make unwarranted assumptions about the past can have serious emotional consequences when these reports form the basis for Damnation of Self. If you have been sexually molested or raped you might have found yourself thinking how you could have resisted or dressed differently, or acted less friendly. But the truth is that you do not know that any of these things would have or could have worked to ward off the perpetrator. Rape is most often a crime of violence and power, not one of sexual attraction, so there is even good reason to suppose that your sex appeal may not have mattered.[4] And, of course, you may not have been strong enough to overpower a man who was significantly larger or more muscular than you. Yet, I have heard women blame themselves for their victimization. Attacking their own jugular for being a victim, they once again make victims of themselves.

Every time you do Could-a/Would-a/Should-a Thinking, you are really reasoning from an assumption to a conclusion. For example, if you say, "Had I not worn that sexy red dress and been flirtatious, then I wouldn't have gotten raped." your reasoning is like this:

- Let's assume that I didn't wear that sexy red dress and act flirtatiously.
- *Then*, I wouldn't have gotten raped (conclusion).

As you can see, this reasoning is missing a premise that is needed to validate your conclusion. Here's the reasoning with the missing premise added:

- Women who don't wear provocative clothes and act flirtatiously don't get raped (missing premise).
- Let's assume that I didn't wear that sexy red dress and act flirtatiously
- *Then*, I wouldn't have gotten raped (conclusion).

The conclusion now clearly follows from the premises. But, I now have one question for you. Is the premise I just added really true?

The answer is, "No!" As I stated a moment ago, rape is usually a crime of violence and power, not of sex.

Here's the moral of the story: Before you screw yourself with could-a/would-a/should-a-ing, fill in your missing premises first, and then take a look-see. As in this case, you may find that you are basing your reasoning on a false premise.

There are two popular ways in which Could-a/Would-a/Should-a Thinking can lead to self-defeating emotions. One is to damn yourself for not having acted differently, as in the rape instance. Another is actually the opposite, namely to vindicate yourself from blame. So, you might tell yourself how you *could have* won the tennis set had you been more rested. This saves you from having to admit that you may not be as good at tennis as your opponent.

But why do you have to resort to such unrealistic thinking in the first place? Unfortunately, I have known many athletes who do this because they have already committed themselves to unrealistic rules of emotion. For example, you think you have to be better than your opponent in order to remain a worthy person. So, to save face, you make an excuse. "Had I gotten more rest," you say, "I would have been the winner." This, however, only shows how one fallacy leads to another. If you dropped the idea that your self-worth depended upon your achievements, you wouldn't have had to resort to this unrealistic Could-a/Would-a/Should-a Thinking in the first place.

"Well," you might ask, "what's so bad about a little bullshitting if it makes you feel better?" I am not saying that a little bit of this can spell big trouble, but, unfortunately, if you are an athlete (or work in some other competitive environment) and you use Could-a/Would-a/Should-a Thinking to save yourself from the perils of Damnation of Self, then you are not likely to escape the full brunt of your problem in this way. If you require victory in order to maintain your personal worth, then it is likely that your life will be a stressful roller-coaster ride in which, win or lose, you must wrestle with the constant threat of being reduced to worthless garbage if you happen to lose. Even when you win, there's always another game in the offing, and another opportunity to fall from grace. This is a lot of needless anxiety! So, you're much better off finding an antidote for your unrealistic self-rating than trying to soothe your aching psyche by rubbing on some Could-a/Would-a/Should-a Thinking.

PERSONIFYING

Did you ever yell to a red streetlight, "Come on, light, change!" or command your ailing auto to start up? Did you ever speak reverently of Mother Nature or wonder why life has treated you so poorly? Did you ever trust Lady Luck or wonder if the hurricane will decide to spare you its wrath? Did you ever proclaim that love is blind or refer to death as the Grim Reaper? While poetry and songs abound with such metaphors about life and the objects that fill it, taking these too literally can sometimes have implications for the way you act and feel.

About a decade ago, the significance of personifying objects and abstractions came to me in a very mundane context. One morning I was preparing a sandwich for lunch, which I intended to eat in my office after teaching my class. I slapped some cold cuts onto a couple of pieces of bread, and thinking how lonely the meat looked on the bread, I decided to do it a favor and add some catsup. So I went to the refrigerator to fetch some catsup, but I could not seem to find it. The longer I gazed into the refrigerator, finding no sign of that familiar bottle, the more frustrated I became. Finally, in desperation, I grabbed one of two old, long-expired breads that clogged the front of the refrigerator and pulled it out from the shelf. Lo and behold, there it was, that familiar shape glaring at me, with its arms firmly at its sides! "That catsup was hiding behind those damn breads!" I exclaimed to myself. Hiding? Damn breads? Wow! I could almost see that bottle, haughtily displaying the word "Heinz," across its chest, scoffing at me as though it had just won a game of hide-and-seek. I grabbed that catsup as though it were a naughty child, punishing it with a quick squeeze as some of its thick contents plopped onto my lonely meat. As it plopped, I felt somewhat relieved at having finally gotten my way over that elusive fugitive.

As I drove to class, thinking silently about the lesson I was to teach my logic students that morning, I suddenly burst out in laughter. Here I was about to speak on logic, after having subdued a bottle of catsup! As I thought more about what had happened, it occurred to me that what had seemed so silly could, in some contexts, have serious implications. "Why did I blame the catsup?" I asked myself. And at once the answer to my query became plain. It was so much easier to accuse the catsup than to accuse myself, so much easier than admitting that I had wasted my own time by failing to organize my own fridge. I have always disliked cleaning out and organizing my refrigerator, so it was much easier to take the catsup to task, than to admit my own irresponsibility. So I blamed the catsup, instead of myself. I even disowned my desire for the catsup by accusing the *meat* of "looking lonely".

I have noticed clients who look upon life as though it were deliberately plotting against them, putting obstacles in their way, preventing their happiness. But life, no more than a bottle of catsup, can deliberately plot against us. By giving it human attributes and then blaming it for your misfortunes, you can conceal your own responsibility for your actions and feelings. In this way, you can fail to take responsibility for your own life. If bad things happen to you, then the world has been cruel to you, and you are merely a passive victim of its evil intentions. As a passive recipient of the wrath of the universe, you are alone, without recourse, at the mercy of life. This picture of reality portends no opportunity to redirect the course of your own life, and to do anything about your plight. When fate, Lady Luck, Mother Nature, the cosmos, or life have spoken, then there's nothing you can do against such a formidable adversary. So you must sit, aimlessly wallowing and stewing in your own misfortune. Right? No!

Antidote: Take responsibility for your life. By blaming abstractions and physical things for your plight, you are not likely to do anything constructive about it. By exercising your reason and willpower, you can exert considerable control over the events in your life. This does not mean that you can defy physical laws or all-knowingly foresee and avert every bad thing that could happen. But, by accepting responsibility rather than renouncing it, you usually have a good shot at improving the state of your life.

NOTES

1. *Ethics*, book 6, ch. 7

2. Walter Lippmann, "Stereotypes, Public Opinion, and the Press," in *Philosophical Issues in Journalism*, ed. Elliot D. Cohen (New York: Oxford University Press, 1992), p. 162.

3. This is an example of a popular fallacy syndrome, which I refer to as the Slippery Slope syndrome. I will discuss fallacy syndromes in greater detail in the next chapter and in part 4.

4. Jeffrey S. Nevid, Spencer A. Rathus, and Beverley Greene, *Abnormal Psychology in a Changing World* (Englewood Cliffs, N.J.: Prentice-Hall, 1994), p. 379; Richard P. Appelbaum and William J. Chambliss, *Sociology* (New York: Harper Collins, 1995), p. 288.

Part 3

How to Identify and Refute Your Faulty Thinking, and Find Antidotes to It

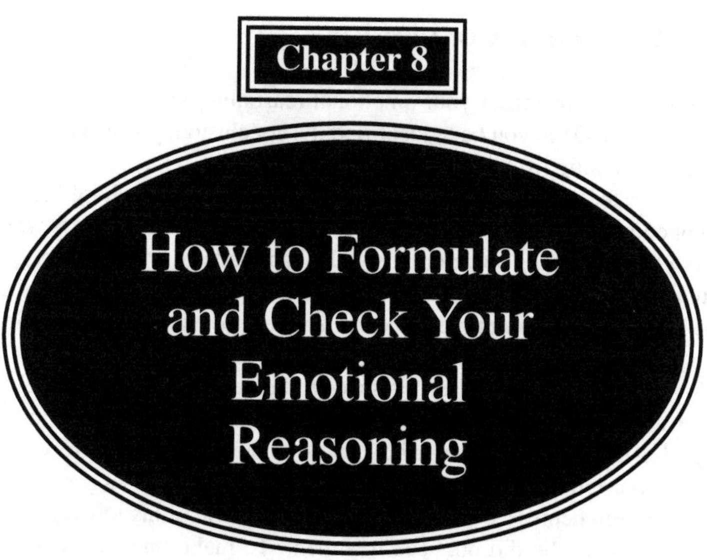

Chapter 8

How to Formulate and Check Your Emotional Reasoning

[Reasoning] is imperfect if it needs either one or more propositions, which . . . have not been expressly stated as premises.

—Aristotle[1]

The reasoning from which you deduce your emotions is not usually perfectly spelled out in your mind. When you are in the middle of having an emotional experience, it is not likely that you will be fully aware of your premises. Think about the last time you were angry. Did you catch yourself mentally filing a *complete* report along with a rule, *fully* expressed? Chances are you had some fleeting glimpses of your premises. You often assume the rule without consciously reciting it. So, you need to sort of read between the lines to fully grasp your emotional reasoning. Once you have done so, you can check your premises for fallacies—such as the ones you have learned about in the last three chapters. This can give you a jump on refuting your fallacious premises and finding antidotes. So how do you read between the lines?

Identifying Your Conclusion

Start with the conclusion of your emotional reasoning, which is either an emotion or an action. Once you have identified the conclusion, you can then go on to build your reasoning from the ground up, so to speak.

To illustrate, take the tragic case of a colleague of mine whose life came to an abrupt end while in his early fifties. At the time of his death, I was waiting to hear from him regarding some criticisms he had made of a manuscript of mine. Unfortunately, the correspondence was never sent. Little did I know, at the time, that my colleague had committed suicide. You see, he had received considerable acclaim for his work in philosophy, and he was highly regarded by his peers, including me. At the pinnacle of his success, he became convinced that he had achieved everything he set out to achieve professionally and that there was nothing else left for him to contribute. So one day, when his wife was out of town, this poor fellow took his own life.

He had been depressed for some time, but because of his low regard for the health care system, he did not seek treatment. To make matters worse, he had talked openly about his desire to kill himself to some of his close colleagues. But not one of them made any effort to help him. Apparently, their somewhat idealized view of him as a great philosopher, combined with the self-confident, strong aura he exuded, made it difficult for them to think of him as incompetent and in need of psychiatric help.

The emotional conclusion this revered philosopher deduced that drove him to suicide was, of course, that of *depression*. But, as obvious as this might have been in retrospect, very intelligent people did not perceive his emotional state as depression. Instead, they simply looked upon his pronouncements about suicide as the philosophical insights of a sage. So, let's clear the air about how to identify an emotion. If you think that I am belaboring the obvious in doing so, you are probably right, but I have come to realize that it is often the most obvious things that people overlook. If this isn't true, then tell me why the fallacies I have discussed in the previous chapters are so popular. Aren't most—or all—of them easy to refute?

So here's a key to *identifying* your emotions. You can do so by considering the kind of *emotional object* your emotion has (see p. 37) and how you *rate* it. See the following working definitions of some of the more troublesome emotions, which are expressed in terms of objects and their ratings. These should help you to identify your own emotions and to expand your reasoning.

- *Anger*: The object of this emotion is something that someone did. You strongly, negatively rate the action itself or the person who did it.
- *Guilt*: The object of this emotion is a moral principle, which you perceive yourself to have violated. You strongly condemn the perceived violation or yourself for the perceived violation.

- *Shame*: The object of this emotion is an action or state of yours, for which you perceive others to be strongly, negatively judging you, your action, or state. You perceive this judgment to be extremely undesirable and also as a reason for you to strongly, negatively judge yourself, your action, or state.[2]
- *Depression*: The object of this emotion is an event or state of affairs that you strongly, negatively rate, and, on the basis of which, you bleakly perceive your own existence.
- *Grief*: The object of this emotion is the loss of someone (a person or animal) whom you strongly, positively rate, and, without whom, you bleakly perceive your own existence.
- *Anxiety*: The object of this emotion is a future event or possible future event, which you think will or might have serious, negative consequences.
- *Fear*: The object of this emotion is a present or possible event, which you perceive as, in some manner, dangerous or threatening to you.
- *Jealousy*: The object of this emotion is a person, or state of a person, who has something that you want but don't have. You negatively rate this person's having that which you lack.

The object of my colleague's emotion was the futility of his attempting to make any further professional contributions, on the basis of which he perceived his own unworthiness to remain alive. So, it is obvious that he was depressed. Once you have the emotion down, you can then go on to file a report.

Filing Your Report

A key to filing a report is to realize that a report is actually a *filling out of the object of an emotion*. Remember I said (in chapter 2) that all emotions have emotional objects? When you have an emotion, it's always *about* something. Your anger is about some action you think was wrong; your guilt is about a moral violation; your depression is about something that you think has devalued your existence; your anxiety, fear, shame, grief, and jealousy are also always *about* something. When you say what you are angry about or feel guilty about or feel depressed about, you are filing your report. When you file your report, for purposes of checking your thinking for fallacies, it's important to provide a *complete* report. That is, you should try to be as precise as possible about what you are angry about, guilty about, depressed about, and so forth. This will make it easier for you to see whether your emotion rests on fallacies. It is also important to fill out your report by presenting the facts, *as you perceive them*. The rating part of your reasoning is primarily in the rule. The report is your take on what has happened; it is *what* you are emotional about.[3] Here's my colleague's line of reasoning so far:

Report: I have done everything that I have set out to achieve professionally and there is nothing left for me to achieve in my professional life.
Emotion: Depression.

So, this is what he was depressed about. But why is this a reason to commit suicide? The answer lies in the unrealistic rating this fellow attached to the furtherance of his professional career. This should provide a clue about the rule of emotion he was assuming.

Finding Your Assumed Rule

Remember the fallacies of emotions we discussed in chapter 5? Here, again, is a summary of them:

1. *Demanding Perfection*: If the world fails to conform to some state of ideality, perfection, or near-perfection, then the world is not the way it absolutely, unconditionally *must* be, and you cannot and must not ever have it any other way.
2. *Awfulizing*: If something bad happens, then it is *totally* catastrophic, terrible, horrible, and awful.
3. *Terrificizing*: If someone appears to have some desirable feature, then this person or thing must be absolutely and *totally* terrific, perfect, and the best of its kind in the entire universe.
4. *I-Can't-Stand-It-Itis*: If you find something difficult or challenging to deal with, then it must be beyond your capacity to tolerate and you *cannot* and must not ever hope to succeed at it.
5. *Damnation*: If there is something about yourself or about another person that you strongly dislike, then you or this other person is *totally* worthless.
6. *I Just Can't Help This Feeling*: If you feel depressed, anxious, angry, guilty, or otherwise upset, then you might as well just accept and go with your feeling because it is really not in your control anyway.
7. *Thou Shalt Upset Yourself*: If you encounter a problem in your life that you deem important, then you have a *moral duty*, yes a moral duty, to ruminate over it, never stop thinking about it, make yourself miserable and upset over it, and demand that others, for whom you also deem it a problem, do the same.

Now look again at the report my colleague had filed and ask yourself if he was assuming any of the above rules. Can you see which of these rules completes the reasoning?

It's Damnation. My colleague's report affirmed the *if clause* of the Damnation rule ("If there is something about yourself . . . that you strongly dislike") and its *then clause* ("then you are *totally* worthless") gave him something to be depressed and suicidal about. So, when you read between the lines, the completed reasoning, which includes a version of Damnation, would go like this:

> *Rule*: If I am no longer able to achieve professionally, then I am *totally* worthless and might as well be dead.
> *Report*: I have done everything that I have set out to achieve professionally and there is nothing left for me to achieve in my professional life.
> *Emotion:* Depression.

Perhaps you are wondering if more than one rule can be assumed. The answer is yes. The truth is, fallacies tend to travel in herds. This Awfulizing rule might also fit: "If I am no longer able to achieve professionally, then it's *totally* catastrophic, terrible, horrible, and awful." And, even taking it one step further, "Since it's so catastrophic, I can't stand to live any longer." So, in refuting and finding an antidote for my colleague's reasoning, it would also make sense to include the Awfulizing and I-Can't-Stand-It-itis rules.[4] Usually, when a certain rule really fits, you will realize it when you think about that rule. If you are really *assuming* it, then it should *feel* right to you. I really mean *feel* here. After all, if the rule is truly driving your emotion, then your body will be saying "Right on!" to it.

Refuting and Finding Antidotes to Your Unrealistic Premises

Once you have identified what your emotional reasoning looks like, then you can go ahead and refute any unrealistic premises. Consider the Damnation rule my colleague assumed. His brand of Damnation makes a person's self-worth *entirely* a function of his or her professional achievements. So, if you are achieving professionally, then you are cool. Otherwise, you are totally worthless.

I confess that I have swallowed a similar kind of Achievement Damnation. In my younger days, I quietly thought and *felt* as though, if I suddenly became unproductive professionally, then I would lose my reason for being, that there really wouldn't be any valuable purpose left in my life. It is good to love what you do professionally, but my passion was self-defeating. When I stopped working, and tried to relax, I felt guilty. When I finished an engaging project (a book, article, research, etc.) and was between projects, I felt disoriented, off balance. I felt as though I were being consumed by a void. I was determined to find something to latch onto before I fell forever from grace. When I vacationed or spent time with my wife and children, I felt like I was betraying my faith. I was an addict going through withdrawals.

I have since come to know well this Damnation infection that had destroyed my ability to relax and kick back. My antidote was really quite simple: "There is more to life than just work, and more to an admirable person than one who is productive professionally." I acknowledge the power of giving and receiving love, and the special place my wife, children, and even my dog have in my life. I know better now, and I keep my knowledge close at hand as I confront the challenges of living.

Still, even with what I now know, there is within me traces of the old hollow feelings that faintly remind me of what it is to be in their grip. I cannot honestly say that I have been cured. I am recovering, not cured. I know that I have the capacity to lapse back if I let myself. I am still an addict, a workaholic in recovery. But my willpower muscle is much stronger now, and my antidote is the controlling rule of my life. I mourn for my colleague, who never got as far as I have gotten personally, even though he was a giant professionally. At the same time, I empathize with his plight, one that is familiar to those of us who think there is something profoundly important about the work through which we find self-expression and self-gratification.

My colleague's report was rife with Overgeneralization. He thought he had done *everything* that he had set out to achieve professionally and that there was *nothing* left for him to accomplish in his professional life. But a profession is a bottomless pit of things to do. When the great philosopher Bertrand Russell died at ninety-eight, he was, at that time, engaged in many projects. It is not possible to run out. As one achieves one goal, there is another behind it. One goal sets the stage for the next, without end. In this sense, it is not realistic to foresee in advance all that you want to achieve in life. To do this, you would need to be like God, omniscient. My colleague was a mere mortal, no more capable of seeing where it all would eventually lead than any other mere mortal. In my early professional days, I never would have thought that my interests would lead me down the roads that I have indeed traveled. Have you not had the same experience? Live and learn—and learn, and learn, to the end or beyond!

How to Read between the Emotional Lines

Here's a summary of the steps to use in reading between the lines in filling out your emotional reasoning:

1. *Identify your emotion*. Your emotion will fit the working definitions provided above.
2. *File your report*. Fill out your emotional object, which is what your emotion is about.
3. *Find the assumed rule*. The report you file will affirm the 'if' clause of this rule, and its 'then' clause will drive your emotion. This rule will probably *feel* (in your gut) like it completes your reasoning.

4. *Refute your irrational premises.*
5. *Find antidotes for the refuted premises.*

Now, when you are in the throes of an emotion, are you really going to put yourself through these five steps? Indeed, you will not *feel* like it. That's just the problem. You probably aren't thinking rationally and are being pressured by your body. This is why your willpower muscle can't be flabby. Don't let yourself be blown about like an object carried off by a strong gusting wind. Push back. Push back hard! Exert that will of yours to let yourself think. Talk to yourself. Think about your thinking! Rise up, brothers and sisters, and set yourselves free! "Wait just a minute," you say to yourself. "What emotion am I feeling?" "What am I so ticked off about?" "What rule am I ticking with?" "Is this realistic?" "Am I screwing myself?" "What's my antidote?"

Here's a hint. If you're experiencing an *intense* emotion (aka stress), then as long as you aren't being attacked by a wild boar or in the midst of some other immediate, grave danger, it is likely that you already have the answers to some of these questions. No, you're probably not being realistic. Yes, you're probably screwing yourself. As you will see, in chapters 12 through 15, certain fallacies are likely to be afoot when you are having certain emotions. And, as you have already seen in chapters 5 and 7, there are certain antidotes that work well with certain fallacies of emotion.[5] In chapters 9 and 10, respectively, I will also provide some useful techniques for refuting your irrational premises and finding effective antidotes to them. This should make your *rational* medicine go down easier. Taking your medicine can be habit forming. Getting into such a habit should be your goal!

Staging a Practice Session

Practice can really help. If you know that you are likely to experience intense emotions in certain situations—for example, eating in a restaurant alone—then you can even stage a practice session. So, close your eyes and *imagine* that it is lunchtime during a workday downtown, and you don't have anyone to eat with so you enter a bustling cafe by yourself and are seated at a central table. You look around and see everybody else in the restaurant with lunchmates, chewing the fat with each other. You glance occasionally at some of the patrons and think that they might be smirking at you. Even though you are really not seated in a restaurant by yourself right now, you can still *imagine* all this. This is what I mean by "staging a practice session."[6]

Now let yourself *feel* the way you normally feel in this situation.[7] So, you say to yourself, "They think I'm some kind of weirdo sitting here by myself. They're probably saying things about me to one another. I don't feel like sitting here making a fool of myself like this. Maybe I should just not eat lunch anymore."

Once you have gotten yourself emotionally up to speed, you can apply your method. While in this intense emotional state, you can say, *What is this feeling?* Well, I guess I feel ashamed.

Ashamed of what? Of not having anyone to eat with, and looking like a weirdo.

So, *what report am I filing?* That these other people are sitting around thinking I'm some kind of weirdo and talking about me.

What rule or rules am I assuming? I think I'm telling myself that, if others think bad things about me, then this must make me an unworthy person. I guess I'm also telling myself that I can't stand to have others say or think bad things about me.

Can I refute these premises? First of all, I'm just Concocting Explanations because I don't even know that anyone here is talking about me. But even if they are, it's irrational to base my self-worth on what others think of me, no less ones who don't even know me; and although I would prefer them not to think badly of me, I really *can* stand it if they do.

So, *what antidotes can I find?* Well, *if* these people are saying nasty things about someone they don't even know, then they're irrational and I shouldn't bother myself with them. I should stick to rating my actions and not myself. I shouldn't underestimate my ability to put up with their bad opinions of me, especially when they're groundless. After all, I do have free will. There's a difference between saying I *can't* stand them talking about me and saying that I *won't* stand it. I can if I want! Anyway, there are other possible explanations about why they may be looking at me. Maybe they're just looking my way and talking about things that have nothing to do with me. Maybe they're actually smiling, not smirking, to be cordial when they see me looking their way. I should base my explanations on evidence, not on some irrational self-defensive fear. So, why deprive myself of nourishment for such stupid reasons. Bon appetite!"

In this way, you can take the edge off your irrational emotion. With your imagination, you can stage the experience just for practice. But if you can manage your emotion on a practice run, you are likely to find it easier to do in the actual situation. Practice staging your own troublesome emotions, and see for yourself.

Checking Out the Reasoning behind Your Actions

Before you act, it is usually a good idea to be tuned in to the reasoning that directs your action. Getting the premises of that reasoning out on the table for inspection first, before you act, can often save you from acting in ways that you will later regret.

I have seen couples wreck the quality of their relationships through their unwillingness to come to terms with their nasty thinking habits. Take the case of

Dan and his wife, Sharon. For many years of marriage, they lived in continuous disharmony with one another. Their Kodak moments were typically interspersed and engulfed by skirmishes, some mild and others severe. To give you an example, on one placid evening after dinner (before the storm), Dan was sitting peacefully in his easy chair speaking politely to Sharon, who sat nearby on the sofa.

"Sharon," said Dan in an upbeat tone, "why don't we go on a cruise to the Bahamas this spring."

"I don't think so," replied Sharon, bluntly.

"Why not?" Dan retorted.

"I don't like boats," she stated.

"Then, why don't we fly to the Bahamas?" asked Dan, in an anxious tone.

"No, I really don't like to fly."

"OK, if that's the way you want it," said Dan, "then I'm not driving to Michigan this summer to visit your parents!"

In a self-defensive tone, Sharon quickly rebutted, "I haven't seen them in three years, and they're not in any condition to come here."

"If you want to see them again," blurted Dan, "then I'd strongly advise you to reconsider the Bahamas. Otherwise, drive to Michigan yourself."

Sharon jumped up from the sofa, "You would let me drive all that way by myself?" she shouted, incredulous.

"That's right, if you're going to be so uncooperative, then what do you expect!"

Unfortunately, the above scene escalated over the next few days to screaming matches and threats of divorce. In the end, the two ended up flying to the Bahamas in the spring and driving to Michigan in the summer. Both trips had their Kodak moments, but they were, as usual, interspersed with more of the same old nasty stuff.

But didn't Dan's "putting his foot down" pay off? After all, he did get his vacation in the Bahamas. Unfortunately, the trip to the Bahamas had an extremely high price tag, despite the fact that the two got a bargain on a package deal including a luxury hotel. It was purchased with their happiness. Things really weren't better in the Bahamas after all!

Can you find the fallacy in Dan's reasoning? Take a look at each of the rules of action below, which I have summarized from chapter 6:

1. *Blackmailing*: If someone is refusing to do something you want them to do or is otherwise uncooperative, then you should withdraw or threaten to withdraw something of value from that person.
2. *Making a Stink*: If you are having a problem being respected, understood, heard, or heeded, then you must kick, scream, yell, or otherwise throw a temper tantrum.
3. *Pity Mongering*: If you are in trouble or having difficulties getting what

you want, then you should cry, sob, weep, pout, mope, whine, or otherwise make yourself look hurt, dejected, downtrodden, demoralized, dejected, rejected, crucified, or otherwise pitiful.

4. *Beating Around the Bush*: If you think someone has made an unreasonable or wrongful request of you, but you feel intimidated to say no, then you should verbally consent while dropping hints of your disapproval.
5. *Poisoning the Well*: If you don't want someone to do or believe something, then you should use strong, negative language to intimidate and dissuade this person from doing or believing this thing.
6. *Getting Even*: If someone does something to you that you think is wrong, then, to get even, you should do something equally as wrong back.
7. *Jumping on the Bandwagon*: If your friends, the popular or trendy guys, your schoolmates, the crowd, the average guy or some other group you admire is acting, thinking, or feeling in a certain way, then you *must* make yourself act, think, and feel in exactly the same way.

Like rules of emotion, each of these action rules has an *if clause* and a *then clause*. The then clause directs an action. For example, the then clause of the Making a Stink rule directs you to kick, scream, yell, or otherwise throw a temper tantrum. This would be the conclusion of your reasoning if you were Making a Stink. On the other hand, the if clause tells you the *circumstances* under which to perform this action. So, if you were Making a Stink, you would be filing a report that says that these conditions are true, which would give you the go-ahead to release the stink.

Well, that's the mechanics. But here's a shortcut you can use to see if you are committing any of these fallacies. Ask yourself each of these questions and see if any ring a bell.

1. Am I Blackmailing anyone?
2. Am I Making a Stink over something to get my way?
3. Am I Pity Mongering by deliberately acting pitiful to get my way?
4. Am I Beating Around the Bush by hint dropping?
5. Am I Poisoning the Well by tactfully using poisonous words?
6. Am I doing something I know is wrong just to Get Even?
7. Am I Jumping on the Bandwagon *just* because others are?

If you say yes to any of these questions then you are deducing your action from an unrealistic action rule. So, did Dan deduce his action from any of these unrealistic rules? Bingo: He was Blackmailing Sharon into going to the Bahamas. Reading between the lines, Dan's reasoning was,

Rule: If Sharon refuses to do what I want, then I'll blackmail her into doing it by holding ransom something she wants.

Report: Sharon is refusing to do what I want, namely go to the Bahamas but she wants me to drive to Michigan.

Action: I'll hold ransom Sharon's trip to Michigan.

Realistically, this was *not* the way to fly! Exerting the willpower to hold back your actions until you have had an opportunity to check out your itinerary of fallacies can save you some hard times. If you have a tendency to commit any of the above fallacies, you should keep this knowledge at the front of your mind, together with an appropriate antidote before you plunge headfirst into turbulent relationship waters.[8]

Fallacy Syndromes

I have said that fallacies travel in herds. Well, one way in which they travel is in *syndromes*. This is a progressive series of fallacies where one fallacy leads to another. There are two or more fallacies in the series.

One very popular syndrome is the Slippery Slope syndrome. In this syndrome, first you Slippery Slope, then you Awfulize, then you give yourself I-Can't-Stand-It-Itis. Let me illustrate with an example.

At age twenty-six Barney earned a doctorate in philosophy from Harvard University. Having graduated from this prestigious Ivy League institution, he had high expectations of landing a job at a top-notch university. But things didn't go as he expected, and he ended up traveling about the country, taking a number of temporary positions (including a one-year, postdoctoral fellowship at the University of Iowa). Barney found himself in a competitive rat race with the nation's brightest minds for a few seats at esteemed institutions of higher learning like Yale, Dartmouth, and Williams, where he interviewed but didn't get hired. Moreover, some of the less highly regarded universities at which he interviewed tended to view him as overqualified and unlikely to remain at their institutions. One interviewer told him, "Ten years ago someone with your credentials wouldn't even apply here." When Barney asked him if he was nevertheless interested in his candidacy, the interviewer winked and said, "You're in the ballpark." But Barney still didn't get the job!

In his struggle to find a permanent position—that is, a full-time, tenure track one—Barney became depressed. He felt like he was just pointlessly going through the motions of trying. He told myself, "Now, all those years of training are going to be wasted. I don't think I can stand it." Barney felt as though everything he had worked for had been in vain.

As you can see, he was exaggerating the consequences of not landing a permanent teaching job in philosophy. Barney was supposing that there wasn't anything else he could do that would utilize his training; and this assumption he made without even exploring alternative job possibilities. Little did Barney realize, at this early juncture in his career, that there could be a gratifying profession of practicing philosophy and that he would become one of its main proponents. Moreover, while in his more rational moments he told himself that, eventually, he would probably get something if he kept trying, this was not an active premise in his emotional reasoning.

Barney was Awfulizing about the perceived consequences of not getting a permanent teaching job in philosophy. He had conceptualized this as terrible, horrible, and awful. And then he told himself how he couldn't stand something so awful happening to him.

As his reasoning was a syndrome, it contained more than one set of premises. There were actually three rules—Slippery Slope, Awfulizing, and I-Can't-Stand-It-Itis—with a report filed under each. This was the basic syndrome:

Slippery Slope: As I haven't yet gotten a permanent job as a philosophy professor, I will never get such a job and all my training will be wasted.
Awfulizing: As I'll never get a permanent teaching job in philosophy and as all my training will be wasted, it's awful.
I-Can't-Stand-It-Itis: As something so awful is happening to me, I can't stand it.
Emotion: Depression about not having gotten a permanent job as a philosophy professor (with thoughts of the futility of all his years of work).

Notice how the above rules all begin with "as" instead of "if." This is a convenient way of indicating that a report has been filed under a rule. For example, the rule, "As . . . all my training has been wasted, it is awful" assumes the report, ". . . all my training has been wasted." Can you see how this use of "as" makes it less complicated to display the reasoning in the syndrome? By building the report into the rule using "as" instead of "if," you don't have to list each report separately.

Notice how, in Barney's thinking, Slippery Slope led to Awfulizing, which, in turn, led to I-Can't-Stand-It-Itis. The one fallacy piggybacked on top of the other. This is what I mean by a syndrome. As you will see in part 4 of this book, such syndromes are very common in self-destructive emotions. The Slippery Slope syndrome is especially popular in anxiety and depression. For every possible fallacy combo, you could conceivably have a syndrome. Like viruses, there are countless mutations.

So, you may find yourself committing syndromes not explicitly discussed or named in this book. If you discover such a syndrome in your thinking, you should give it a name, preferably one that is catchy or easy for you to remember, and will help you to identify the syndrome when you commit it.

Well, I imagine you want to know what happened to Barney. He spent a few years taking temporary jobs, including putting together part-time teaching work at different colleges and universities to earn enough to survive. His perseverance did eventually pay off, and he got a tenure track position as a philosophy professor at a highly progressive, state community college located in sunny California. True, it wasn't the Ivy League as he had hoped, but he enjoyed working there nevertheless. Equally true, he could have accomplished the same thing with considerably less emotional stress. As a result of the Slippery Slope syndrome, Barney lived in academicians' purgatory, and it needlessly felt like hell!

Notes

1. W. D. Ross, ed., *Prior Analytics*, trans. A. J. Jenkinson, vol. 1 of *The Works of Artistotle* (New York: Oxford University Press, 1966), book 1, ch. 1.

2. I am defining "shame" broadly enough to encompass embarrassment. A narrower definition of shame would restrict the negative judgment to a *moral* judgment.

3. The rule always rates an emotional object. The report may sometimes do its own rating. For example,

> *Rule:* All bastards should burn in hell.
> *Report:* John is such a bastard for lying to me like that.
> *Emotion:* Anger toward John (with the hope that he burns in hell).

In including in your report that John is a bastard, you have not merely described what John has done; you have also rated him. So, in such cases the report is not purely factual or descriptive.

4. When fallacy rules piggyback like this, you get what I call "fallacy syndromes." This more complex form of reasoning will be discussed later in this chapter and also in part 4.

5. I will also expand on these antidotes in chapter 10.

6. Also known as "rational-emotive imagery." See, for instance, Susan R. Walen, Raymond DiGuiseppe, and Windy Dryden, *A Practitioner's Guide to Rational-Emotive Therapy*, 2d ed. (New York: Oxford University Press, 1992), pp. 65–66.

7. I don't know if you really have a problem with dining out alone, but many people do. I will use this situation for illustration but you can always substitute your own imagery when you stage your own practice session. For example, if you have strong anxiety about getting up in front of a group of people to give a speech, you could imagine yourself on stage in a large crowded auditorium about to give a speech.

8. I have already suggested some relevant antidotes to fallacies of action in chapter 6. I will also provide a list of such antidotes in chapter 10.

Chapter 9

How to Refute Your Faulty Thinking

That some reasonings are genuine, while others seem to be so but are not, is evident. This happens with arguments, as also elsewhere through a certain likeness between the genuine and the sham. . . . So it is, too, with inanimate things; for of these, too, some are really silver and others gold, while others are not and merely seem to be such to our sense. In the same way, both reasoning and refutation are sometimes genuine, sometimes not, though inexperience may make them appear so; for inexperienced people obtain only a distant view of these things.

—Aristotle[1]

Now that you know some major fallacies to look for in your premises, you are already ahead of the game in refuting reasoning that only *seems* genuine, but is really a sham. "Ah," you say. "There I go again, telling myself that I'm a stupid jerk, devaluing myself, making a nothing of myself. That means that I'm still resorting to that old standby of mine, the Damnation of Self Rule. What a waste of brain cells! What's really stupid is berating myself because I think I did something stupid."

See what I mean? By applying the repertoire of fallacies you learned in this book, you can spot these infections and hopefully kill them before they multiply. But, let's face it: Your mistakes might not always be so obvious to you, and you might have to dig a bit to expose them. Sometimes, you may even uncover a mistake that doesn't fit neatly into your repertoire of fallacies.

Knowing how to refute an irrational way of thinking can help you to weaken the emotional appeal it may have for you. It's like unclothing the proverbial wolf in sheep's clothing. "Ah," you say. "And to think that I thought that was really a rational idea. Now I see it for what it really is, a fallacy." This is where it can be useful to have some techniques for unclothing the wolf. In this chapter, I will discuss some of these techniques.

Checking for Counterexamples

I used to naively think that all dogs were warm, cuddly, and friendly, including all big black Labs. Well, one day, I was taking a stroll with my wife and a large black Lab charged at us, like a hound out of hell, growling and snarling viciously. "Fear not," said I valiantly to my beloved damsel in distress. "Just stand perfectly still," said I, quite calmly, confident that this big show-off would run up to us, smell us, slobber all over us, and bid us good tidings. To my chagrin (and pain), this dashing pooch took a substantial piece of flesh out of my leg, and there I stood, dripping with blood. Alas, an indisputable counterexample to my incredulity!

A counterexample is an example that disproves a rule or generalization. Take the popular belief that, whenever you say something false, you are *lying*. Can you think of a counterexample? Well, what if you really *think* that what you are saying is true? Are you still lying? Not necessarily. When a witness gets up on the stand in a court of law, he is guilty of the crime of perjury if he deliberately tries to deceive the court. But, it is no such crime if he is merely mistaken.

Let's try another one. Many people think they should never break a promise. Well, is it really *always* wrong to break a promise? What if that's the only way to save someone's life?

Many people also damn themselves or others because they or others have done something bad. "I'm a bad person because I lied to my mother," you say. Well, can you think of a counterexample to the assumed rule that says a bad act equates to a bad person? It's not very difficult. Did your mother ever do anything bad or unworthy, even tell a big fat lie? Unless she's infinitely better than Mother Teresa, she sure did. So, unless you want to condemn your own mother *and* everybody else's, you should get off your own back.

Learning to look for counterexamples can help you to avoid tunnel vision in confronting reality. If you are suffering from the blues, they can be eye-openers. So, let's suppose you had a doozy of a fight with a significant other and you now feel like giving up the ghost. "What's the point to being alive anymore," you think. "I might as well be dead." Your reasoning:

> *Rule*: If I have a serious falling out with my significant other, then I might as well be dead.
> *Report*: I had a serious falling out with my significant other.
> *Emotion*: Depression (with thoughts and images of dying).

Can you remember the last time you had a fight like this and felt the same way? Well, you got over it, right? That's the counterexample to your nutty rule. It portends more meaningful life to come. Like a rainy day, this too shall pass.

CHECKING FOR EVIDENCE

Evidence is to an irrational premise as daylight is to a vampire. Where the one is, the other is not. Both work in the darkness. Irrational premises, like vampires, perish in the light. Subject an irrational belief to evidence and see how quickly it begins to deteriorate and turn ugly. "Where's the evidence?" Keep this weapon handy. The pus of infected thinking dries up under its direction.

Where's the evidence that you are *entirely* worthless if you screw up on the job? Where's the evidence that your arriving late will have catastrophic consequences? Where's the evidence that the guy in front of you deliberately tried to infect you with an exotic disease? Where's the evidence that the person you admire so much is perfect in every way? Where's the evidence that you couldn't stand to live on your own? Where's the evidence that you must have the approval of others? Where's the evidence that you have a duty to make yourself crazy? Where's the evidence that, no matter what you do, you are fatalistically doomed never to find a mate? Where's the evidence that your spouse will suddenly stop abusing you, even though neither of you have made nor intend to make, any significant life changes? Where's the evidence that blondes have more fun?

Under the weight of such evidence, the "unreason" of your faulty thinking is exposed. In issuing such a call, you can, at once, refute your irrational premise and pave the way for a powerful antidote to work against it. In asking yourself the question, "Where's the evidence?" you assume that your beliefs *should* be backed by evidence. You put the credo of evidence to work as an antidote against your irrational thinking.

I have often called upon the power of evidence to deflate my own self-defeating thinking, and have advised my clients and students to do the same. Let me illustrate this with a blast from my own past. One not-so-glorious evening about fifteen years ago, en route in my trusty, metallic-blue Cougar to teach an evening class, I came to a busy intersection, indeed one that I had crossed many times before. My radio resonated with the sounds of Diana Ross and the Supremes, playing a favorite oldie of mine, "You Can't Hurry Love." In the midst of making my left-hand turn on green, which turned to amber and then to red, a motorcyclist quickly approached the intersection. Well, he did not stop when the light turned red, and I did not get out of the way fast enough. It took only an instant for the event to play out in which the motorcyclist hit my Cougar broadside, totaling the car, ejecting him into the air and projecting him over my car. I watched him stand up, walk a few feet, and then lay back down on the ground. It was all quite surreal, like a motion picture playing out at a crawl. I could see the front wheel of the cycle swaying back and forth as it came closer, closer, and closer. I could hear Diana Ross singing, "No you just have to wait" (how fitting!) and inch by inch, he moved closer as I helplessly awaited the inevitable.

Well, fortunately, we both survived. While the cyclist suffered some broken bones, I suffered primarily from You-Can't-Hurry-Love flashbacks. After the accident, whenever I heard this song, the accident would play out in my mind, complete with the feelings and images I had then experienced. A favorite oldie of mine had become a blast from the past that unearthed my mortal fear of dying. In fact, whenever the song came on my car radio, as I drove, I expected to be struck by an oncoming vehicle. The song had, in my mind, taken on the power to cause traffic accidents. I quickly shut it off before it could work its mischief.

Now, I ask myself what sounded so ridiculous to my intellect, but which was quite serious emotionally. Where's the evidence that Diana Ross's song caused the accident? Where is it? "No evidence for such," I told myself repeatedly. But the feelings and images of that gloomy evening still hung on.

Nonetheless, the call for evidence, with its clear answer, "No evidence whatsoever," rebounded loudly and forcefully in my mind and paved the way for me to stand up against my bodily inclinations. "Act on evidence," I antidotally declared to myself. "Don't let a groundless, irrational fear control you." So, I stopped shutting off the tune, and flexed my willpower muscle to listen through the end as I drove. The more I listened without getting into another accident, the more counterexamples I gathered against the irrational connection. The more I disregarded the fear, the fainter it grew.

Many years later, I can listen freely to this song as I merrily drive along. Upon hearing the song, I am still reminded of the accident. While I don't enjoy the tune quite as much as I used to, it does not excite fear in me, and I don't expect to be mowed over by a motorcycle when it comes on the radio.

Checking for Self-Defeating Consequences

What would happen if people had to resolve all of their headaches before they could be happy? Well, few, if any of us, would ever be happy. What if you had to be certain about things before doing them? Then you would never do much, if anything, in your life. What if doing something bad made you a bad person? Then everyone, yes everyone, would be bad. What if parents had a duty to sacrifice their happiness for their children's happiness? Then, if their children had children, they too would have to sacrifice their happiness. What if you were a passive receiver of your ideas and emotions? Then you would have to give up the idea that you are capable of controlling your own life. What if everyone dictated reality? Then no one would get along. What if, whenever someone did something wrong to a person, the person did something wrong back? Then there would be an endless generation of wrongs. What if you just perceived things in terms of black or white? Then you would miss all the possibilities in between. What if you treated others as stereotypes? Then you would not get the opportunity to know them. What if you fatalistically expected the future to be like the past? Then you would not do anything about your situation and, consequently, you would fulfill your own prophesy.

Most of us who drive have had automobile accidents. The last time somebody ran into you, did you call him a stupid idiot or other damning name? If you did, then your rule would be something like, "People who cause automobile accidents are stupid idiots."

Well, did *you* ever cause an accident? If not, *could* you ever cause one, that is, are you capable of causing one? That would also make *you* a stupid idiot, or at least a potential one. Is your mother or father a stupid idiot or a potential one? Is *everyone* a stupid idiot or at least a potential one? That would be the consequence of this rule if it were true.

Here's my point. Irrational ideas generally have self-defeating consequences. Getting used to exploring these consequences can often help you to see just how muddled the idea really is. So, before you go with an idea, ask yourself what it portends. Realizing its implications can be an important step in stopping the idea from subverting your happiness.

Take the case of Allison and her husband, Leonard. Allison suffered from intense anxiety, which manifested itself in a frequent desire to confront Leonard with "problems" she perceived to require immediate attention. When one problem was laid to rest, another was likely to be raised very soon after. In fact, there were very few occasions in the time they spent together that were not occupied with Allison's presenting a new problem. Whether it was a problem with children, health, work, finances, or the state of the world, Allison invariably found something to focus upon that she perceived as problematic. Often, the problems came in twos. "Leonard," she would way, "I have two things to discuss with you." Leonard's role was often one of respondent, whether he wanted to be in this role or not. Frequently, Allison played devil's advocate with Leonard's responses, trying to find holes in his proposed solutions to the problems she raised. Often, Leonard's forced participation in this activity of problem solving resulted in his becoming angry, and this, in turn, added to the tension existing between the two. On the other hand, Leonard's own concerns were squeezed in between Allison's, and they usually received a minute or two of lip service.

Can you guess what emotional rule Allison was using? It was a version of the old "Thou Shalt Upset Yourself," namely,

- I must constantly be on the lookout for serious problems so that none slips by me unnoticed. If I find what looks like such a problem, I have a *moral duty* to sound the alarm, ruminate, and disturb myself over it until it is satisfactorily resolved, and demand that others close to me (namely Leonard) do the same.

Well, Allison was quite willing to admit that this was, indeed, her rule. It was one upon which she had arranged her life. Emotionally, it was as though she stood guard over the floodgates of hell. With all the feelings, thoughts, conscience, and sense of one bound by moral duty, she kept a constant vigil, cautiously watching that no evil got through. From her emotional standpoint, it was incomprehensible how Leonard could refuse to cooperate. In her mind, this was mutiny. Such uncompromising dedication to her rule of life placed considerable strain on the happiness of both.

In fact, the slavish and dutiful manner in which she enforced her rule made the couple's happiness together a virtual impossibility. Good times were fated to dry up with the emergence of a new problem that needed immediate attention. Leonard described the situation as a series of "dark tunnels." Finding a way out was in vain, for there were only a few moments of basking in the sunlight before the couple was once again submerged in a new dark tunnel, crawling anxiously about in the darkness looking for a glimmer of light.

The self-defeating nature of Allison's rule was quite obvious. She stood guard against the evils that might destroy happiness, consumed in the very act of standing guard. So, a strong refutation of her rule was how it defeated the very point that it was supposed to serve.

What to do about breaking this vicious, self-defeating cycle? Since Allison's moral compass was off, it seemed to me that she needed to be reoriented, morally. This did not mean dictating morality as much as it meant placing her back in touch with the moral rules to which she herself subscribed.

Perceiving the self-defeating character of her rule made it easier for Allison to see how much she had strayed from her own moral codes. There were three moral rules that Allison professed to accept, but they were plainly at odds with her self-defeating "duty" to upset herself. For one, by her slavish, blind adherence to this bogus duty, she had failed to respect a rule of *respect for personal dignity and autonomy* by trying to force Leonard, against his will, to live within her bleak underworld of dark tunnels. Second, she had violated a rule of equity by unfairly setting the agenda for both partners. Third, she had violated one of her most serious rules to *do no harm* by creating a stressful environment for them both.

Here are some helpful antidotes for cases like Allison's: Instead of trying to force-feed significant others, you should treat them with dignity by respecting their right to self-determination. Instead of dominating the relationship, strive for a relationship of mutuality and sharing. Avoid polluting the headwaters of the relationship by looking for problems. Instead, look for more fulfilling, enjoyable, and intimate ways of relating.

These are more realistic moral rules than the self-defeating, fallacious rule that Allison had mistaken for moral duty. The reason why these are more realistic is that they have a much better track record of promoting personal and interpersonal happiness. But they have not gone down easily for Allison, who still presently has a strong emotional attachment toward performing her bogus duty. Suspended in a state of cognitive dissonance between her realistic moral rules and her pseudomoral duty, she has had to put her inner pedal to the metal. She has had to flex her willpower muscle to deliver actions against the rough terrain of her bodily inclinations. For her, it still feels right to proactively seek out those evil problems that might otherwise seep through a weak line of defense. But every time she does, she loses sight of the very rules of morality that she seeks to preserve.

I know that Allison has tried hard to defeat these deeply entrenched tendencies that defeat her purposes. I also know that it remains an uphill battle for her, which may not always be won. But you can lose some of the battles without losing the war! Better to fight your tendency to live unhappily and to irregularly defeat it than to passively and slavishly remain in its grip.

Checking for Double Standards

Irrational rules about the treatment of others are hard to *consistently* apply. By accepting such rules, there is a good chance that you will find yourself adopting two standards, one for yourself and another for everyone else.

To help you to see if you have adopted a double standard in relating to others, you can ask yourself this question: "How would I like it if others did the same thing to me?" For instance, how would I like it if:

- Others refused to recognize my preferences as legitimate but insisted that I honor theirs?
- Others demanded of me that I never make any mistakes?
- Others called me damning things, like shithead, asshole, and so forth?
- Others blackmailed me?
- Others tried to get their way with me by kicking and screaming?
- Others tried to manipulate me by Pity Mongering?
- Others tried to intimidate me into doing what they wanted by Poisoning the Well?

- Others insisted that I join them in sitting around, obsessing and aggravating myself over something that I was not especially inclined to worry about in the first place?

I am not saying that having one consistent standard for yourself and others will mean that you are being reasonable. You are not being reasonable merely because you are quite willing to have others demand perfection of you, call you damning names, manipulate and intimidate you, blackmail you, kick and scream at you, and even needlessly insist that you suffer. Consistency in applying your rule to self and others is not all you need to be rational. Yet, it does seem to be at least one necessary condition of rationality. As the logician will tell you, it is impossible to have *p* and *not-p* at once. If you don't think so, then try peeing and not-peeing at the same time!

Asking yourself the question, "How would I like it if others did the same thing to me?" can be a useful way to confront such incoherence in your thinking. Take the case of Daniel and Sandy, married twelve years. The same age, the two went together in high school and were married the year they graduated. Although Sandy was valedictorian for her high school class, Daniel enrolled in college as a math major while Sandy took a job as a waitress. For four years, she faithfully waited tables to put Daniel through college. One month after Daniel graduated, he landed a high paying job in industry. Two months later, Sandy gave birth to a bouncing baby boy.

For the next five years, Sandy stayed at home with the little boy, cleaned house, did the shopping, and faithfully had dinner on the table when Daniel arrived home from work in the evening. Sandy, however, began to express a desire to go to college to become a teacher. Although Sandy also had reservations about going to college while she cared for an active five-year-old, Daniel encouraged her to go. So, reluctantly, she enrolled in classes at a local college and began taking classes toward her degree. During this time, Sandy remained primary caretaker for their child as well as homemaker. Although Daniel helped care for their child occasionally and did some of the shopping, the bulk of such domestic activities still rested with Sandy. Because Daniel's career was very demanding, he often worked long hours, taking his work home with him, even on weekends. So, Sandy found herself juggling three full-time roles—housewife, mother, and student—with occasional assistance from Daniel.

When Sandy finally graduated after five years, she was offered a job as a high-school teacher. Very excited about her career prospects, she still had reservations about her ability to handle the job while remaining a good mother to her now ten-year-old son. Daniel, however, was very encouraging, and convinced her to accept the job offer.

As job pressures mounted amid inevitable parental crises and the usual stock of parental responsibilities and household chores, Sandy began to feel overwhelmed by the demands placed upon her. So, she began to ask for more help from Daniel, who, by now, had climbed to the status of an executive in his firm. Tension between the couple brewed, as Sandy attempted to delegate more domestic responsibilities to Daniel.

Daniel summed up his position in these words. "I can't afford to be doing women's work when I have a job to do. There's just not enough hours in a day to do what she wants me to do."

Well, it was very clear what Daniel's rule was, namely:

- Cooking, cleaning, shopping, and taking care of children should be the province of women, not men, and I should not be expected to do these things when I have a (real) job to do.

I asked Daniel to consider how *he* would feel if he were in Sandy's shoes. "Here you are, trying to hold down a job, take care of most of the domestic chores including being primary caretaker to your child, and, when you ask your wife for help, she tells you, 'Sorry, I have a *real* job to do and don't have time.' How would you *feel*?"

I asked Daniel to try to get inside Sandy's subjective world, and to experience the frustration of being treated according to such a double standard. The more he empathized with Sandy's plight, the more apparent his double standard became. Along with this insight, the poverty of his rule also became clear. And the antidote became just as clear!

Sharing of domestic responsibilities and mutual cooperation was a rational solution for two partners who, for so long, had lived according to a double standard. This was not so easy for Daniel to emotionally accept. His rational side said "Yes," but his bodily feelings, images, and deeply ingrained ideas about the roles of men and women screamed out an emphatic "No!"

Nevertheless, Daniel took the challenge. Flexing his willpower muscle to work against these currents that eroded the couple's happiness, he began to take on more domestic responsibilities. In time, he began to feel more comfortable with these new activities. The last I heard, this couple was resonating with mutual cooperation on the domestic front while they both prospered in the workplace!

Refuting Faulty Thinking and Finding Antidotes

Many popular approaches to dealing with irrational thinking such as Rational-Emotive Behavior Therapy (REBT) and Cognitive Behavior Therapy (CBT) emphasize the usefulness of finding and refuting irrational beliefs. As I have stressed, these are very important aspects of defeating your counterproductive beliefs. But these aspects are stage setters. They set you up to come in for the kill by discrediting your irrational lines of reasoning. The kill is often in the antidote.

Antidotal reasoning redirects your behavior and emotions. Without the antidotal *shoulds* and *shouldn'ts* that counter your irrational (absolutistic) *shoulds* and *shouldn'ts*, you are likely to continue to act and feel in self-defeating ways. So, your happiness very much depends upon the antidotes you find against your irrational lines. In the next chapter, I will address this important aspect of improving your personal and interpersonal happiness.

NOTE

1. *On Sophistical Refutations*, in *The Basic Works of Aristotle*, ed. Richard McKeon, trans. W. A. Pickard-Cambridge (New York: Random House, 1941), ch. 1.

Chapter 10

How to Find Antidotes to Your Faulty Thinking

[W]e should not know what sort of medicines to apply to our body if some one were to say 'all those which the medical art prescribes, and which agree with the practice of one who possesses the art.' Hence it is necessary with regard to the states of the soul also, not only that this true statement should be made, but also that it should be determined what is the right rule and what is the standard that fixes it.

—Aristotle[1]

Remember the steps I gave in chapter 8 for formulating and checking your emotional reasoning? Let's list them, briefly:

1. Identify your emotion.
2. File your report.
3. Find the rule you are assuming.
4. Refute your irrational premises.
5. Find antidotes for your refuted premises.

In chapter 8, I discussed steps 1 through 3. In chapter 9, I discussed step 4. In this chapter, I'm going to focus on step 5, finding antidotes for your refuted premises. Let's start with some important *dos* and *don'ts* of finding antidotes.

ANTIDOTAL *SHOULDS* AND *SHOULDN'TS*: SOME HOT TIPS

What do these rules have in common?

- If you prefer something, then it is the one true reality, and, therefore, everybody else *should* also share your preference.
- People who care about you *mustn't* ever treat you unfairly.
- You *must* upset yourself whenever you have a problem in your life.
- You *shouldn't* ever act on a decision unless you are absolutely certain about it.
- If you have had bad luck in the past, then you *should* simply resign yourself to the same in the future.

Well, for one thing, each is irrational. Second, each commands, demands, dictates or prescribes something by using such words as *should, shouldn't, must,* or *mustn't*. Third, each makes an *absolutistic*, uncompromising demand. As you have seen, if you live according to such irrational, absolutistic demands, you are likely to live unhappily.

A major purpose of antidotes is to defuse such destructive *should*s, *shouldn't*s (*must*s and *mustn't*s) by correcting them with more rational, less rigid *should*s and *shouldn't*s. So, in a very real sense, your happiness may depend on how well you handle your *should*s and *shouldn't*s. In particular, if you can't tell the virulent ones from the helpful ones, then you are likely to live unhappily.

In the last chapter, you saw some basic ways to refute irrational premises. These methods of refutation can be used to distinguish the virulent (irrational) *should*s and *shouldn't*s from the helpful ones. The virulent ones can be disproved by showing that they admit of counterexamples, lack evidence, have self-defeating consequences, or involve double standards. On the other hand, the very point of finding antidotes to these irrational ideas is to address such defects.

Beware! In trying to fix one irrational idea by finding an antidote to it, you can end up saddling yourself with another irrational demand. For example, I have not infrequently encountered clients who demanded perfection about Demanding Perfection. "I should not be Demanding Perfection at this stage in counseling, and after all my progress too!" proclaimed one of my clients after catching himself in the act of whining over having made a mistake at work. This client's antidote to Demanding Perfection was to demand that he never Demand Perfection! Well, he had to go back to the drawing board to come up with a more realistic antidote, one that cut him some slack, and gave him permission to be human.

So, here's an important antidote to irrationally and absolutely swallowing your antidotes. You shouldn't assume that your antidotes are beyond refutation or that they are perfect and cannot be improved. Honing your antidotes by checking them for counterexamples, evidence glitches, self-defeating consequences, and double standards is a useful way to guard against rigid, absolutistic thinking in the very process of trying to avoid this type of thinking. Keeping this antidote in mind might save you from jumping from the freezer into the frying pan!

Even useful antidotes may not work in every situation. For example, a useful antidote for improving intimate relationships such as marriage is to be open and honest about your thoughts and feelings. But, what do you do if your spouse is a domestic abuser and openness and honesty about your intention to seek asylum would probably get you killed?

As Aristotle stressed, problems of everyday life are not like math problems where there is a formula that works once and for all. Instead, in applying antidotes to your self-destructive, emotional reasoning, you should be mindful of exceptional circumstances under which even a generally effective antidote may have contraindications.

But don't get carried away with making exceptions. Not everything is a special case. For example, while avoiding serious harm can be a legitimate exception to openness and honesty in intimate relationships, getting back at somebody by "clamming up" is not. This is just the irrational rule of Getting Even in sheep's clothing.

It is easy enough to fall into a routine of making bogus excuses for not pushing yourself hard enough to overcome your irrational ways. This can take the form of telling yourself that your present situation is a true exception to a rational rule when it really isn't. "Why should I be honest with that son of a bitch," you protest, "when he's been so dishonest with me. I shouldn't give him the right time of day!" In making such a damning excuse, you can end up exchanging a rational rule for an irrational, self-defeating one. Instead of improving your relationship, you can make it worse. It's true that in some unusual cases, what is ordinarily rational medicine can turn out to be poison for your happiness. But before you go downing poison in a medicine bottle, look carefully (at your rules) before you swallow!

Antidotes that make ironclad, unconditional, absolutistic demands are not likely to be antidotes at all. Fighting absolutistic thinking with absolutistic thinking, like fighting fire with fire, is likely to do more damage, at least in the long run. This is why the language you use to formulate your antidotes should avoid the appearance of being rigid and inflexible. As Albert Ellis and his disciples have repeatedly stressed, issuing prescriptions by using *must* and *mustn't*, especially when followed by "always," "never," or "ever," usually signify absolutistic thinking.[2] These words imply necessity, and what is necessary is unconditional.

On the other hand, *should*s and *shouldn't*s do not *always* imply ironclad necessity; nor, in some common uses, do they signify absolutistic, inflexible thinking. This is true because these words can also be used to *recommend* or *advocate* rather than command, dictate, insist, or demand.[3] So you *should* (I strongly recommend that you) stick to using *should*s and *shouldn't*s in expressing your antidotes rather than *must*s and *mustn't*s. And you *should* (I strongly recommend that you) avoid the qualifiers "always," "never," and "ever." In this way, in finding antidotes for your irrational thinking, you can decrease the chances of becoming rigid and inflexible about your rigidity and inflexibility.

Here's another useful tip, which comes from Aristotle's cabinet of rational medicine. Antidotes generally aim at counteracting extreme or absolutistic thinking with a Golden Mean. This is moderate thinking, thinking that avoids extremes. Here are a few examples:

- Demanding Perfection of yourself or others is one extreme; Damnation of yourself or others is another; but accepting yourself as an imperfect person is rational.
- Perceiving an absolute duty to upset yourself over your problems is one extreme; avoiding responsibility entirely is another; but doing what you reasonably can about your problem and then leaving yourself alone is rational.
- Using deceit, threats, pity, blackmail, and other manipulative devices to get your way is one extreme; failing to assert yourself is another; but treating yourself as well as others as rational, self-determining persons is rational.
- Magnifying Risks of bad things happening in your life is one extreme; underestimating dangerous situations is another; but accurately assessing the probabilities is rational.
- Awfulizing about events in your life is one extreme; denying that bad things happen is another; but putting the bad things in your life into perspective in relation to other aspects of your life is rational.

Need I say more? Rational antidotes to your unhappiness generally aim at counteracting extreme or absolutistic kinds of thinking with more moderate ones. This is Aristotle's aphrodisiac, his key to emotional and behavioral bliss: moderation satisfies. Aristotle wouldn't tell you to party 'til it hurts.

How Refutation Can Help You Find Antidotes

Strictly speaking, antidotes are about *your thinking*. They tell you how to correct a flaw in your thinking. No, more exactly, *you* tell yourself how to correct a flaw. They are you talking sense to yourself. They are *self-talk*. They are you talking yourself *out of* what you have irrationally talked yourself *into*.

By refuting your irrational thinking, you will, in effect, have a road map of what flaws to correct. Suppose you are telling yourself that you must be perfect at whatever you try. Well, a refutation might consist of realizing that a consequence of this rule is that perfect human beings exist. But, quite obviously, they do not. That perfect human beings exist is plainly false to fact. Have you ever met any? I dare say not! There is just no evidence to prove that such people exist. So your rule that tells you to demand perfection of yourself must also be unrealistic. To conclude otherwise would be illogical.

Now, how does this point you toward an antidote? Easy. Once you see the flaw in your thinking, you can see what might remedy it. In the present case, your flaw is in your assumption that human beings can, indeed, be perfect. So an antidote to your irrational rule is simply to give yourself permission to be human. This means that you should give yourself permission to make mistakes. Cut yourself some human slack, and take a load off!

PUTTING YOUR ANTIDOTES TO WORK

So, here again is a general strategy to improve your life: *Refute your irrational premises by exposing their flaws and find antidotes to correct those flaws.* But, remember, finding antidotes and putting them to work are not the same. To put them to work requires exercise of willpower. You will have to flex that muscle to think, feel, and act in the ways directed by your antidotes.

Willpower will also be behind the scenes even in your very effort to formulate and correct your emotional reasoning. In the midst of an intense emotion, it is not easy to stop and take a careful look. You will need to say to yourself, "Time out! I should look at my reasoning first, before carrying this any further." This is the "mother" of all antidotes! Without flexing your willpower to comply with this very basic antidote, you will never get started. More likely, you will act first and regret it later.

Doing your thinking after the fact is better than not at all, and by looking at your thinking after the fact, when you have calmed down, you can prepare yourself for the next time you find yourself responding irrationally. But even here, when you become emotionally aroused again, you must still tell yourself to wait a minute and to look at your thinking. You will still need to recognize your irrational premises. Having your refutation and antidote ready to use against these irrational premises can save you time and effort, but it will not eliminate the need to exercise your willpower. Having an antidote ready to use does not guarantee that you will in fact use it. You will also need to flex your willpower long enough to recognize the need for it, and hard enough to overcome the sway of your irrational tendencies.

Fallacies of Emotion: Refutations and Antidotes

There is no way to formulate in advance all of the irrational premises that you may harbor, all of their possible refutations, and all of their antidotes. Nevertheless, as you have already seen, there are commonplace fallacies that, in one form or other, frequently infect emotions and actions.

Below, I have summarized the fallacies of emotion that were discussed in chapter 5. For each, I have provided a brief refutation exposing the rule's flaws, and I have also suggested some antidotes that address these flaws. I am not saying that the antidotes I have provided are the only possible ones for each rule, but they can nevertheless be very useful ones in fighting off the many virulent strains of these commonplace irrational rules. They also provide clear examples of the process of finding antidotes for your irrational premises. Once again, your success will also depend upon the amount of willpower you are able to muster on behalf of your antidotes.

Demanding Perfection: If the world fails to conform to some state of ideality, perfection, or near-perfection, then the world is not the way it absolutely, unconditionally *must* be, and you cannot and must not ever have it any other way.

Refutation: The assumption that ideality, perfection, or even near-perfection is humanly possible in this earthly universe is false to fact.

Suggested Antidotes:

- You should make a reasonable effort to achieve your goals and to get what you want, but you should be realistic in the goals you set.
- You should be prepared to tolerate disappointment.
- You should change your absolutistic, unrealistic *must*s and *should*s to preferences.

Awfulizing: If something bad happens, then it is *totally* catastrophic, terrible, horrible, and awful.[4]

Refutation: There are increasing degrees of badness in the universe, and they can increase ad nauseam, but the idea of a *totally* catastrophic, terrible, horrible, and awful thing is a fiction for which there is no evidence.

Suggested antidotes:

- You should put the badness of something into perspective by looking at it in relation to much worse possibilities (e.g., being beheaded on a guillotine).
- You should avoid the use of superlatives such as "terrible," "horrible," "awful" and "worst," and instead use nonsuperlatives such as "tough break," "unfortunate," "bad," and "very bad."

Terrificizing: If someone appears to have some desirable feature, then this person or thing must be absolutely and *totally* terrific, perfect, and the best of its kind in the entire universe.

Refutation: The idea that there are totally terrific, perfect, and, ultimately, the best things in the entire universe is a fiction for which there is no evidence.

Suggested antidote:

- You should view people and things in the world according to both their desirable and undesirable features.
- You should neither idealize nor demonize people and things.
- You shouldn't make your love, admiration, or respect for people depend upon an assumption that these people are totally terrific, perfect, or the best.

I-Can't-Stand-It-Itis: If you find something difficult or challenging to deal with, then it must be beyond your capacity to tolerate and you *cannot* and must not ever hope to succeed at it.

Refutation: If people never tried to overcome difficult or challenging things and instead retreated from them by telling themselves that they couldn't stand them, then there would be few human accomplishments worthy of pride, since all or most human accomplishments worthy of pride are made in the face of adversity.

Suggested antidotes:

- You should change the "I can't" in your refusal to stand challenging or difficult things to "I won't" or "I choose not to" stand it. In this way, you should stop hiding behind "I can't" and accept responsibility for not standing it and freedom *to stand it.*
- You should exert your willpower muscle to tolerate short-term frustration for the sake of greater, long-term satisfaction.
- You should look upon difficult or challenging things as opportunities to grow through the experience of trying, rather than as occasions for failing.

Damnation: If there is something about yourself or about another person that you strongly dislike, then you or this other person is *totally* worthless.

Refutation: Doing something worthless doesn't equate to *being* totally worthless. Otherwise everyone, or almost everyone, would be worthless.

Suggested antidotes:

- You should stick to rating *actions* (yours and others) and not persons.
- You should view your self-worth as a constant and not a variable that changes with successes, failures, or the approval and disapproval of others.

- You should choose a philosophical basis of your constant self-worth with which you are comfortable, and you should remind yourself of it (such as, for example, that you are a child of God; a human being; a remarkably complex creature with the capacity to reason, know, recall, enjoy, desire, hope, dream, will, and act; an autonomous, free, self-determining being; a being with inalienable rights to life, liberty, and the pursuit of happiness; a conscious, experiencing, self-aware being as opposed to a cauliflower or moss).
- You should view your past mistakes as learning experiences, and you should resolve to use the acquired knowledge to make positive changes in the future.

I Just Can't Help This Feeling: If you feel depressed, anxious, angry, guilty, or otherwise upset, then you might as well just accept and go with your feeling, because it is really not in your control anyway.

Refutation: If you couldn't exert any control over your own emotions, then you would be a biological machine that responds to stimuli automatically. There would be little difference in kind between your knee-jerk responses and your emotions. Both would be fully determined and completely out of your control. If so, then it would be a waste of time to even try to overcome your irrational emotions by finding antidotes to them and exerting your willpower, because your emotions would always be beyond your control anyway. But this is plainly false to fact because many people do, indeed, succeed in overcoming their irrational emotions in this way. And if others can regulate their emotions, what makes you think that you can't? Why the double standard? Is that not really a cop-out?

Suggested antidotes:

- You should change *I can't* in "I can't help my feelings" to an emphatic *Yes, I can*. This means acknowledging your own freedom and responsibility in regulating your emotions instead of making excuses for yourself.
- You should *prove* your freedom to yourself—prove to yourself that you are more than just some preprogrammed biological mechanism—by resisting your emotion, flexing your willpower muscle, holding back on acting and feeling the way your body inclines you, telling yourself that you *can* do it, and then *doing* it, taking back control over your body and mind.
- You should hold yourself accountable for your emotions according to the same standards that you apply to others.
- You should avoid the use of terms that deny responsibility for your feelings, such as "you made me angry," "you upset me," "you pissed me off," and "you aggravated me," and use instead the responsibility-bearing mode such as "I made myself angry," "I upset myself," "I pissed myself off," and "I aggravated myself."

Thou Shalt Upset Yourself: If you encounter a problem in your life that you deem important, then you have a *moral duty* to ruminate over it, never stop thinking about it, make yourself miserable and upset over it, and demand that others, for whom you also deem it a problem, do the same.

Refutation: A moral duty to make yourself and/or others miserable and upset whenever you encounter what you perceive to be a significant life problem is not part of any recognized social, religious, or moral code; nor can it be justified by any philosophical theories of ethics. It cannot be derived from the promotion of human happiness, pleasure, alleviation of pain and suffering, respect for rational self-determination, obedience to God, nature, or any other philosophical standard that has been used to justify human duties. In fact, such a demand is inconsistent with and contrary to these rational standards.

It is also unrealistic to demand perfect certainty in resolving your practical problems before you can stop thinking about them. This is true because the reports you file in practical reasoning are always tentative and, at best, only probable.

Suggested Antidotes:

- You should give yourself permission, and, indeed, affirm your moral right to be happy and not to suffer even if something seems wrong or doesn't go your way.
- You should make a *reasonable effort* to resolve your life problems and shouldn't ruminate about them once you have made this effort.
- You should seek *reasonable and probable solutions* to your life problems, and, therefore, shouldn't demand that they be perfect solutions or that they provide absolute certainty before you accept and act on them.
- You should *do* what you reasonably can do about your problem and then leave yourself (and others) alone.
- Instead of ruminating about your problem, you should exert your willpower to go on with your life by doing things you like to do or think would be productive.

Fallacies of Action: Refutations and Antidotes

In chapter 6, you found out how fallacies of action can mess up your interpersonal relationships. Finding antidotes to them can therefore help you to fight off self-destructive effects upon very intimate aspects of your life. Below, I have summarized the self-destructive rules of action that I discussed in chapter 6; and, along with each rule, I have provided a brief refutation and some useful antidotes that address the exposed flaws. Feel free to use these as guides to constructing antidotes to versions of these rules that may be destroying your interpersonal relationships.

The-World-Revolves-Around-Me Thinking: If you prefer something, then it is the one true reality, and, therefore, everybody else should also share your preference.

Refutation: Your preferences and tastes cannot be validated by factual evidence any more than those of anyone else's. For example, what facts prove that your preference for action thrillers is more valid than someone else's for romantic comedies? So, there is no more validity to your preferences than to those of the other person. This also points to a double standard, one for yourself and one for others. While you disregard the preferences of other people, you expect others to accept yours.

Suggested antidotes:

- Because there is no valid empirical way to establish your personal preferences over anyone else's, you shouldn't assume that your preferences must somehow be more valid or truer than another's.
- Instead of picking the other person apart according to your own preferences, preconceptions, and personal biases, you should put yourself in his or her subjective shoes, and try your best to understand his or her perspective.
- You should seek and exercise your willpower to make and keep equitable compromises with others on matters of preference.
- Where mutually agreeable compromises cannot be reached, you should still exercise tolerance for the other person's perspective by respectfully agreeing to disagree.
- In assessing what's right or good for others, you should look at their particular circumstances instead of judging them according to your own circumstances (e.g., just because you can eat fattening foods without putting on weight, or read and study with the TV on, doesn't mean other people can or should).

Blackmailing: If you want something from someone, then you should get it by withdrawing or threatening to withdraw something of value from this person.

Refutation: This treats others like objects manipulated for your own purposes. Insofar as you would not want to be treated in this way yourself, you have a double standard in your treatment of others. Since relationships based upon such treatment are not usually worth maintaining, blackmailing others is likely to destroy the very relationship you seek to maintain. In attempting to establish relationships based upon blackmail, you also degrade yourself by implying that the only way to get what you want is through coercion rather than through mutual trust and respect.

Suggested antidotes:

- You should recognize that you are a rational being with the unique human capacity to use rational argument to get what you want.

- You should push yourself to *use* this rational capacity of yours as the primary means to get what you want.
- You should also treat *others* as rational beings, rather than as mere objects. This means fully informing them of what you seek, and then letting them decide on the basis of your rational argument, rather than on the force of coercion.

Making a Stink: If you want to be respected, understood, heard, or heeded, then you should kick, scream, yell, or other sundry manner of throwing a temper tantrum.

Refutation: This not only involves a double standard, it is likely to work in reverse. The more you kick and scream, the less respectable and credible you are likely to appear.

Suggested antidotes:

- You should make rational arguments instead of the stinky gas of self-defeating, self-degrading tantrums.
- You should push yourself to maintain rational control over your skeletal muscles. No kicking, jerking, scowling, teeth clenching, growling, screaming, foot stamping, fist pounding, arm flinging, or other wild body movements, please!

Pity Mongering: If you are in trouble or are having difficulties getting what you want, then you should cry, sob, weep, pout, mope, whine, or otherwise make yourself look hurt, dejected, downtrodden, demoralized, dejected, rejected, crucified, or otherwise pitiful.

Refutation: By making yourself look pitiful, you weaken your own credibility and imply that you do not have any independent, rational basis upon which to be judged. You also forfeit the chance to rationally and *empathically* discuss your desires with others, and to model, build, and share in a more mutually gratifying, trusting, and respectful form of relating.

Notice that empathy is not the same as Pity Mongering. People can empathize with you only when they understand how you are really feeling, by entering your subjective world, and walking a mile in your shoes.[5] Unlike Pity Mongering, it is an honest sharing of your feelings and does not involve manipulating or deceiving people into feeling sorry for you.

Suggested antidotes:

- You shouldn't exploit the human capacity for pity to get others to do for you what *you* wouldn't rationally do for them.
- Instead of putting on a show intended to manipulate others into feeling

sorry for you, you should discuss your feelings with others in a candid, honest way, and encourage genuine, empathetic understanding.
- In trying to get others to empathize with you, your goal should be to help them *understand* how you are feeling so that they can take this into account in deciding whether to do what you want them to do.

Beating Around the Bush: If you perceive someone as having made an unreasonable or wrongful request of you, but you feel intimidated to say no, then you should "save face" by verbally consenting while nonverbally dropping hints of your disapproval.

Refutation: By giving mixed signals about your true wishes, you risk misleading others, leaving them with false impressions, going along with something to which you may have reasonable objections, or unnecessarily putting off having to set the record straight. In this way, neither your wishes nor those of the other person to whom you have given mixed messages are likely to be satisfied.

Suggested antidote:
- Instead of agreeing to something you don't reasonably want to do, you should politely and diplomatically refuse, and then explain your reasons for refusing.

Poisoning the Well: If you don't want someone to do or believe something, then you should use strong, negative language to intimidate and dissuade this person from doing or believing this thing.

Refutation: This treats others as objects to be manipulated. Insofar as you want others to treat you as a rational, self-determining person, you are acting on a double standard by attempting to treat others like objects. In resorting to the manipulative use of language rather than using it to present evidence, you provide no rational basis for doing or believing as you wish.

Suggested antidotes:
- If you want someone to do or believe something, then you should respectfully argue your case on the evidence before you.
- You should avoid the use of strong negatively charged emotional language in presenting your case. (Don't ask, "Are you still going out with *that bum*?")

Getting Even: If someone does something to you that you think is wrong, then you should do something equally as wrong back so that you even the score.

Refutation: When you add one wrong to another, you get two wrongs, not one right. Visiting one wrong with another tends to generate further retaliatory strikes, leading to a progression of regrettable attacks and counterattacks. This is self-defeating, making things worse, not better. For these purposes doing something wrong to another should be distinguished from harming another in self-defense, which may, in exceptional situations, not be wrong or self-defeating.

Suggested antidotes:

- If you feel disposed to get even, then you should stop and objectively consider the consequences of your action first, and then ask yourself whether your action would really be worth it in the end.
- If you perceive another to have done something wrong to you, then you should, whenever reasonably possible, explain to this person why you think what he or she has done is wrong.
- You should listen to the other side of a disagreement, discuss your differences, and try for a mutually agreeable resolution.
- If you have reason to think that you are unable to reason with someone whom you perceive to have done something wrong to you, then you should take constructive actions to avoid further encounters with this person.
- You shouldn't confuse harming someone in self-defense with Getting Even.

Jumping on the Bandwagon: If others such as friends, popular or trendy folks, schoolmates, the crowd, or average people are acting, thinking, or feeling a certain way, then you too should conform.

Refutation: This means that you should discount evidence and instead run headfirst into the water without first seeing if it is infested with hungry sharks. It implies blind obedience. This is likely, sooner or later, to land you in considerable hot water!

Suggested antidotes:

- You should look before you leap, carefully examining the consequences (negative as well as positive) of conformity, before Jumping on a Bandwagon.
- In deciding whether or not to follow the pack, you should consider its possible negative effects on your personal autonomy, individuality, authenticity, and potential for creative living.
- You shouldn't allow peer pressure or other forms of subtle coercion to lead to blindly Jumping on a Bandwagon.
- Before following the advice of others in areas requiring special knowledge or expertise (e.g., health, legal matters, stocks and bonds), you should consider whether such people are qualified to dispense such advice (have documented, relevant training or education in the field). If they don't have

documented expertise, then you should avoid acting on their advice, unless confirmed by others who are relevantly qualified.

FALLACIES OF REPORTING: REFUTATIONS AND ANTIDOTES

In chapter 7, you saw some of the common ways you can mess up the filing of reports. Reports that contain fallacies are unfounded or false to fact, and the point of trying to refute them is to show that they really are so. Like fallacies of rules, these fallacies often go undetected in your premises. They are quite common among humans. Stereotyping, Black-or-White Thinking, Magnifying Risks, and the rest are often built into popular culture. Questioning them may be like questioning mother and apple pie, so you may be inclined to leave them alone.

Take these, for example:

- All men are after just one thing.
- Women, you can't live with them, and you can't live without them.
- If anything can go wrong, then it definitely will.
- Life is like a box of chocolates; you never know what you are going to get.
- Either you're a friend or a foe.
- Whatever happens to you—past, present, or future—is a matter of fate, so there's really nothing you can do about it.

With all respect due to Forrest Gump, life is not always like a box of chocolates, and, while you don't have *total* control, you can have considerable control over what you get. In addition, some people are neither your friends nor your foes. Some women can be quite congenial to live with, and sometimes we can be happy being single. And, while *some* men may have excessive interests in sex, all humans, including men, have more than one drive.

In practicing refutations of the reports you file, you can avoid acting on such groundless and false assumptions that, like the tenets of a religious faith, may receive the blessings of popular culture. I have accordingly summarized, below, some main fallacies of reports and their refutations, and I have provided some useful antidotes. This account should give you a good idea about how to go about refuting and finding antidotes for fallacies that may be infecting your reports.

Overgeneralizing: Putting things into a general class or category in a manner that is false to fact (for example, "All men are after just one thing").

Refutation: These reports speak in absolutistic language (such as *all, none, always, never, any, ever,* and *only*) about groups of people, places, things, and events. When you try to make one size fit all, the result is usually a bad fit! When you Overgeneralize about people (stereotype them), you miss the opportunity to get to know them as distinct individuals. When you oversimplify reality or make decisions based on clichés, you ignore facts and situations, which could have serious, self-defeating consequences.

Suggested antidotes:

- You should be on the lookout for false and unrealistic uses of words like "all," "none," "always," "never," "any," "ever," and "only" in your reports; you should replace these with more realistic word choices such as "some," "sometimes," and "more often than I would prefer."
- You shouldn't generalize about all or most members of a group, based on just a few members, unless you have evidence that these members are *representative* of all (or most) of the other members. (For example, you shouldn't conclude that all men cheat on their wives just because your ex-husband cheated on you, since you have no good reason to think that your husband is representative of men in general.)
- You shouldn't assume that what's true of the part must also be true of the whole. (For example, that there is evil in the world doesn't mean the world as a whole is evil; that a person said or *did* something stupid or bad doesn't mean the person himself is stupid or bad.)[6]
- You should judge people on their own merit instead of stereotyping them.

Black-or-White Thinking: Seeing things in terms of opposites and forgetting about the shades of gray.

Refutation: Logically, something can be neither black nor white. There are many shades in between. So, by thinking that things *must* be either black or white (good or bad, true or false, loved or hated, and so forth) you reason from a false premise. In so doing, you are likely to miss other shades of reality that may be potentially important to you in dealing with your problems or making your decisions.

Suggested antidotes:

- You should be on the lookout for opposite terms like *good or bad, true or false, loved or hated, friend or foe* (etc.); and, if you find them, you should look for realistic options lying in between which you might have missed (e.g., between friends and foes are neutral, impartial persons).
- In an effort to make reality manageable, you should resist reducing complex issues without definite answers into simple matters of yes or no, true or false, right or wrong (e.g., many moral problems, philosophical questions, and life decisions don't have just one simple right or wrong, yes or no answer).

Magnifying Risks: Exaggerating the chances of something undesirable happening.

Refutation: Risk assessment depends on evidence, not on how bad you think something is or how afraid of it you are. For example, the risk that it will rain does not depend on how much you don't want your picnic to be rained out. It can be assessed in relation to meteorological information. Moreover, the fact that something bad *can* happen does not mean that it *will* happen (the infamous "Murphy's Law"). It is easy enough to find counterexamples. Just imagine something very bad that could have happened yesterday, but didn't. Finally, it is false to fact that the future is predetermined by a form of cosmic cement known as fate, which keeps you stuck in your unhappy condition. There is no evidence that such a force exists, and cases abound of how people changed their futures (in a positive way) by making constructive changes in their present lives.

Suggested antidotes:

- You should check out the evidence for something before jumping to conclusions about how likely it is.
- To reduce the chances of something going wrong, you should avoid acting blindly and impetuously. This means getting the facts straight, reaching an informed decision, exercising the willpower to overcome irrational fears and impulses, and putting your decision into action. (This is Murphy's Law made rational and constructive!)
- Instead of telling yourself that your future *must* fatalistically and unfortunately resemble your past, you should take constructive action, in the present, to increase the likelihood of future prosperity.

Wishful Thinking: Unrealistically believing what you want to be true instead of looking at the evidence.

Refutation: There is no evidence suggesting that wishes alone can resolve your problems. On the contrary, by telling yourself that things will be different, without any concrete evidence, you are likely to stay just where you are. So, Wishful Thinking is self-defeating because it keeps you from doing anything to *really* change your situation.

Suggested antidotes:

- Unless you want history to repeat itself, you shouldn't ignore the evidence of the past.
- You shouldn't expect things to be different unless you have evidence to think that something has changed or will change that will improve your situation in the future.
- Instead of just telling yourself that things will be different, you should

exert your willpower to overcome your inertia, and *do* something about your situation.

Concocting Explanations: Trying to account for *why* something is true in a way that is not adequately supported by the facts.

Refutation: People usually seek explanations to obtain leverage over a problematic or bewildering situation and to relieve themselves of anxiety and frustration. For example, if you can explain why your car keeps stalling out, then you may be able to fix it. On the other hand, concocted explanations are based on flimsy evidence or on fears or other subjective states of mind. These explanations usually mislead and add to anxiety and frustration instead of relieving it. So, in Concocting Explanations you are likely to defeat your very purpose for seeking an explanation in the first place.

Suggested antidotes:

- In explaining a problematic or bewildering situation, you shouldn't panic or prematurely jump to conclusions. ("OK, he should have been home an hour ago but that still doesn't mean something bad happened.")
- You should generate a creative list of possible explanations. (Well, maybe he's working late, maybe he stopped off at the store, maybe he's stuck in traffic, maybe he got into an accident, maybe he's having a drink with his buddies, maybe he's having an affair, maybe he's been abducted by space aliens, or . . .)
- You shouldn't choose the explanation you fear the most just because you fear it the most. ("Right now I don't have any more reason to think he's gotten into an accident than to think that he's working late, so I'll withhold judgment until I check things out.")
- Faced with several competing possible explanations, you should check out, first, the explanation that's easiest to check out. ("I'll just call his office to see if he's still there.")
- You should go with the explanation that fits the facts the best after you have checked things out. ("I called Samantha and she said her husband, who happens to be my hubby's best friend and coworker, hasn't come home yet either. She also said that her husband told her that he and his work buddies were going to stop off on their way home to shoot some billiards. Now that I think about it, I remember that my husband stopped off to play billiards once before without telling me. So, I think he's probably at the billiard hall. I'll wait a while longer before putting out an APB on him!")

Could-a/Would-a/Should-a Thinking: Making unprovable claims about what could have, would have, or should have happened.

Refutation: When you make unrealistic or unjustified assumptions about what could-a/would-a/should-a been, you are likely to defeat your own purposes. If your point is to teach yourself or someone else a lesson, then you fail to do this because your reasoning is flawed. If your point is to cast or escape blame or responsibility, then, again, your claims are unfounded. Often, such unrealistic talk is really a setup for Damnation ("Had I dressed less provocatively, he wouldn't have raped me; that makes me worthless trash") or excuse making ("If I hadn't been under such pressure at work, I wouldn't have hit you and broken your jaw; so you should forgive me").

Suggested antidotes:

- Before drawing conclusions about what you could-a/would-a/should-a done, you should state all your assumed premises and examine each to see if it holds water. ("I'm assuming that rapists are motivated by how women look and dress, and that rape is a sex crime. But rapists are generally motivated by power and control, not by sexual attraction. Since rapists sometimes attack eighty-five-year-old women wearing house dresses, how do I know he wouldn't have attacked me even if I wore something less flattering to my figure?")
- If, after examining all of your assumptions, you find your conclusion about what could-a/would-a/should-a been to be possible but not really justified, then you should qualify it with a "maybe" and "maybe not." ("*Maybe* I would have been financially better off today had I bought that stock but *maybe not*.")
- If you find yourself making unrealistic claims about what could-a/would-a/should-a been, you should be on the lookout for other active, virulent strains of thinking such as Damnation (of Self or Others).
- If you find yourself making unrealistic claims about what could-a/would-a/should-a been, you should consider whether you are using such a claim as an excuse (a cop-out) for accepting responsibility for your actions.

Personifying: Giving nonhuman objects (like a bottle of catsup or "life" in general) human attributes and blaming them for your misfortunes.

Refutation: By transferring responsibility and blame from yourself onto nonliving objects and abstractions (bottles of catsup, cars, traffic lights, life, fate, etc.), you appease yourself but continue to make the same mistakes and suffer the same negative consequences. The *literary* or *fictional* use of personifying ("The black clouds looked angry") should be distinguished from the *literal* or *real-world* use of Personifying ("It deliberately rained because I made plans to go to the beach"). The literary use has literary value; it allows you to use metaphor in order to paint a picture in words in a vibrant, colorful way. But, by taking such usage literally, you can allow yourself to be misled into discounting your responsibility for your real-world decisions.

Suggested Antidotes:

- You should accept responsibility for your decisions rather than blaming them on nonhuman objects when things don't go the way you want them to go. This means taking constructive actions to improve your situation or learning from your past mistakes to avoid repeating them in the future.
- In making your *real-world* decisions, you should avoid literally treating nonhuman objects as though they were actual persons.
- You should be on the lookout for the language of Personifying such as applying properties of human minds ("stubborn," "cruel," "fickle") to nonhuman objects or abstractions ("my car," "life," "fate").

How Antidotes Can Work Together

As you can see by my suggested antidotes, there are a number of different responses antidotes direct. For example, some antidotes tell you to change your language. Others aim at constraining, changing, expressing, examining, performing, or recognizing an action, emotion, or belief. Others tell you to exert your willpower to do or stop doing something. Some antidotes tell you to look for certain related fallacies. Others tell you to accept responsibility.

Some of the antidotes I have listed use the word *should* while others use *shouldn't* or the equivalent (for example, you *should avoid*). The *should* antidotes can be useful because they give you *positive instruction* about what *to do* rather than what *not to do*. The *shouldn't* antidotes can often be useful because they clear the way for a *should* antidote. For example, a *shouldn't* antidote for coming up with an adequate explanation is that, "You shouldn't panic or jump to conclusions." But this does not tell you how to come up with an adequate explanation. On the other hand, the *should* antidote, "You should generate a creative list of possible explanations" tells you what to do to begin to formulate an adequate explanation.

Sometimes one *should* antidote clears the way for another. For example, the first of the below *should* antidotes gets you ready for the second:

1. You should recognize that you are a rational being with the unique human capacity to use rational argument to get what you want.
2. You should push yourself to *use* this rational capacity of yours as the primary means to get what you want.

Learning to use *should* antidotes and *shouldn't* antidotes systematically in such ways can be an important skill. Let me give you an example.

Fred and Alan, a gay couple, were living together for one year in a monogamist relationship. Fred was a radiological technician at a local hospital and Alan was a sales manager at a large department store. While the two had remained faithful to one another, Alan had become disenchanted with the way Fred was treating him. For example, in company, Fred sometimes corrected his grammatical mistakes, spoke in jest about personal matters such as Alan's compulsive checking of his alarm clock before going to sleep, and sometimes ridiculed his rather conservative political outlooks. On one occasion, the two were having dinner with another gay couple when Alan accidentally, audibly passed gas. While the other couple tried to act nonchalant about the event, Fred burst out hysterically. "Oh Alan," he declared, "you're really full of hot air tonight!" The three chuckled a bit as Alan sat there silently. The rest of the evening was strained as Alan woodenly interacted.

That night, Alan slept in the guest room with the door locked and refused to talk to Fred. The next morning, Alan continued to ignore Fred, despite the several apologies Fred attempted to launch. So, the two went to work without any resolution.

After work, Alan stopped off at a gay bar, met another man and the two struck up a conversation. After a few drinks and friendly conversation, the man invited Alan back to his apartment for some "snacks." Alan declined, but he took the man's phone number.

A few days later Alan and Fred were still in a cold war. This is when Alan came to see me and told me about his situation. We talked about his relationship with Fred. While it was apparent that Alan still loved Fred, he also had a burning desire to *get even* with him for what he perceived to be his insensitivity. Feeling hurt and resentful, Alan pondered the idea of having an affair with the man he had met in the bar just to "teach Fred a lesson."

As the thought ran through Alan's mind, there was a sweet feeling of vengeance that invited him to pursue this counterattack. But what was Alan ultimately going to prove? I asked Alan to take a hard objective look at the consequences of cheating on Fred first, before allowing himself to be seduced by the fragrant scent of revenge. Herein was an antidote of cardinal import:

- If you feel disposed to get even, then you should stop and objectively consider the consequences of your action first, and then ask yourself whether your action would really be worth it in the end.

The more we talked about the implications of such a drastic measure, the more Alan came to realize that he would be defeating his own purposes. Alan ultimately wanted Fred's devotion and care, but, by having an affair, he would be likely to chill, if not completely destroy, the prospects for gaining these affections.

So what would be a more fruitful approach? Once Alan realized the self-defeating consequences of having an affair, he was able to appreciate a further antidote, which had previously escaped his noticed:

- If you perceive another to have done something wrong to you, then you should, whenever reasonably possible, explain to this person why you think what he or she has done is wrong.

Such common sense as this could not possibly have escaped any intelligent human. Right? Wrong! Under the direction (spell!) of Getting Even, Alan did not sense the obviousness of this antidote. After accepting the futility of having an affair, Alan realized the bogus nature of Getting Even. The first antidote—to first consider the ultimate consequences of getting even—cleared the way for this second antidote to be understood and embraced. It challenged him to take constructive actions rather than to get even. Although the thought of a possible affair continued to appear and reappear with the intermittent allure of Getting Even, Alan flexed his willpower muscle on the side of reason, and fought off this seductive musing. He never did have "snacks" with the man he met in the bar!

It has been about two years since Alan and Fred had their heart-to-heart about the importance of respect for privacy and personal dignity, and the relationship is still evolving. Fred still sometimes forgets and acts insensitively. But the two are very much in love and have managed to stay together in a largely supportive and caring relationship. The pressures of being gay in a heterosexual society open another can of worms, which I will address in the next chapter.

Notes

1. *Ethics,* book 6, ch. 1.

2. Albert Ellis, *Overcoming Destructive Beliefs, Feelings, and Behavior* (Amherst, N.Y.: Prometheus Books, 2001); Susan R. Walen, Raymond DiGuiseppe, and Windy Dryden, *A Practitioner's Guide to Rational-Emotive Therapy*, 2d ed. (New York: Oxford University Press, 1992). Some uses of *must* and *mustn't* do not signify absolutistic thinking. For example, "If you are to remain alive, then you must have oxygen" asserts a biological necessity.

3. The idea that language can also be used to *pre*scribe as well as *de*scribe was introduced by J. L. Austin in his important little book, *How to Do Things with Words* (Cambridge: Harvard University Press, 1975). Austin referred to the use of *should* to recommend as an "exercitive," which, he said, was "the giving of a decision in favour of or against a certain course of action, or advocacy of it. It is a decision that something is to be so, as distinct from a judgment that it is so: It is advocacy that it *should* be so, as opposed to an estimate that it is so . . ." My italics, pp. 155–56.

4. This rule does not explicitly use the words *should* or *must* but the words *terrible, horrible*, and *awful* nevertheless imply them. If something is terrible, horrible, and awful, then you *should* or *must* be horrified by it, terrorized by it, and feel awful about it. It is this prescription implied in the rule that can direct self-destructive emotions.

5. Elliot D. Cohen and Gale S. Cohen, *The Virtuous Therapist* (Belmont, Calif.: Wadsworth, 1999), pp. 61–64.

6. This means that Damnation can also be considered a form of Overgeneralizing. I have elsewhere referred to this type of mistake as the *Fallacy of the Whole* (sometimes, more technically dubbed the Fallacy of Composition). The reverse fallacy is the *Fallacy of the Part* (sometimes also called The Fallacy of Division). This is when you assume that what's true of the whole must also be true of the part. For example, because the world is good, everything in it must be good; or because you are a rational animal, each of your actions must be rational. See my book, *Caution: Faulty Thinking Can Be Harmful to Your Happiness.*

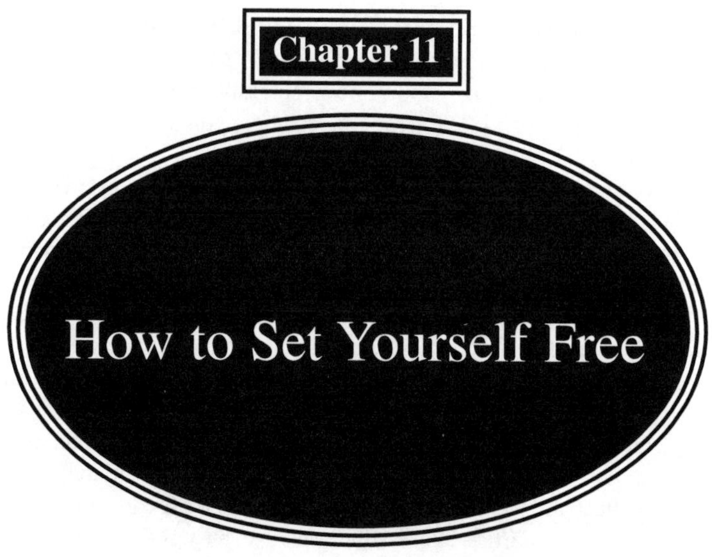

Antidotes to an Oppressive Upbringing

[A]ctions and states of character are not voluntary in the same way; for we are masters of our actions from the beginning right to the end, if we know the particular facts, but though we control the beginning of our states of character the gradual progress is not obvious, any more than it is in illnesses.

—Aristotle[1]

In my experience, many emotional problems stem from a lack of development of personal freedom and autonomy. You can unknowingly become a "willing slave" to social practices and expectations that leave little room for cultivation of personal growth. In such cases, exposing and refuting these self-destructive social rules hidden in the premises of your emotional reasoning and finding antidotes to them can help you gain greater control over your emotions and your life.

Two Willing Slaves: The Case of Anne and Bob

Here's a case that should show you just how repressive and dysfunctional socialization can be, and how antidotal reasoning can help you to reclaim lost freedom and autonomy.

Bob and Anne, a middle-class couple, had been married for three years and were in their late forties. Bob had been married once before and, after a marriage of nineteen years, his wife had divorced him. He had three grown children, was a manager in a large firm, and held a graduate degree in business management and an undergraduate degree in theology. Raised in a very strict religious home, he had been expected to become a clergyman. And although he had practiced as a minister and pastoral counselor for some time, he later gave it up for a career in business.

Anne had been married twice before and had one daughter from her first marriage, which ended after seventeen years with the death of her husband. Her first marriage had been a rather traditional one; Anne was a mother and homemaker and her husband "wore the pants," as she said. Her second husband, whom she described as a con artist, clandestinely had seven wives (simultaneously!). During the time he had been married to Anne, he had beaten and mentally abused her and had also succeeded in swindling her out of a considerable amount of money. After ending this abusive relationship, Anne sought out pastoral counseling to work through some of her issues related to the abuse. However, after beginning a sexual relationship with her therapist, therapy was terminated. Subsequently, she married the therapist, who was none other than Bob.

My first session was a joint meeting with both Anne and Bob. It had been Anne's idea to seek counseling. As she saw it, her marriage was suffering from a "lack of communication." Bob, on the other hand, displayed a good deal of resistance to counseling, and was just going along with it because "this was what she wanted." As time went on, Bob became more amenable to the idea of counseling and began to open up more. However, for reasons I will explain, we never did fully overcome the obstacle of his resistance.

In later sessions I talked with Anne about her thoughts on a woman's status in marriage. She explained how Bob enjoyed telling jokes at functions and how she herself tried not to say anything humorous for fear that she might overshadow him. She tried her best to "stay in the background" so that he would not resent her. As time went on, however, she became more aware of the self-defeating nature of such behavior. She observed that, when she was submissive, Bob was less respectful of her (speaking sarcastically and criticizing her) than when she asserted her autonomy.

I also continued to meet with Bob, sometimes privately, sometimes with Anne present. In private sessions, Bob spoke more openly about his feelings and was less defensive. In joint sessions, there was the clear aura of a wall he had erected between himself and his wife.

At times it looked as though relations were improving between the two. In retrospect, however, I realize that this was just an illusion. Gradually, the situation worsened. Bob began to drink heavily and the wall began to thicken.

By the last session I had with Bob (this was a joint session), he was displaying the greatest amount of resistance ever. He denied having any drinking problem and rationalized his drinking as his way of "getting back" at his wife for smoking, a habit of Anne's that he detested.

It seemed evident at this point in counseling that there was an important piece missing from the jigsaw puzzle of Bob's life—a piece that was needed to satisfactorily explain his present marital problems. There was something important Bob was not telling anybody. Realizing the hopelessness of the situation so long as Bob's resistance persisted, I decided to confront him, knowing full well that I might alienate him further. I indicated to him that the excuse he gave for his excessive drinking (to get back at his wife for smoking) was probably just a smokescreen for some more important underlying concern of his.

Suspecting that socialization, especially gender role issues, had played a part in the problems this couple had experienced, I gave each client an edited excerpt from John Stuart Mill's *Subjection of Women*.[2] This classical treatise discussed the adverse effects of traditional gender role socialization on both genders, especially women. Mill argued that women have been socialized into a kind of "willing slavery" according to which they are brought up to be submissive and yielding to the control of others, to live for and through others, and to cultivate affection instead of intellect. On the other hand, men are brought up to be just the opposite, and, in Anne's words, "to wear the pants." Hoping that this essay would encourage reflection on their individual belief systems, I asked each to read this selection and then to discuss it with the other.

Although Bob refused further counseling (on the grounds that he really did not need any), I continued to meet with Anne. At the next session, I talked with her about her reaction to Mill's essay. She told me that she was particularly struck by Mill's point that women are socialized into becoming "willing slaves," and that what Mill had said applied to her own case. As she left my office that day, she turned toward me, looked me straight in the eyes, and said, "No more willing slave." I can recall seeing the determination in her eyes. The willpower that I have repeatedly spoken of in this book seemed to reveal itself to me in her powerful expression, like a ghost lying dormant inside her, suddenly materializing before my very eyes. My faith in her native power to thrust off those emotional shackles that bound her was affirmed in that unearthing look!

During that same session I also had learned from Anne of another breakthrough. Although Bob did not identify the problem, he had revealed to Anne, in a letter, that he had a "problem," that it was a "bad" one, and that she would not remain married to him if she knew what it was.

One week later, the "problem" surfaced: Bob was gay. He explained to Anne that he had been having homosexual relations since the age of ten. When he married Anne, he thought he could leave this life behind him, but he had been mistaken. On a weekly basis, he would meet other gay men in the back of an X-rated bookstore to engage in sex.

The circumstances were compounded by Anne's reasonable fear of AIDS. She had had sex for the past three years with a homosexual man who had had multiple sex partners, and who had not, so far as she could determine, taken any precautions. In helping her explore her options, I suggested that she and Bob get tested for HIV (the virus that causes AIDS). Both eventually were tested. Whereas Anne tested negative, Bob's results were less sanguine and indicated need for further testing.

Anne's initial response to her finding out about Bob's homosexuality was one of self-pity, particularly over what she perceived to be the deceit he had perpetrated on her. But despite these very deep hurtful feelings she still had a desire to remain with him. She expressed fear about supporting herself financially without Bob's help; she proclaimed that she loved him even though she also hated him; she still held out hope that he might be able to leave his homosexual past behind him; and she expressed bewilderment about how he could favor another man over her.

At this time, Bob and Anne had been living under the same roof, but this arrangement ceased when one night he got drunk and beat her. She suffered bruises, scratches, and a torn ligament in her foot. Although she called the police, she could not "bring herself" to press charges. As with her second marriage, she was once again the subject of abuse.

In the weeks that followed, I continued to talk with Anne about the importance of taking control of her own life. Although I did not tell her *what* to do, we explored some of her options such as getting a job. Shortly after, Anne enrolled in a college course, got a job, prepared her house for sale, and filed for a legal separation. The last time I spoke to her, she told me that, although she "had her moments," she "felt good" and "in control of things." She also told me that she kept her copy of Mill's *Subjection of Women* handy, and that she was still underlining things in it!

What about Bob? At the time of the couple's separation, Bob rented an apartment, and papered his walls with pictures of naked women. Eventually, Bob met another woman and moved out of the area with her.

AUTONOMY

As I have explained, you can make your own emotional and behavioral headaches by deducing them from irrational premises. By exposing, refuting, and finding antidotes for these premises, you can overcome such self-destructive emotions and behavior and attain considerable control over your life. This means that you have the ability to determine your own happiness. This is what I mean by autonomy.

You're not just some inert piece of matter. You're a person with a remarkable power of self-determination. This is what philosophers dub your "free will."

I am not saying that you have free will in some deep metaphysical sense in which your will exists apart from the biochemical and neurological processes in your brain. For example, the French philosopher Rene Descartes thought that the power needed to move your body came ultimately from your immaterial soul. Well, what if you really don't have an immaterial soul, and your mind is really just a highly complex organic computing machine (hardware) with a very intricate program (software)? Would that mean that free will is just a popular myth?

I think not. You can have free will regardless of whether or not you have an immaterial soul. Not that I think you don't, but that's really not the point. And here's why: You have the remarkable ability to think about your own thinking, to expose and refute your irrational premises, to find antidotes to them, and to use these antidotes to overcome and redirect your self-defeating emotions and behavior. Whether or not this process is entirely biochemical does not change the fact that you have this capacity, and are, therefore, capable of self-regulation. To the extent that you *use* this capacity you are free. To the extent that you allow yourself to be stifled by self-destructive rules, you are *not* free. Unfortunately, this is the sense in which Anne and Bob were, to a large extent, "willing slaves." Let's take a look at this idea by listening to the words of philosopher John Stuart Mill.

Socialization

In 1861 Mill wrote,

> All men, except the most brutish, desire to have, in the woman most nearly connected with them, not a forced slave but a willing one, not a slave merely, but a favorite. They have therefore put everything in practice to enslave their minds. The masters of all other slaves rely, for maintaining obedience, on fear—either fear of themselves or religious fears. The masters of women wanted more than simple obedience, and they turned to the whole force of education to affect their purpose. All women are brought up from the very earliest years in the belief that their ideal of character is the very opposite to that of men; not self-will and government by self-control, but submission and yielding to the control of others. All the moralities tell them that it is the duty of women and all the current sentimentalities that it is their nature to live for others, to make complete abnegation of themselves, and to have no life but in their affections. And by their affections are meant the only ones they are allowed to have—those to the men with whom they are connected, or to the children who constitute an additional and indefeasible tie between them and a man.[3]

Times have undoubtedly changed since Mill spoke these words, and women living in the "free world" have achieved greater opportunity for self-determination than ever before. Women have greater opportunities for education and job prosperity, and such arrangements as sharing child rearing responsibilities equally between spouses has made a showing. Nevertheless, the socialization of which Mill speaks provides a good example of how free will and personal autonomy can be quietly thwarted without even your awareness. This appears to have been true in Anne's case (and also in Bob's, as I will discuss). Let me illustrate.

During a session in which Bob was not present, Anne told me that, although she should be able to offer her husband advice, it is her husband who should have the final say in family matters. When I asked her why she felt this way, she said that it is *the man* who should "wear the pants." I filled out Anne's reasoning like this:

Rule: The man should wear the pants, that is, make all the final decisions.
Report: My husband is the man.
Action: I let my husband make all the final decisions.

Seeing Anne's reasoning fully spelled out, with both rule and report made explicit, allowed me to better focus upon the *premises* of her reasoning. My next move was to question her rule.

"Why," I asked, "do you think the man should wear the pants?"

She responded, "It's in the Bible; it's God's will."

Anne's response generated more reasoning:

Rule: Whatever God wills should be done.
Report: It's God's will that the man wear the pants—make all the final decisions.
Action: I let the man make all the final decisions.

Quite clearly, it was not my place to try to poke holes in clients' religious beliefs and values. Still, it is not uncommon for clients to take refuge in their religious convictions as a way of short-circuiting further rational exploration. The rule that "whatever God wills should be done" is a version of what philosophers of religion call the "Divine Command Theory,"[4] and has in fact enjoyed a respectable place in the annals of philosophy. On the other hand, Anne's report piqued my curiosity. "Why," I asked, "would God will that the man wear the pants?"

Anne responded, "Men are better than women at making decisions." And this generated still *further* reasoning:

Rule: The one who is better at making a decision should make it.
Report: Men are better than women at making (all) decisions.
Action: I let the man make all the decisions.

The rule stated here was a rule of fairness according to which the most qualified person is the most deserving. Obviously, Anne had a right to this perspective on fairness just as she had a right to her religious values and philosophy. So I didn't press her on this rule.

But take a look at her report. This is not a respectable religious or moral theory. It is instead an Overgeneralization, a confusion of "some" with "all." Sure, some men are better than some women at making decisions. But where's the proof that *all* men are better than *all* women at making *all* types of decisions? This was a no-brainer! So I asked Anne if there was *anything* she was more qualified at than her husband, and with a moment's reflection she confessed: "I know more about real estate and investment. Bob doesn't know very much about these things." So, I packaged this confession into a further bit of reasoning and presented it to her:

"Well, you say that those better at making decisions should wear the pants. Is that correct?"

"Yes," she responded.

"And you say that you are better at making financial and real estate decisions. Is that also correct?"

"Yes."

"Then who should be making *these* decisions?"

The answer to my query was inescapable. "I should be making them," she responded, with a clear note of discovery in her tone.

Here was the antidotal reasoning to match the bogus reasoning directing her absolute obedience to the rule of men.[5] An antidote drawn from her very own theory of fairness: "Let the authority be vested in the most competent among us for the task at hand, be that male or female." This was an equitable antidote, or at least not a sexist one!

Here was a moment of revelation for Anne that derived from her native power to look logically upon her own thinking. Perhaps, for the first time, she was able to get above her own thinking, like a pilot in a surveillance helicopter hovering over a wooded area, looking for a crime suspect. Insulated from her own socialization by the power of logic, she hovered over her own thinking long enough to discover the source of her subjection. There, hidden in the thicket of her premises was a groundless overgeneralization, a myth propagated within a male-dominated society, programmed into her from her earliest days. There she was, face to face with this source of so much pain and confusion in her life. Shrouded in a veil of holiness, this insidious generalization about the inferiority of women to men worked its mischief like a corrupt law enforcement officer hiding behind a badge of honor in the commission of egregious acts. It was, after all, a sacrilege to question the will of God. But God doesn't make false-to-fact generalizations, *people do*!

Anne's "willing slavery" was now revealed. The insidious nature of such servitude is that its chains are invisible and the slave does not realize her own enslavement. Anne's logical excursion into the factually bogus roots of her own enslavement was a first step toward asserting her freedom and autonomy.

I dare not say that she was thereby liberated. Anne's battle was the uphill one of asserting the willpower necessary to overcome her prior socialization. The more we worked at exposing her premises, the stronger her awareness grew of their self-destructive nature. Anne's stage of awareness graduated to what I have earlier described as cognitive dissonance. Backed by bodily feelings and sensory images, the reasoning that kept her a willing slave still had strong undercurrents.

A strong antidote against these seductive forces of socialization was the assertion of autonomy through action. The French philosopher, Jean-Paul Sartre, once said that a human being "exists only to the extent that he fulfills himself; he is therefore nothing else than the ensemble of his acts, nothing else than his life."[6] This is the thought I tried to convey when I urged Anne to take constructive action to change her life circumstances. Telling her *what* actions she should take would have been self-defeating. It would have destroyed her opportunity to decide *for herself.* While we did discuss options, the decisions had to be hers.

I have always had great admiration for the courage that Anne showed in confronting the forces of socialization that held her down. As you can see from the case description, this was no easy matter. Anne vacillated between two opposing lines of reasoning, one directing her to seek out another man and live through him, the other directing her to follow her own lights. The efforts she made to enroll in a college class and to get a job were important steps toward freeing herself from an oppressive socialization, and reversing the emotional undercurrents that bound her.

In case you're wondering if I think that all women should burn their bras and resign their posts as mothers and homemakers, let me be clear. I am *not* using Anne's plight as representative of women in general who choose to be mothers and homemakers. A key word here is *choose*. Anne had not perceived her situation as one open to choice. From her perspective, this was just the way it *had* to be. It was not until she began to examine the premises instilled in her through a rigid socialization that she became aware of her power to choose.

Second, there is a difference between being a willing homemaker and mother, and being a victim of domestic abuse. Anne's history of physical and emotional abuse fits into a common pattern consonant with being a willing slave but not with being a free agent. Social workers have sometimes used the term "victim mentality" to describe domestic abuse victims' emotional acceptance of a rule that says, "I should be (indeed, I deserve to be) subjected."[7] Anne's emotional reasoning seemed to embrace this rule.

The Self-Evidence Fallacy

A case in point was when Anne found out that Bob was gay. While, at first, Anne expressed indignation over her husband having deceived her, this emotion gradually gave way to expressions of insecurity, helplessness, and guilt. In fact, at one point, she openly blamed herself for her husband's preference for men. Here, her rule appeared to be, "If a husband prefers other men to his wife, then it must be the wife's fault." So, from this rule together with the report that her husband was gay, she deduced guilt.

I suspect that this perceived shortcoming gnawed away at her womanhood under the direction of a rule that went something like this: "If your husband prefers other men to you, then you must be a failure as a woman." But why would it be the wife's fault?

I have heard this expressed before by female clients who seem to assume that the function of a woman is to keep their men sexually satisfied. On this way of thinking, failure here strikes at the heart of what it means to *be* a woman. That is, these women seem to hold a rule like this one:

- If a woman does not keep her man sexually satisfied, then she's a complete failure as a woman.

This rule tries to define what it *means* to be a woman in terms of her ability to attain and sustain the approval of her man through her sexual performance. I suspect that this rule played a significant role in directing Anne's self-doubts. It is a form of Damnation of Self, one that appears to be prevalent in women like Anne who have been socialized to be willing slaves.

Writing in the early fifties, the feminist philosopher Simone de Beauvoir maintained that there is a double standard in the socialization men and women receive. According to de Beauvoir, for women, being with a man goes to the heart of *being* a woman, indeed of being a person at all. Without a man, she is nonexistent, says de Beauvoir; without a man, she is "a scattered bouquet." On the other hand, for men, the beloved woman is only one value among others; they wish to integrate her into their existence and not to squander it entirely on her."[8] He can exist away from her, and still remain an autonomous person in his own right, but she cannot.

Is keeping your man sexually satisfied *really* part of what it means to be a woman? Does being a woman *require* having (and keeping) a man? Women like Anne, enslaved by their indoctrination, have been inclined to say yes or at least to *feel* like saying yes!

But to see exactly why this is crazy, consider this parallel question. "Is being unmarried really part of what it *means* to be a bachelor?" Of course it is. You can't even conceive of a *married* bachelor. This would be self-contradictory, like trying to pee and not pee at the same time. But you *can* conceive of a woman who's not good in bed. A woman who does not sexually satisfy her man or who is unattached does not thereby lose her womanhood like a bachelor loses his bachelorhood when he gets married. When something is part of the meaning of a word, it is self-contradictory to deny it. You cannot say that a figure is triangular, and then add that it doesn't have three sides. But you *can* surely conceive of a woman with a sexually disgruntled husband or a woman who is single. A woman, by definition, is a *female, adult human being*, and there are many single, unattached, female adult human beings living in the world. They are still women, and they can be *happy women*!

Statements like, "All triangles have three sides," "All bachelors are unmarried," and "All adult, female human beings are women" are sometimes referred to as *self-evident*, because all you have to do is understand what they mean in order to see that they're true. Just by thinking about them, you can verify them. Such statements don't need any independent proof because they make *themselves* evident. You don't have to go out and look at many bachelors to confirm that they are all unmarried; just your knowledge of what the word *bachelor* means is enough to see that a bachelor *must* be unmarried.[9]

In contrast, a statement like, "The earth is round (or spherical)" is *not* self-evident because you can't discover its truth merely by knowing the meaning of words. It took sailing around the world to discover the truth of this statement. (We used to think the earth was flat.) Similarly, statements about the causes of things are never self-evident. Instead you verify them through experience. For example, in order to find out if fire will burn you, you or someone else must first get burned. No amount of analysis of the meaning of the word *fire* will substitute for this experience.

Unfortunately, if you are not careful, you might confuse statements that require evidence, and which even might be false to fact, with statements that are really self-evident. This can happen if you assume that a rule you were brought up to accept, such as the one requiring a woman to sexually satisfy her husband, is true by definition and therefore beyond inspection.

If you assume it's self-evident that a woman must keep her man sexually satisfied, then you won't even question it. "That's just the way it is" is what I frequently hear folks say about their socialized rules. They don't stop and question them because they think that they're self-evident. But this is a crock, and a potentially dangerous one. If you don't look at what you're buying, then sooner or later you'll get hurt.

If you're looking for profound truths, then you're going to have to dig for them. Profound truths are rarely if ever self-evident. And self-evident truths are rarely if ever profound. Hey, did you know that frisky frogs are frisky or that all cows are cows or that all green apples are green? Duh! That's the sort of stuff that's self-evident. Statements that are self-evident are typically either true by definition as in, "All triangles are three sided" or they are empty truths like, "All trees are trees."

"Well," you ask, "aren't there at least *some* profound truths that are self-evident?" Maybe, but as soon as you try to say what they mean, you end up qualifying and defending them anyway. "We hold these truths to be self-evident . . . All men are created equal . . ." says the Declaration of Independence. Well, isn't that more profound than, "All triangles are three sided" and "All frisky frogs are frisky"?

Yes, but what does it really mean? If taken literally, it seems false. Are all men (and what about women?) the same size and shape, and are they equally as intelligent? Well, maybe it really means that they are all equally entitled to life, liberty, and the pursuit of happiness. That sounds more promising as an interpretation, but notice that, as soon as you try to make practical sense of this meaning, you end up making qualifications and arguing for them.

Should a fetus have exactly the same right to life as an adult human being? Should we acknowledge and protect a serial murderer's right to life? Should you have the right to assisted suicide if you are suffering from an incurable, irremediable disease? Should you have the right to smoke marijuana in the privacy of your home? Should homosexuals have the right to adopt children? Should you have the right to drive your car without a seatbelt or ride your motorbike without a helmet, if that's what makes you happy? What happens if your pursuit of happiness interferes with someone else's? Answers to such controversial questions are far from self-evident. Yet these are what give practical meaning and import to talk about rights to life, liberty, and the pursuit of happiness. As the history of controversy in our courts shows, answers to such questions rest on open-minded, sensitive, rational debate, not on preconceived, absolutistic, self-evident recipes.

So here's a major antidote. Don't just assume that something is self-evident. If it seems to say something important, something that has impact on your life, then chances are that it's not self-evident and therefore requires defending. Question the things you were brought up to believe. Don't just accept them as though they were self-evident.

So, you should ask yourself, "Why am I any less of a woman if I don't have a spouse or boyfriend? Why do I *have to* have a man to be happy? Why do I *have to* satisfy my husband sexually in order to be a real woman? The definition of "woman" is a *female, adult human being*, and you can *really* be this with or *without* a man. There is no contradiction in that. You *can* be a woman in your own right. Neither logic nor language dictates otherwise!"

The dynamics of living happily, singly or married, and of having a mutually successful sexual relationship are complex issues that can't be settled simply by tending to the meaning of words. Those who profess to have self-evident truths about these matters are likely to be selling you snake oil. So beware! If you accept your rules of action or emotion without questioning them, then you have committed what I call the *Self-Evidence Fallacy*. This is the fallacy of assuming that you don't have to look before you leap because your beliefs are immune to looking. This is a bad idea. Most beliefs worth looking at are not immune to looking. Truths by definition ("All bachelors are unmarried") and empty truisms ("All bachelors are bachelors") are immune but do not give you any guidance. On the other hand, rules of emotion and action are not immune to careful questioning. In fact, I will go out on the limb and say that, insofar as such rules give you practical guidance (for better or for worse), they are *never* self-evident. This means that they are *always* open to inspection. They are *never* immune!

Here's a further example of the Self-Evidence Fallacy. Several years ago, I taught a practical reasoning course in the women's program of a community college. The students in this class were all displaced homemakers—women who were recently divorced or widowed, and whose children were grown. I challenged these individuals to examine some of the rules of emotion and action that they were brought up to believe, and to which they religiously adhered. Many of these women embraced a line of reasoning throughout their adult lives that went like this:

Rule: If I do anything for myself instead of my children or husband then I'm being selfish, and I shouldn't be selfish.
Report: Going to college or getting a job would be doing something for myself instead of my children or husband.
Action: I don't go to college or get a job.

I challenged the group to explore their rule, only to be met with much resistance. The women responded to the challenge as though I were asking them to defend why a mother was a female parent, or a daughter a female offspring. They didn't even recognize the need to provide evidence for their rule because they assumed it was self-evident. This assumption made their rule irrefutable for them. Because they thought it was beyond question, they *never bothered* calling it into question!

I asked these women to tell me what they meant by the word "selfish." Unanimously they responded, "Doing something for myself." This definition of selfishness certainly did make at least part of their rule true. If I do anything for myself, then I do indeed do something for myself! That's certainly self-evident, and quite trivial at that. The problem was that their definition was flawed.

Here's why. When you do things like eat and sleep you are doing things for yourself, but are you necessarily being selfish? Of course not! I pointed out that there is a difference between being selfish and being *self-interested*, and we all agreed that you could be self-interested without be selfish. Eating, sleeping, even breathing, are self-interested activities but that doesn't mean that you are selfish if you do them. So we next pursued the question of what else you needed to do in order to act, not only out of self-interest, but also selfishly. In the end, we agreed that you act selfishly when you do for yourself *without due regard for (the rights of) others*.

Were these women violating anybody's rights by going back to school or by getting a job? No! They would certainly not be violating the rights of their adult children by pursuing these goals. But, these women never even thought to raise the question, not now and not in their married, child-rearing days. For them, the question didn't arise because they thought that if they did *anything* for themselves, yes anything, they would necessarily and irrefutably be acting selfishly.

Even after these women came to see the fallacy in their thinking, the emotional clout of their irrational rule still persisted. They still felt guilt and shame about making a life for themselves independently of their family. There was still a *feeling* that they were doing something wrong, and it made their rational adjustment to a new way of life much harder.

In this state of cognitive dissonance (which, for several of the women, included other, related forms of unfinished business, such as grieving), an effort of will was needed to cast off the shackles of their oppressive socialization that made them slaves and conduits to the happiness of others. Inside, they *felt* like obsolete equipment that had outlived its usefulness. The thought of redefining themselves through a new life plan was frightening—it defied familiar bodily feelings and sensory images. It took much courage to cross this unfamiliar, formidable terrain. For some of these women, it also took the encouragement of family members. For most, I doubt that the specter of these old feelings was ever completely eradicated. But these women now had an antidote to the emotional residue of their oppressive socializations.

If you find yourself feeling compelled to follow old, familiar rules of action or emotion that you never really inspected because it never occurred to you that they *needed* any proof, then you may be in the same boat as the women I just discussed. What to do? Pay attention to the meanings of words. Does doing something for yourself really *mean* the same as being selfish? Does being a woman really mean sexually satisfying your husband? Does being a woman mean having a man? Does being a man really *mean* not crying? Does being a man *mean* being able to have an erection? You delude yourself if you assume the answers to such questions without exploring them. Male genitals do not fall off when a man cries or if he is unable to have an erection; and women do not cease to be women (or persons in their own right) if their husbands divorce them or they never find a suitable mate. These things are not self-contradictory, like imagining a triangle without three sides or a married bachelor or a dog that isn't a dog. The rules you have been brought up to accept, and which guide your actions and emotions, are not self-evident, and you can challenge them without contradicting yourself. This is exactly what you *should* do. Challenge them; try to refute them! While you may find that some of these rules are reasonable and work quite well, you may find that others are self-defeating and oppressive and have insidiously been undermining your happiness.

Social Conformity

The serious consequences of failing to challenge and refute these oppressive rules are well illustrated in Bob's case. Unlike the cases of Anne and the displaced homemakers, Bob's rules were so sealed off from his rational consideration that there could be little progress toward personal freedom and autonomy.

Bob's own history reflects a form of victimization that I suspect played a significant role in his adult life. As I have previously described, Bob had come from a very strict, religious background, which demanded his allegiance to biblical injunctions, including the sinfulness of homosexuality.

In one private session, Bob recounted how, as a child, he came to be sodomized on a number of occasions by a man who performed various other sexual acts on him. Bob told me that it was really not so bad, and that he actually liked it.

I won't get into the thorny psychological issue of whether Bob's homosexuality was a learned response or was somehow part of his natural sexual inclination, or some combination of these. More important is the fact that Bob was a powerless victim of this man's acts. As a child, Bob had neither competence nor maturity to consent. As a result of his powerlessness and vulnerability, he could exert no control. Nor could he protest due to the sinfulness ascribed to homosexuality by his parents and by his own religious indoctrination. His homosexual experiences had to be kept tightly under lock and key.

Psychologist Eric Berne uses the term "life script" to describe childhood decisions that are carried into adult life. According to Berne, these decisions are characteristically acted out in a gamelike fashion, and can often destroy the prospects of autonomous living.[10] I believe that Bob was so scripted because of a childhood decision made in response to his extreme circumstances. I believe that Bob came to view himself as damaged goods. From his seedy one-night stands in the back of X-rated bookstores to the inevitable failure of two marriages, he repeatedly set himself up for hell and damnation. He was the abominable sinner, and his life was the outpouring of unrealistic rules of action and emotion that were rooted in the oppressive socialization he received. The more he played the game, the more abominable he became in his own eyes, the more comfortable he *felt* with this self-deprecating image of himself, and the more reason he had to continue to deduce his own demise:

Rule: All homosexual sinners must be damned.
Report: I am such a sinner.
Emotion: Shame (with thoughts of deserving hell and damnation)

In a homophobic society that indoctrinated him to accept these premises, Bob kept up his game with the support (blessing!) of society.

Yet, I also believe that there was another, approval-seeking line of reasoning that directed Bob to do what society expected of him:

Rule: I must have the approval of others.
Report: Conforming to societal expectations gets the approval of others.
Action: I conform to societal expectations.

Bob's actions of decorating his walls with pictures of naked women, and his continuation of the cycle of seeking out monogamist, heterosexual relations with yet a third unsuspecting woman seemed part of a systematic effort aimed at conformity to social rules. Unfortunately, the more Bob tried, the more "damnable" he became in his own eyes.

It was probably Bob's rule of conforming to the will of others (as he perceived it) that ultimately motivated his vicious cycle of self-deprecation and deceit. Society condemned him for his sins, and so did he. Society expected him to live a monogamist, heterosexual lifestyle, and so did he. His pathology was that of blindly willing what he perceived to be willed by others. He was *Jumping on the Bandwagon*! In so jumping, he forfeited personal freedom and opportunity to develop an independent, authentic self.

I'm not saying that all social conformity is pathological or commits this fallacy. As Aristotle said, human beings are "social animals," and we could not live together in a society without some common rules. For example, we need rules against killing and plundering. But the amount of social conformity that we need to live happily together is often exceeded by the rules of society. The social stigma attached to homosexuality is a clear example where society has gone too far. If a person is openly gay, then he or she must be prepared to withstand the disapproval, ridicule, and persecution of a biased social system. It takes courage and strong character to be willing to pay this price.

This should not excuse Bob's misdeeds, however. As Sartre reminds us, people make themselves cowards (and heroes) by their actions.[11] When bodily feelings and sensory images associated with social ostracism and rejection surge, it takes willpower to counter the inclination to retreat or hide. Bob's plight is a good example of what can happen to you if you recoil from exerting your willpower. In hiding out within the safe and secure environment of accepted social rules and expectations, Bob paid the price by losing himself.

Mind-Sets and Stereotyping

Bob's blind acceptance of social rules could also be seen in his strong tendency to *stereotype* people. On one occasion, he told me that Anne had a "union mentality." When I asked him what he meant by this, he said that she expected to get paid for whatever she did.

On another occasion, he used a regional stereotype to characterize Anne. "My wife has a New England mentality," Bob proclaimed.

I asked, "Does your wife come from New England?"

"Yes," he declared.

"What do you mean by a New England mentality?" I inquired.

In a defensive tone, Bob retorted, "People from New England are crude; they just say whatever is on their minds without first thinking about what they are saying."

Here he was making this broad generalization about *all* New Englanders, so I wondered about how representative his sample was. "Have you known many people from New England?" I queried.

"No," he said. "But the ones I've known have been like that."

I cringed at the meagerness of his evidence! In a perplexed tone, I asked, "How can you say, then, that *all* people from New England are like that on the basis of such a small sampling?"

And, in an even more defensive and resolute intonation, he proclaimed, "All right, maybe not all of them are like that; but Anne is one of the ones who *is* like that!"

As you can see, I attempted to refute Bob's overgeneralization that all New Englanders are crude by showing that it was hastily derived from an insufficient sampling of New Englanders. But Bob stubbornly held onto his stereotype. Instead of conceding to my objection that he didn't know very many New Englanders, he proclaimed, "All the ones I've known are like that." When pressed further about his lack of support for generalizing about *all* New Englanders, he proclaimed, "Anne is one of the ones who *is* like that."

The tenacity with which Bob held fast to his stereotype made refutation very difficult. This is not unusual. If you harbor a stereotype it is likely that you will try to hang onto it even in the face of contrary evidence. Why might this be the case?

In chapter 7, when I talked about stereotyping, I mentioned Walter Lippmann's idea that we "define first, and see later." Bob's case is a good example of what Lippmann meant. As is often the case with stereotypical thinking, Bob's stereotype of New Englanders never was the result of careful inspection. I would venture to say that Bob had learned it from others, perhaps his parents. This is how stereotypes are usually transmitted, not by direct experience but by indoctrination. While Bob softened the literal expression of his stereotype, it continued to operate with full *emotional* support. Bodily feelings and sensory images rallied around the stereotype and sanctioned it. It *felt* right even if, from a rational perspective, it was groundless.

In such cases where you adhere to a generalization in spite of your lack of evidence, you can be said to hold it as a *mind-set*. It is resistant to evidence. This is the earmark of a mind-set. No matter what evidence you are given against the generalization, you are likely to persist in applying it, drawing the same conclusions from it as though it remained undaunted by its refutation. You know the old saw about the bigoted white guy who meets a black guy who doesn't fit his stereotype: "Oh, he's just an exception, not like all the rest of 'um!"

Abandoning your mind-sets can be hard. In order to realize that you have a mind-set, you can't *have* a mind-set in the first place, which winds you in a circle. The best antidote I have for you is this: You should cultivate a habit of proportioning your belief to the degree of available evidence. See yourself as having a *responsibility* (to yourself and others) to believe on the evidence. This responsibility follows from the fact that believing on the evidence tends to promote human welfare—yours and others. For example, if you dismissed all members of the opposite gender because they were all after just one thing—sex, or your money, or whatever—then you would never form bonds of friendship or intimacy with any of them.

If you cultivate such a habit of believing on the evidence, then a mind-set is likely to stand out from the rest of your beliefs. If you have trouble defending your generalization or find yourself eager to dismiss evidence, then you should take these as signs that you have formed an emotional attachment that does not really have a logical leg to stand on. Here is where your willpower must kick ass!

In Bob's case, I tried working with him to become more evidence conscious. I explained to him that it's hard to see Anne as an *individual* when she is seen instead as a "New Englander" with a "New England mentality."

Rather than seeing each other as instances of some general class, I emphasized that both Bob and Anne had to work on seeing each other as individuals in his or her own right. In the immortal words of Sartre, each had to realize that, for human beings, "*Existence precedes essence.*" Just what does this strange-sounding statement mean?

Let's let Sartre speak for himself: "It means that, first of all, man exists, turns up, appears on the scene, and only afterwards, defines himself."[12] This is the reversal of the stereotyping process described by Lippmann in which we "define first, and then see." In defining the person first in terms of a stereotype, you are likely to miss the opportunity to get to know the person as a distinct "existence" (as an individual).

One way in which I tried to encourage Anne and Bob to view each other as individuals was to ask each to make a list of things they liked about each other and another list of things they disliked. The lists were to be prepared independently and I then was to meet separately with each to discuss them.

Both clients prepared lengthy lists. Anne concentrated on negative aspects of Bob's character, as she perceived them, such as his temper, moodiness, put-downs, and his lack of respect for her belongings. But, she also came up with some *perceived positive* features such as his intelligence, good looks, love-making, morals, willingness to work hard, and ability to function in business. These lists helped each client to view the other as a distinct individual instead of some fixed "essence" or stereotype (such as "New Englander" or "union mentality") and they helped to discourage unwarranted inferences from some negative aspect of the person's character to Damnation of the *entire* person.

So, Sartre's advice is also a useful antidote against that formidable emotional rule, Damnation. And here it is: Do not assume that the "essence" of a person comes before his or her "existence." Adopt, instead, the philosophical viewpoint, which says that people are not like manufactured products (such as scissors or paper clips) whose essence (nature, purpose, function) is already determined in advance by its design. A paper clip does what it is designed to do, namely, clips paper. People, unlike paper clips, *design themselves*. This includes New Englanders, Midwesterners, Middle Easterners, Europeans, Africans, whites, blacks, women, men, teenagers, senior citizens, and so forth. View people as distinct individuals rather than as members of fixed, rigid classes. Work on overcoming the emotional inertia that directs you to avoid people whom you have stereotyped. Push yourself to get to know them first.

Feeling Free versus Being Free

I have often thought about the plight of Bob as I live and work. It's easy to think that you are free when your thoughts and deeds resonate with your sensory images and bodily feelings. Subtly, and with the blessings of feeling and imagination, we can embark upon a life fraught with frustration. Without knowing why, the cycle perpetuates, with the same self-defeating reasoning directing our responses, with feelings and sensory images making our premises *feel* right. And onward we march, spinning like a top, not knowing precisely why our lives are in such disarray.

The tragic consequences of being a willing slave in such a vicious process are underscored in the saga of Anne and Bob. They signal the value, indeed urgency, *to think about your thinking*: to stand apart from the particular premises and conclusion to which you are inclined bodily. Armed with a stable framework for exposing, refuting, and finding antidotes for your irrational rules and reports, you can then assess the faulty thinking that perpetuates a vicious cycle of self-destructive behavior and emotions. Here lies the occasion for the assertion of free will, without which we can become willing accomplices to a self-perpetuating, vicious cycle of pain and frustration.

I believe that the power to rise above such determinism was inherent in the nature of Anne and Bob all along, untapped for the most part, but nevertheless part of their human endowment. When you vacillate between alternative courses of action (think of your last choice of a snack from a snack machine), when you wrestle with even the most mundane decision, the feeling of a future yet not run and genuine options still open, tells you that you have power to effect change. As a philosopher, I cannot say that this feeling of freedom can ever prove a will that is not completely determined by environmental, genetic, and/or biological conditions. But, as a human being, who often wrestles with decisions, I cannot help but *feel* that I am free.

Perhaps this feeling is one that has evolved for purposes of motivating us toward actions aimed at survival. Without it, trying to decide a course of action (shall I do this or shall I do that?) would feel like an exercise in futility. Without *feeling* free, you wouldn't *act* as though you really were. Yet, if this subjective sense of freedom is taken to be identical with the willpower needed to affect genuine behavioral and emotional change, then this feeling can be misleading. Bob may have felt free as he acted and emoted in line with a socialization that kept him in a vicious, self-defeating cycle of pain and frustration.

The truth is that Bob was not free in the sense that I have defined. He was more like a preprogrammed computer. Compiled and hidden from his inspection, the code (the premises) that drove his program directed him on a dysfunctional course of living. Genuine freedom meant accessing the code, editing the defective lines, and implementing the revised program. In human terms, this meant having the courage and willpower to confront and change a system of premises, conclusions, feelings, sensory images, and behavior that subverted his happiness.

The case of Anne and Bob is an example of how our lack of control over our own lives can escape our consciousness. Anne and Bob both knew that they were not happy. What they did not know was why. They did not miss their freedom because they did not realize that they did not have it. When Anne looked me straight in the eyes and said, "No more willing slave!" the fact that she was such a slave, in the first place, was a revelation to her. Part of Bob's tragedy was that he never seemed to realize how much in bondage he really was.

I'm not saying that you should fix something if it isn't broken. The exercise of willpower to redirect bankrupt reasoning is not necessary if the rules are working for you. Yet, I have sometimes found in myself the need to stand above my rules of living, look at them, and denounce them.

When I was a young man, engaged to my wife, I can recall feeling very upset (in fact, angry) at her suggestion that she might keep her own last name or at least retain it as her middle name. I thought that this meant that she was not devoted enough to me to take my last name. I have long since thought about how irrationally I had behaved. My socialized rule prescribed that a wife take her husband's last name, but I had never really carefully thought about why I believed this in the first place. Now I see that this rule, which had my emotional support, was part of a system of belief that treated women as possessions, a socialization that had contributed to Anne's unhappiness. The fallacy in my thinking was a form of Jumping on the Bandwagon sometimes dubbed the "Appeal of Tradition."[13] This amounts to *blind* adherence to tradition, regardless of whether or not there is a basis for upholding the tradition.

Whether I was right or wrong in my judgment is really not the issue (although I do believe now that this tradition is bankrupt). The issue is that I *thought* I was freely standing up for my name, when, in reality, I was merely a cog in a deterministic social machine. I now regret the unhappiness that I generated by having been such a cog.

You should not underestimate the amount of willpower it can take to resist and overcome irrational social rules aligned with feelings and sensory images that have spun your wheels for many years. The "pushing" you may have to do from inside yourself to redirect your life is a challenge that cannot be trivialized. Yet, as the plights of Anne and Bob suggest, the heaviness of the burden can be worth its weight in happiness.

NOTES

1. *Ethics*, book 3, ch. 5.

2. John Stuart Mill, "The Subjection of Women," in *Philosophers at Work: Issues and Practice of Philosophy*, ed. Elliot D. Cohen (Belmont, Calif.: Wadsworth, 1999).

3. Ibid., p. 148.

4. John Hick, *Philosophy of Religion*, 2d ed. (Upper Saddle River, N.J.: Prentice-Hall, 1965).

5. Formally, this antidotal line of reasoning went like this:

Rule: The one who is better at making a decision should make it.
Report: I am better than Bob at making real estate and financial decisions.
Action: I make (all) the financial and real estate decisions.

Note how the conclusion of this antidotal reasoning contradicts the irrational reasoning to which it is an antidote. Since she was now torn in two directions, she now needed to summon the willpower to take her antidote and overcome her irrational reasoning.

6. Jean-Paul Sartre, *Existentialism and Human Emotions* (New York: Philosophical Library, 1985), p. 32.

7. Janice K. Wilkerson, "The Philosopher as Social Worker," in *Philosophers at Work,* pp. 155–65.

8. Simone de Beauvoir, "Women in Love," in *Philosophers at Work,* p. 138.

9. The *must* here is legitimate. It is what philosophers call "logical necessity." A statement is said to be logically necessary when there is a contradiction in denying it. You should not confuse this type of *must* with the ones found in irrational, self-destructive rules of reasoning. These are not *must*s of logical necessity. They are false impersonators of the real McCoy!

10. Eric Berne, *Games People Play* (New York: Ballantine, 1964).

11. Sartre, *Existentialism and Human Emotions*, p. 34.

12. Ibid., p. 15.

13. Elliot D. Cohen, *Caution: Faulty Thinking Can Be Harmful to Your Happiness* (Ft. Pierce, Fla.: Trace-Wilco, Inc., 1992), p. 58.

Part 4
Zeroing In on Some
Troublesome Emotions

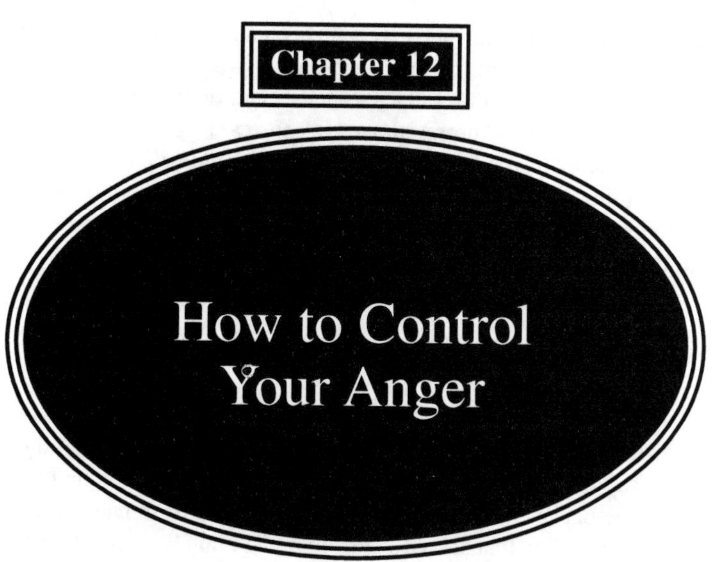

Chapter 12

How to Control Your Anger

Anger seems to listen to argument to some extent, but to mishear it, as do hasty servants who run out before they have heard the whole of what one says, and then muddle the order, or as dogs bark if there is but a knock at the door, before looking to see if it is a friend; so anger by reason of the warmth and hastiness of its nature, though it hears, does not hear an order, and springs to take revenge. For argument or imagination informs us that we have been insulted or slighted, and anger, reasoning as it were that anything like this must be fought against, boils up straightway.

—Aristotle[1]

As Aristotle astutely saw, it is an irrational rule of the kind, "Anything like this *must* be fought against," that can lead a person to "boil up straightway" and to "take revenge." Behind the heat of irrational anger lies such a rule that demands perfection of a person and a report that says this person has failed to mete up. The result of such a "disconnect" (inconsistency) between your perceived reality and what you think *must* be is anger ranging from quiet simmering to violent, destructive outbursts.

Your anger can enlist other fallacies such as Getting Even and take the form of "revenge"—as Aristotle noted above. It can team up with Damnation and come out as a vicious assault on a person, verbally and/or physically. It can do both of these things and more. The bottom line for most of us who get caught up in uncontrolled anger is (at least ultimately) serious regrets. So how can you control your anger and save yourself a whole lot of trouble?

A Love Consumed by Flames: The Case of Peter and Fran

You can "listen to argument" more carefully and less hastily before you jump the gun and destroy what you may value most. Take the case of Peter and Fran, who met at a college dance. He was a sophomore and she a freshman. After the first date, somehow he knew that she was "the one." To Fran, he was the first boy she had ever met who shared so many of her own views.

From their very first dance, the two became an item, and were virtually inseparable. Both had a strong interest in art, and they would talk for hours about great works. On weekends they would be together, going to restaurants, movies, the theater, art museums, the beach, and studying together. The following semester, they began taking classes together. It was a relationship "made in heaven," except for one thing.

They often became embroiled in bitter quarrels. It didn't take much to get them started. Sometimes the genesis of the quarrel was a disagreement about a social issue. For example, once they became embroiled over whether sex was a necessary part of love. Fran claimed that you could love someone without having sex; Peter became furious. Not infrequently, their quarrels stemmed from criticisms by each about the other's parents. One quarrel faded into the next and quarreling became almost a daily event. Usually, they would end by threatening to break up, and they would part company. Then, within hours, he would phone her, or go over to her house to "make up."

One cold winter evening, when he was visiting her at her home, they became embroiled in a quarrel; he ran out of her house in protest, and sat in his car parked out in front of her house; for hours, he waited for her to invite him out of the bitter cold back into her house. Instead, she drew the shades and he finally went home.

They dated for two years and then married. In fact, on the night of their wedding, the two were not on speaking terms. When those sacred words, "You may kiss the bride" were uttered, the two were at war!

Their honeymoon, which was spent in the Bahamas, ended rather abruptly when Peter announced that he wanted to return home early to study for a history exam. Fran became hysterical. Crying, she told him that she wanted an annulment.

Nevertheless, the two "made up" and remained together. As a result of their marriage, new occasions for quarreling emerged. Unlike before, he could not "go home" and "cool down" when they had quarrels, so the quarrels became more intense, and occasionally escalated from verbal to physical confrontations, ushering in a new dimension to their mutual hostility. Sometimes, in the midst of a heated quarrel, Peter would try to escape Fran's fury by seeking shelter in another room, locking the door behind him. Fran, however, would usually follow him, stand outside the door, pounding violently on it, trying to break it down. In an effort to prevent her from destroying the door, he would open the door and attempt to restrain her. This, in turn, led to further physical altercations. They would invariably scream at each other at the top of their lungs, blurting out profane and vile remarks calculated to "push the other's buttons."

Their sexual relationship was also a precipitating factor. While they had satisfying sex, they would often quarrel after having it. From Fran's perspective, Peter became "cold" and "unfriendly" after sex. When she confronted him on this, he would get angry, and this would ultimately lead to further exchanges of aggression. She started to avoid having intercourse with him. Peter began to tell her that she was "frigid," and this in turn led to further quarrels.

Nevertheless, the two felt strong attachments to each other. When one was ill the other was there. When one was worried about something, the other tried to listen and seemed to care. But as soon as the worry implicated the other in some negative way, for example, if Fran were upset over something Peter said or did, the expressions of care would turn to animosity. When they had a mutual problem, they would generally quarrel and scream at each other before finally speaking rationally about resolving it. In the end, they usually worked things out successfully but not without quarreling first. Sometimes, after a quarrel, they would "kiss and make up," and reaffirm their love for one another. A nervous tension pervaded their lives, even during their happy times.

Peter became a banker and eventually attained the status of vice president. Fran became a TV anchor for the nightly news and was highly regarded by her colleagues, and extremely popular with her viewing audience. To the outside world, they looked like the "ideal couple."

Fran and Peter were in their early thirties when they came to see me. They didn't understand why their personal lives were in such turmoil. Each professed to love the other but wondered how they had so easily managed to sabotage their professed love. Although they had previously decided not to have children, they were also reconsidering this decision as Fran's biological clock was running down. They didn't know if this would be such a good idea, and thought that a philosophical perspective might help.

Sometimes I met the two clients separately, and other times together. On one occasion, Fran told me that she gets angrier with Peter than anyone else.

"When he does something wrong," she said, " I hate him more than if anyone else did the same thing."

"Give me an example," I said, looking for something concrete to grab onto.

"Last Saturday we had tickets to see one of my favorite rock groups. We had the tickets for almost a month, and one of his friends at the bank invited us over on Saturday evening, the same time as the concert, and he told his friend that we'd come. He didn't even ask me and then he told me about it on Saturday morning. He claimed that he forgot about the concert, but I don't know. I felt like tearing his head off. If anyone else did that to me, I don't think I could possibly have gotten so angry. I don't know what it is about him!"

"So you didn't believe him?" I asked.

"No, I think he really didn't want to go, so he conveniently forgot."

"What do you mean by 'conveniently forgot'?"

"I think he didn't want to go and just didn't care enough to do it for me. And he didn't even have the decency to ask me before agreeing to his friend's invitation. Can you imagine?"

"Are you saying that he deliberately tried to get out of going by agreeing to his friend's invitation without consulting you; that he deliberately did this to get out of going to the concert?"

She paused a moment, and then responded. "I really don't think that he consciously forgot" she said in a pensive tone. "I think that it was really very inconsiderate. It's that he didn't even care enough about me to remember and even to ask me first before consenting for me. How inconsiderate is that!"

"So you think that he if he really cared about you, then he wouldn't have been so forgetful and inconsiderate?"

"Yes," she said impatiently.

"Well, I think I have your premises straight. Your rule is that if Peter really cares about you then he mustn't act inconsiderately toward you, and you think that what he did to you was very inconsiderate. Do I have it right?"

"Yes," she conceded.

"OK, suppose he really did these things that he really mustn't do if he cares about you. Is that a bad thing?"

"Yes, it's a bad thing!" she said excitedly. "Its really an awful thing when someone so close to you like your husband, who's supposed to care about you more than anyone else cares about you, treats you like that."

"I see," I said. "But, if he weren't your husband, would it have been so awful?"

"No!"

"Why is it so much worse when your husband, instead of, say, a friend, does this? Do you regard this as some kind of betrayal?"

"That's exactly what it is. He betrayed me!"

"So I guess that's why you get more angry at him than anyone else. You hold him to a higher standard than anyone else. Since he's you're husband, he must care for you more than anyone else in the world does and must, therefore, *never* act inconsiderately toward you. If he does, then it's awful because he's betrayed you. And if he really betrayed you, then I suspect that explains why you wanted to tear off his head. We *do* hang people for treason! Do you think he deserves capital punishment?"

She laughed. "No, I still love him, but I feel like getting him back for doing something so rotten to me!"

"What would you like to do to him?"

She smiled, knowingly. "I'd like to torture him until he breaks down and cries. I think that would get him back for being such a bastard."

"So you think he's a bastard?"

She paused for a moment. "Well, that's what I thought when he first did it. But he can be sweet sometimes too. I don't think he's always a bastard, just sometimes."[2]

The Getting-Even Syndrome

As you can see, Fran's thinking included several unrealistic rules, piggybacking on one another to deduce anger. Here's a bird's-eye view of the syndrome:

- *Demanding Perfection*: As my husband must always care more for me than anyone else in the world cares for me, he must never betray me.
- *Awfulizing*: As my husband must never betray me and as he *has* betrayed me (by being inconsiderate), what he's done to me is awful.
- *Damnation of Others*: As my husband has done something awful to me, he's a bastard.
- *Getting Even*: As my husband's a bastard, I must get him back (by breaking him down).

Action: I get even (by breaking him down).

Look at how these rules follow a definite logical sequence. As my husband treated me in a manner in which he *must never* treat me (Demanding Perfection), what he has done to me is *awful* (Awfulizing); which means he's a *bastard* (Damnation of Others); which means I must *get even* (Getting Even). This is what I call a fallacy syndrome. As I mentioned in chapter 8, this is when two or more fallacies follow a patterned logical sequence, one fallacy setting the stage for the next.

Notice the "disconnect" or inconsistency between Fran's demand for perfection in the first premise—Peter must never betray her—and her report of reality in the second premise—Peter *has* betrayed her. Fran's demand that Peter never betray her and her perception of his inconsiderateness as betrayal, is what tees the anger syndrome off. Fran deduces all the other fallacies in the syndrome—Awfulizing, Damnation, and Getting Even—from these premises. Such a perceived conflict between what you think *must* be and what you think *is* appears to be at the root of all anger syndromes. The above sequence of fallacies is a very popular anger syndrome: the Getting-Even Syndrome.[3]

As you can see, fallacies do indeed travel in herds. One fallacy sets it up for the next and so on. The next time you get really pissed off, take a look at your thinking while you're still pissing. There's a good chance you'll catch yourself going with the flow of these malignant rules.

One antidotal logic is to attack irrational anger at its roots. So how do you do that? Well, as long as Fran kept on Demanding Perfection of Peter in his treatment of her, she was likely to go to the Awfulizing stage, then to Damnation, and then on to Getting Even. But if she changed her absolutistic *must* to a preference and instead said to herself, "Oh well, I would have preferred if Peter hadn't behaved inconsiderately to me, but what am I gonna do, he *is*, after all, human," then, with some effort of will, she might have halted the progression of her anger.

If you have strong tendencies to experience intense anger, the amount of effort sufficient to overcome these tendencies can be considerable. Cognitive dissonance, especially in the case of anger, can be a tough nut to crack. Intense angry feelings and bodily urges that support and are supported by irrational thinking can quickly surge in response to a perceived insult or unwelcome action, even if you know you are being overly sensitive.

As mentioned earlier, it is usually easier to halt an *action*, which falls under voluntary (skeletal muscular) control, than internal visceral churnings and feelings, which are largely autonomic. Using this logic, I decided to work with Fran on refuting her Getting Even rule, from which she deduced emotionally torturing her husband.

"But he really has it coming!" she said, which signaled to me that her Awfulizing circuits were still on.

"Do you think that emotionally torturing your husband until he breaks down and cries is likely to help improve your relationship?"

She thought a moment and replied, "No, it never has in the past. It usually creates hard feelings. Peter's like me. When I do something he doesn't like, he gets angry and does something nasty back."

"And that really defeats your purposes, doesn't it? If you're out to improve your relationship—and you wouldn't be here if you weren't—then it makes sense to avoid this kind of tit-for-tat stuff, right?"

"Philosophers are so logical," she said with a chuckle.

"I hope you're convinced," I said with some doubt seeping out from my gut. "So let's talk about some antidotes you can use against this tit-for-tatting."

"OK," she said in an unusually congenial tone.

"Well, if you get the urge to get even with him for screwing up last Saturday or for something else he might do next, then what do you suppose you could do?"

"I don't know," she said, with a smile. "Shoot him?"

"Not exactly!" I said. "Remember what you just said about how getting back at Peter can cause hard feelings?"

"I'm not senile," she quipped with a note of condescension.

"OK, so that's your antidote. Stop and consider the consequences. Use your common sense! Just ask yourself if it's really worth it in the end. Then use your willpower. You do believe in free will, don't you?

"Yes, I believe in free will," she said self-defensively.

"So, prove it!" I exclaimed. "Keep yourself from doing something you're likely to regret. All right?"

I could recall her bright smile that lighted up the room. She seemed to like the idea of feeling and really being in control of her own life. And she actually complimented me, I think!

"All right!" she said. "I used to think that philosophers were weird, like the ones in Gulliver's Travels who were philosophizing while their wives were doing it right under their noses. Thanks."

Encouraged by her positive response, I suggested these other antidotes that I thought would be helpful to her:

"Talk to Peter," I said. "Don't reprimand or degrade him. You're two reasonable, free agents, so that's not necessary. Explain to him how disappointed and let down you were. Then listen to what he has to say. Maybe you can reach some mutual understanding about how he could make it up to you. Maybe he could get tickets for another concert, or plan a romantic dinner for two. You could turn this into a positive thing if you take a rational approach."[4]

Fran was amenable to my proposal and it worked! Peter got tickets for a Sister Hazel concert and made reservations for dinner and a room at a fancy hotel for Saturday evening. The two ended up having a romantic evening; and it was fight-free. Well, almost fight-free—except for a small disagreement about taking too long to find a parking space.

The case of Fran and Peter shows how, once you get into an irrational mode of relating, there can be a buildup of momentum to keep relating in this way. As Aristotle stressed, the more you behave in a certain way, the stronger becomes your habit. On the other hand, if you work on relating rationally, this too can build up its own momentum. So you should exert your willpower to keep yourself going on a rational keel. The longer you keep it up, the more stable it is likely to become. This doesn't mean that you have to be perfect (a screwup here and there is human), but you should try your best to keep a good thing going. After a while, you are likely to begin to *feel* less comfortable with your old ways.

The Grudge Syndrome

One common way to keep anger burning is to carry a *grudge*. This was what both Peter and Fran did, although Peter seemed at times to be the greater offender of the two. Sometimes the embers would be simmering for days before they reignited. The two would quarrel, make up, and a few days later, Peter would still be angry. Peter offered this description:

"When we make up, it feels better temporarily, but then I start to think more about what she said and I start to feel alienated from her."

On the surface, he would appear to get mad about something new, but on closer inspection, it was really a flare-up of an underlying brushfire that was never fully eradicated. The new event simply added some fuel to the old fire. For example, on one occasion Fran went grocery shopping on her way home from work and forgot to buy the dessert Peter requested.

"I'm sorry," said Fran apologetically, "with all that I had on my mind, I wanted to get home, and I forgot."

Peter snarled, "You remember things when you want to!"

"I'll go back and buy it if you want! OK?" said Fran, trying to quell his frustration.

"No, forget it! If you couldn't get it straight the first time, then don't even bother," said Peter in a cold tone.

"Why are you making such a fuss over this?" asked Fran indignantly. "You'd think you were going to die if you didn't have marble cheesecake!"

As the dialogue gradually escalated to a shouting match, the topic was diverted from marble cheesecake. "If anyone's a pompous asshole, it's you!" shouted Peter, referring to a remark that Fran had made to him three days earlier.

"You can't let anything go, can you? Maybe I was right all along!" said Fran, launching her counterattack, seeking revenge.

You can see how the words, "pompous asshole" were used like tactical weapons by each client. In Peter's case, retaliation was preceded by an interim period of silent brooding.

In this period, the two were, on the surface, friends, and they were prepared to let bygones be bygones. But that was just on the surface. Beneath that flimsy veneer the fire was still simmering, and it didn't take much fuel to rekindle it. The disposition to continue the war was still there.

If you find yourself rekindling the old wars, it is likely that the scars they left were not completely healed. Why not?

Quite often, we irrational humans revisit the scene of the crime and prevent ourselves from moving on. We end up holding grudges. Here are the usual steps in the Grudge Syndrome: First, you Demand Perfection of the other person; second, you Awfulize about not having it; and, third, Thou Shall Upset Yourself—you tell yourself that, because the other person did something so awful to you, you have a moral duty not to let it go. You have to, and I mean *have* to (it's obligatory to) keep it up. To let it go and stop thinking about it would be to cop out on the inestimable horror of what had happened—in the present instance, having been degraded by the one person whom you believe *must* hold you in highest regard. "No," you declare, "I simply cannot just let this ride." So you ruminate until the occasion arises to release some of the pressure.

In Peter's case, he had stubbornly refused to allow Fran to think ill of him. How could someone who loved him so much think of him as a pompous asshole.

This *must* never be; but it *is*. How horrible and terrible that what must never be is. So, how could he just forget it? This was what ran through Peter's mind when anger filled the void of the missing marble cheesecake.

But forgetting *is* what common sense recommends. Forget it. Forget the venom that poisons interpersonal relationships. If you love your partner, then exert your willpower to love and let yourself be loved. Forget self-defeating and stubborn adherence to ghostly moral duty that promises only pain and frustration without redemption.

"Holding it inside isn't good either," you may protest. No it isn't, but the "it" that you hold inside does not really have any substance. *It* is the unrealistic and exaggerated response to the fact that people, no matter how important they are to you, will never treat you perfectly. In fact, you are not likely to always agree about what perfect treatment really is in the first place.

So how do you forget about it? Give up your Demand for Perfection. Instead of saying that "she must never call me a pompous asshole," be contented with preferring that she doesn't do it again. And, if you still have an emotional predilection to say how awful it is that she did, think about something a lot worse, like how wasteful it is that potentially precious moments are being eroded and reduced to stressful moments by irrational Demands for Perfection and irrational distortions about how bad it is that she's not perfect. Face it, she's not. Neither are you.

A Case of Explosive Rage

Peter and Fran frequently had what might be called "galloping anger." They would get into quarrels that sometimes even ended as brawls. But seldom did one suddenly explode at the other. Instead, their anger reached a crescendo. The "back and forth" manner of aggression they displayed generally built up to a concert pitch but rarely got there by a sudden explosion. The most severe and challenging case of explosive rage that I ever confronted was the case of Jennifer, a twenty-year-old college student.

Jennifer had a habit of easily exploding when others said or did anything with which she didn't agree or which frustrated her desires. As a result, Jennifer's relationships with her friends and parents suffered, and she found it difficult to hold a job without getting herself fired.

When I asked her about this she stated, "That's just the way I am; when someone talks shit to me, I say things back. That's just the way I am."

What interested me, for openers, was the "talks shit" part. "What," I asked, "do you mean by 'talking shit'?"

Jennifer rolled her eyes and looked at me like I was from Mars. "Talking trash," she impatiently replied, "and trying to fuck with you."

"Oh," I said, wondering if she had just talked trash.

Well, it really didn't take much to tick Jennifer off. This was no more apparent than in her relationship with her parents. On one occasion, her mother asked her to pay for a phone bill that included several lengthy long-distance calls she allegedly made. Jennifer immediately became irate.

"Fuck you, bitch," she screamed in a bloodcurdling voice. "I wasn't the only one who made calls!" And then she proceeded to go on a tirade against her mother, telling her that she was a failure, that she walked bent over like a cripple, that she was cheap, that she was ugly, that she hated people like her, that she reminded her of a former friend whom she hated, and on and on.

When the dust settled, Jennifer was sorry; but with great predictability, she was soon provoked again, and exploded with rage. There seemed to be no end in sight. With small brushfires erupting in between, large explosions seemed to occur for one reason or another on an average of every four days.

I asked Jennifer why she thought she got so angry when her mother requested payment for the phone bill. This very question unseated her anger. "Because it's not fair!" she said raising her voice. "I'm not the only one who uses the phone. My mom also uses it. And she had the nerve to ask me to pay for them!"

"OK," I said. "So you think it was unfair for her to ask you to pay the entire bill. Maybe you're right. But why did you get so angry?"

Jennifer looked at me with astonishment and in a condescending tone she uttered, "Duh. Because a mom is not supposed to treat her daughter unfairly?"

"Does this apply to other people too, besides your mom?" I probed.

"Yes, but especially parents. They're supposed to take care of their children, not try to steal their money."

"So you think that, in asking you to pay the phone bill your mom was stealing from you?"

"Yes!" she exclaimed. "Why should I have to pay the whole thing if I wasn't the only one using the phone."

"That sounds reasonable to me. If you really weren't the only one who ran up a bill, then it would make sense to share the costs. So let's suppose that your mom was treating you unfairly by ripping you off."

"Then that's disgusting!" she blurted. "Imagine a mother trying to steal money from her own daughter. Yuck!"

"So are you saying that a mother must never rip off her daughter, and if she tries to, then that's really pretty awful?"

"Yes," she affirmed, with self-assurance.

"Well, why didn't you just refuse to pay and tell her why?"

"I did!"

"But, according to your mom, you screamed at her and berated her too. Is that true?"

"Yes, I admit that, and I told her that I was sorry, but I really couldn't help it."

"You *couldn't* help it?"

"Well maybe I could have but I didn't. I can't stand to be treated like she can walk all over me because she pays my college tuition and stuff. She doesn't show me any respect."

"I think I understand your reasoning. You think that your mother shouldn't act unfairly or in other ways disrespectfully towardsyou, and if she does, it's so awful that you really can't stand to put up with it. Not only that, you seem to be telling yourself, at least at the time you get angry, that you really can't help your anger. You think it's what your mom does that makes you angry. So, you're not really taking responsibility for your anger. You think your anger just happens to you. Someone mistreats you and you explode, just like what happens when you strike a match and get a flame. You have no part in what happens. That would make you as helpless as the match!"

"It really *wasn't* my fault. My mom was the one who started up with me!"

As you can see, Jennifer was very resistant to taking responsibility for her own emotions. This was the bottom line of her rage. In effect, she gave herself permission to explode by telling herself that she wasn't in control anyway. As a result, she felt very much out of control. The more she tried to control her life, the more she exploded, and the less in control she felt. This was a vicious cycle, which could be broken only by realizing her syndrome of faulty thinking and then working on overcoming it.

The Short-Fuse Syndrome

Well, as you can surmise from our discussion, Jennifer was assuming several unrealistic rules of emotion in her thinking, each of which piggybacked on the other. Do you know what they were?

Here is my shot at formulating her syndrome:

- *Demanding Perfection*: My mom must never treat me unfairly or disrespectfully.
- *Awfulizing*: As my mom must never treat me unfairly or disrespectfully, and as she *did* so treat me, it's awful.
- *I-Can't-Stand-It-Itis*: As it's awful how she treated me, I can't stand it.
- *I Just Can't Help This Feeling*: As I can't stand how she treated me, I can't help but lose my temper and shouldn't even bother trying to control myself.

Emotion: Rage (with the perception of powerlessness over her emotion)

This is what it means to have a *Short Fuse*: First you ignite your own fuse by *Demanding Perfection*. Then you *Awfulize* about not getting it. Then you tell yourself how you *Can't Stand* to put up with something so awful. Then you let your fuse burn down and blow your cool by telling yourself that you *Just Can't Help It*.

The most success I had in helping Jennifer to confront this complex syndrome was in helping her to address the last rule, just before the explosion—I Just Can't Help this Feeling. I told her about three antidotes that she could use against this rule:

- Change *I can't* in "I can't help my feelings" to an emphatic *Yes I can.*
- *Prove* your freedom to yourself by resisting your emotion.
- Avoid use of terms that deny responsibility for your feelings, and use responsibility-bearing terms instead.

I suggested that she try these when she felt the anger beginning to swell inside her. She was a swimmer and took much pride in her athletic ability and fine-tuned body. I told her how, like her body muscles, her willpower muscle also needed exercising to become stronger.

As an athlete, Jennifer well understood the idea that she had to work up to it. So I advised her to concentrate on practicing self-control in response to smaller frustrations first, working up to the bigger challenges later.

When Jennifer's friends said things to her that she didn't like, she usually responded with hostile, jeering, or mocking remarks. Yet, her responses to her friends' perceived offenses tended to be less intense and vicious than her responses to her parents'. So, I advised her to concentrate on practicing self-control with friends' perceived minor offenses, and to work up to dealing with the big enchiladas, such as major confrontations with her parents. But, before she could do this, she had to acknowledge her ability to control her anger. So I encouraged her to change *I can't* in "I can't help my anger" to an emphatic *Yes I can.*

To do this, she had to speak to herself differently when she felt her bodily currents rising. Instead of saying, "Since *you* are ticking me off, I *can't* help but get ticked" she could say, "Since *I'm* doing my own ticking; I *can* help getting ticked."

The *can* here is itself empowering. It is extremely important to tell yourself that you *can* resist your bodily feelings and inclinations. In speaking the word, "can," at such times, you *prescribe* your own freedom. You disavow yourself of being a passive object, and instead affirm your internal power of self-control. This affirmation is itself liberating because it *feels* liberating. It is a spur toward resistance and change. And when you actually do resist, you *prove* to yourself that this feeling of freedom is *really* freedom.

In Jennifer's case, this was potent medicine. The more she controlled herself in confronting minor day-to-day frustrations with friends, the more free she began to feel. As her confidence in her freedom increased, so did her actual freedom, and she became more tolerant of both friends and family.

It would be an oversimplification to say that this was *all* Jennifer needed to do to be happy. She still had to work on the other irrational rules that fueled her short fuse, especially her Demanding Perfection, which made the burden of self-control strenuously heavy for her. Nevertheless, it appeared that by telling herself that she had power over her anger—that she didn't *have to* fly off into a rage when she was treated unfairly—the less power her other irrational rules seemed to have in directing her anger.

In showing herself that she *could*, after all, help her feelings, she was, in effect, refuting her other rules from which she deduced her anger. Here's an analogy that might help. If having measles means having spots, and you can show that you don't have spots, then you can show that you don't have measles. Well, the anger is the telltale spots of the Short-Fuse Syndrome. If you can prove that you can control your anger, then you can show that you don't have the syndrome. If you don't have the syndrome, then this means that you are not committing all of the fallacies in it. For example, you might be telling yourself that what someone did to you was not so gosh darn awful that you can't stand to put up with it. This is a healthy sign. The main symptom of the Short Fuse is explosions of anger. No explosion, no Short Fuse!

Rational Anger

As you can see, controlling your anger can make an important contribution to your happiness and to the happiness of the people who may mean the most to you. I am not saying, however, that it is always unacceptable to get angry, for not all anger is irrational. Indeed, passively accepting maltreatment is also not a viable route to happiness. As I have emphasized in chapter 11, willing slaves are not happy campers either.

Aristotle's idea of seeking the Golden Mean and avoiding extremes applies well here. Docility is one extreme—a deficiency in anger. Volatility is another—an excess of anger. Both should be avoided. But, if you were to lean in one of these directions more than the other, Aristotle would recommend leaning more toward the deficiency. The philosopher speaks:

> The man who is angry at the right things and with the right people, and further, as he ought, when he ought, and as long as he ought, is praised. This will be the good-tempered man, then, since good temper is praised. For the good-tempered man tends to be unperturbed and not to be led by passion, but to be angry in the manner, at the things, and for the length of time, that the rule dictates; but he is thought to err rather in the direction of deficiency; for the good-tempered man is not revengeful, but rather tends to make allowances.[5]

As Aristotle suggests, being prepared to make allowances and reasonable concessions in living can make a useful contribution to living happily with others. Giving the *benefit of the doubt*, especially to significant others, instead of getting angry straightaway, can be a healthy allowance.

As you have seen in the cases discussed in this chapter (and no doubt in the context of your own life), the things people become embroiled about are often hardly worth the effort. Not perturbing yourself over relatively minor issues can make a *major* difference.

NOTES

1. *Ethics*, book 7, ch. 5
2. The *focus* of an emotion appears to be the dominant thought on your mind when you're experiencing an emotion. When Fran's focus was on Peter's action, she was thinking, "How awful!" When it was on Peter, she was thinking, "What a bastard!" When it was on getting him back, she was thinking, "Torture the bastard!"
3. You could also have this syndrome without going to the Damnation of Others stage. Recall that Fran was still thinking about Getting Even, even when she no longer thought that he was a bastard. This less complex variant would then move to the beat of *Demanding Perfection/Awfulizing/Getting Even.*
4. These are abbreviated versions of antidotes given in chapter 10. For the complete formulation, see chapter 10 in the section on "Fallacies of Emotion: Refutations and Antidotes."
5. *Ethics*, book 7, ch. 5.

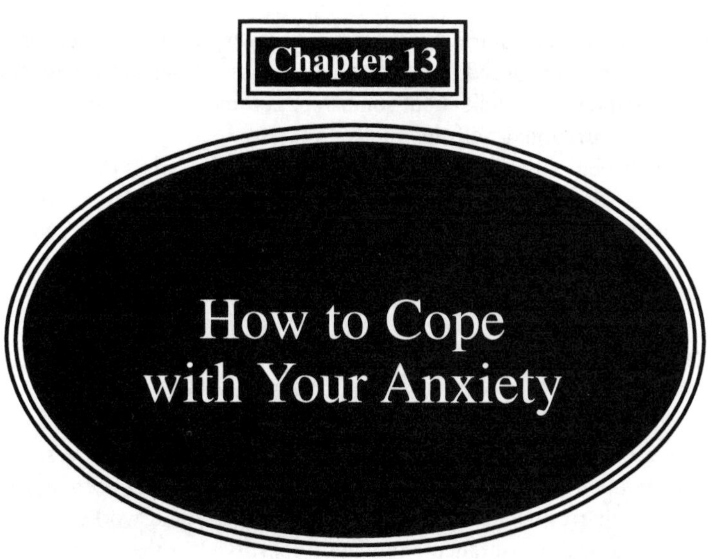

Chapter 13
How to Cope
with Your Anxiety

[P]eople . . . define fear as expectation of evil. Now, we fear all evils, e.g., disgrace, poverty, disease, friendlessness, death . . . But it is possible to fear these more, or less, and again to fear things that are not terrible as if they were. Of the faults that are committed one consists in fearing what one should not, another in fearing as we should not, another in fearing when we should not.

—Aristotle[1]

Anxiety involves a state of emotional tension about a future event or possible future event. Some emotional tension about the future can actually help to keep you alert and out of danger. If you are crossing a busy street, or in the path of an oncoming Mack truck, then let's hope you get keyed up enough to watch out! The human propensity to experience nervous tension about perceived dangerous, future possibilities appears to be part of our evolutionary, protective endowment.

Unfortunately, much of the anxiety you may experience may be neither realistic nor useful. When it is deduced from irrational premises, it can really mess you up!

In this chapter, I will talk about some very common human concerns that are often objects of irrational, self-destructive anxiety.

One such object is human mortality. Realistically, it is safe to say that, at some point in your future, you and those whom you love are going to die. How you deal with this fact can have significant implications for how you live and how you feel. Let me begin by telling you about the case of Vicki.

The Search for Meaning: A Case of Confronting Your Own Mortality

Vicki was a beautiful, twenty-nine-year-old woman who lived in a small, one-bedroom apartment with her Jack Russell terrier. Never having been married, she held a degree in art history from Columbia University and worked as a claims processor for a health insurance company. Vicki lived in the same town as her parents and often visited and confided in them. She had an active social life and dated many men, but never developed an intimate relationship with any of them. When a man tried to get serious with her, she stopped dating him.

Vicki was intelligent, sweet, petite, and vivacious, and her smile could light up a room. Although she was raised as a Christian, she did not embrace Christianity, and in fact was agnostic. She did not believe that Christ was immaculately conceived and that he died for the sins of all humankind.

Without any sense of where she was going in life, where she had come from, and what her prospects might be after her mortal demise, she came to see me, a lost soul, anxiously awaiting a future, which, for her, had no meaning.

"What point is there to life anyway if you're just going to die. How could anything you do even matter if you die?" This question had gnawed at her psyche since her childhood. Lying in bed awake at night, on her back, staring up at a dark, vacant ceiling, she became conscious of the tenuousness of her own existence. The silence of night and the void of darkness contributed to her feelings of emptiness, and the grotesque image of her own futile demise as well as that of her parents arose from the dead of night to haunt her: "There is no meaning of life. We're born into the world and we die. There is no meaning and purpose. We just are. And then we are not." This replayed over and over in her mind, as she lay awake, sometimes for hours, in the still of night. And, it would sometimes strike her in the course of her waking hours.

Death was what she feared most in life, and her inability to dismiss, disprove, or cope with it continued to frustrate her happiness. She avoided movies with macabre themes in favor of romantic comedies, and felt uncomfortable when others talked about "morbid things." The prospect of death hung over her, no matter how hard she tried to escape it. The more she tried, the more frustrated she became.

Defining Your Own Meanings of Life

It seemed that, in order for Vicki to find meaning in life, she first demanded *assurance* that life was not in vain, that there was some ultimate, cosmic purpose and goodness to life. If life just ended with death, then there would be no consolation in living. "Maybe if I believed that a God existed who was looking out for me and others I love, I could find consolation in living," she said. "But I don't know if there really is such a God. I sometimes try to tell myself that there is, but I just don't know."

Vicki's view of life reminded me of something one of my undergraduate professors once said in a lecture. He professed that the cook's job is futile because what he creates turns to feces in the end, anyway. This always seemed to me to be unnecessarily pessimistic.

"OK," I said, gathering my thoughts after a moment. "What if there really isn't any God and you won't live past your last mortal breath, and no one else will either. Does that mean that your life and everybody else's life is without meaning?"

"Yes, I think so. What's the point of living if that's all there is to it!"

I peered into the eyes of this beautiful, young woman, who kept herself in a jar, and I wondered how common sense could have so tragically escaped her. Then I spoke. "The philosopher, Nietzsche, said that "God is dead," but he never said that life is without meaning. The meaning that life has is, instead, the meaning that you bring to it. You don't have to have the assurance of God's existence to go out and do your own thing. And even if God really does exist, nothing changes. You still have to go out and live in order to give meaning to your life."

In chapter 11, I talked about Jean-Paul Sartre's idea that "existence precedes essence." Well, this is one way of saying that human beings define their own purposes ("essences") through their own lives ("existences"). You are, says Sartre, the sum total of your actions. You are not defined by your dreams and expectations. No, you define yourself through what you *do*.[2] This is good advice for those who think that life is inherently without meaning.

Still, Vicki resisted Sartre's antidote. I believe her resistance was largely due to Demanding Perfection, which pervaded her life. She demanded that there first be some preestablished, cosmic meaning of life before she could have any meanings of her own. She demanded that she have absolute knowledge of God's existence before she could find consolation in living. She demanded that she and those she loved live forever, and that evil rarely, if ever, happen. So, anxiously awaiting the unknown, thwarted by her own utopian demands and expectations, she lived without a sense of meaning to her life.

"I never did anything with my degree in art history," she once told me in confidence. "I feel like I just wasted my education, even though I went to an Ivy League school."

"Do you enjoy art?" I asked.

"I rarely look at any," she said. "I used to paint, and I was pretty good at it, but I haven't picked up a brush since I graduated college."

Sartre's advice to this forlorn client was deafeningly clear. Do what's meaningful *to you*. Some people do what they think others want them to do. They become doctors or lawyers or go into the family business because they think that this is what they are *expected* to do. Some people live vicariously through their children. The father who never was a professional ball player, but wanted to be, now grooms his son for the career he never had. The bored housewife who once had aspirations of being an actress now sits at home and watches the stars on TV. These people don't live authentically, according to their own lights; and they define themselves negatively, as disappointed dreams and expectations.

Philosophers have written books that profess *the* meaning of life. But there really is no meaning of life worth living except the meaning of life that is meaningful *to you*. This is the antidote I tried to convey to this unhappy woman.

"Why don't you take up painting again," I asserted in a matter-of-fact tone.

"I guess I could, but it's really hard to start. I haven't done it in so long that I might not be very good anymore."

"Again, you want assurance before you do something!" I exclaimed. "Why don't you just do it!"

"OK," she said, reluctantly. "I'll try it."

The next time I saw Vicki, her beautiful smile spoke a thousand words, as did the painting she showed me. It was a picture of the ocean. The waves appeared to roll in calmly against the background of a gray sky. The vast grayish waters subtly blended into the sky so that the horizon was only faintly visible. A picture of constraint, it had a hidden power and fury that I could not miss. And I wondered if this picture captured her life. The vague boundary between the water and sky gave a sense of venturing out in life with only a misty future ahead, and no infallible compass to guide you through the grayish vista. Yet, subdued, and compliant with the darkish skies from which it could not fully distinguish itself, the ocean still held within it fathomless possibilities. The gray would inevitably turn to blue and the waters would reflect its beauty. The waves would crash against the shore with a fury that was now only hinted at. There was a life in this sea that was only temporarily constrained. The dark sky suggested a storm brewing, yet the waters were still calm. Nevertheless, it was a sad kind of peacefulness that concealed a life of vitality. I was convinced that she had expressed the qualities of her own peaceful life that concealed her own vitality. It was now time to unleash her endless possibilities.

Vicki was inspired by my praise of her work. The spark of light that kindled inside began to glow with the radiance of her smile, and we went on to explore some of her endless possibilities.

Did she eventually want to meet someone to share her life with or live singly? Did she want children? Was she satisfied with her present line of work?

Did she want to take up art professionally? These and many other possibilities, hidden in the depths of the sea of life, began to surface in our discussions.

"Do you want to marry and have children?" I asked.

"Yes, I'm really envious of my friends; most of them are married and have kids."

"So why do you suppose that you haven't been able to find someone?"

She thought for a moment. "I don't know. I have gone out with lots of guys. Some of them have tried to get serious."

"What happened when they got serious?"

"I broke it off."

"Why?"

She paused for a moment. "I guess I was scared," she confessed.

"Scared of what?" I asked.

"I started to think that they might not be the right one. And then I got this horrible feeling like nothing would be the same."

"Nothing?" I asked.

She frowned. "A lot of things!"

"Like what?" I quipped.

"I don't know. It's kind of frightening."

It seemed clear that what Vicki feared was change itself. She felt safe living in her little jar. It was, after all, familiar, and she had grown accustomed to it. She had relied heavily upon her parents for consolation, and, like a babe in the arms of her mother, there was a kind, warm security in this. Venturing out into that sea of life had risks. Staying on shore was safer.

In this regard, I thought about something the philosopher Thomas Aquinas once wrote. He said that if the ship captain wanted to be safe, he would keep his ship in port. But, of course, this would not be consistent with being a ship captain. A ship captain defeats his purposes by staying on shore. And so too, Vicki was defeating her own purposes by playing it safe. In doing so, she was preventing herself from experiencing a life she desired. Once again, the demand to live life risk free kept her in a state of constant anxiety about meeting the "right" man.

I wondered what Vicki meant by the "right man." So I asked her how she could tell if the right man ever came along.

"Everything would just feel right. Everything would just click," she authoritatively stated.

I wondered what she thought would make a man "click." "What are you looking for in a man?" I asked, and she responded with no hesitation.

"I want someone who's kind, likes to dance, likes art, and has similar views on things as me, especially politics. I would never marry a Republican. He has to be tall, strong, and good looking, and he has to be very intelligent."

"What would happen if he had different political views than you?"

"We wouldn't be compatible. We would never get along."

Alas, here was another irrational rule that kept this woman from carving out a meaningful life for herself:

- Since others, especially those who are significant in my life, must always agree and never disagree with me, the right man for me *must* therefore always share the same views as I do, and must never disagree with me."

As you can see, this is a version of *The-World-Revolves-Around-Me Thinking*: You demand that your own preferences define reality for others.

I suggested to her that it would get boring living with someone who always thought like her. I also pointed out how people's worldviews are constantly evolving and how partners with different perspectives could help each other to grow. While she conceded that the right man could disagree with her, she still maintained that this guy needed to agree with her on "the important issues." When pressed to say what she meant, it appeared that "the important issues" simply meant "anything about which I feel strongly."

"Do you think you'll ever find a man who will meet up to your demands?" I asked.

"I don't know," she responded. "I haven't so far."

I tried to convey to her that, if the cards were stacked against her, that she was the one doing the stacking. The right man for her was, after all, the right man for her only when she decided he was, and she was the one laying down the standards. These standards were of her choosing, not some objective reality. Yet, I doubt she appreciated the tremendous amount of freedom (and responsibility) she had in defining these standards.

I was here reminded of an ancient myth Plato recounted about finding your soulmate. Long ago, human beings were split in half and scattered about the earth as a punishment for their defiance to the gods, so that finding your "other half" was literally just that![3] Unfortunately, the idea that there is just one person out there intended for you can be used as an excuse for not taking responsibility for your decisions. If you wait around for your other half to come along, you are likely to be waiting for all of eternity.[4] At some point you will have to say, this man is right for me because I have determined it to be so.

I believe that Vicki's absolutistic demand that people live forever made taking this plunge formidable to her. On several occasions she told me that she didn't feel like an "adult inside," that she still "felt like a child," and that she didn't really "want to be an adult." I think that her irrational fear of her own mortality kept her clinging to her childhood. For her, since people *must* live forever, it would be *awful, horrible*, and *terrible* if they didn't. Given this irrational rule, it is not surprising that she suffered intense anxiety about getting older. It felt safer living in a world where she never grew up, but she could purchase this feeling only at the expense of remaining largely unfulfilled.

Vicki's challenge was that of overcoming the momentum of her emotional attachment to this safe, but sorry existence. It takes willpower to make changes, despite the uncertainty of growing up and venturing out into the unknown regions of the sea of life.

The last time I saw Vicki she was still struggling with this challenge. She had met a man who proposed to her, and she was seriously considering accepting his proposal. She still suffered intense anxiety in confronting the tenuousness of life and her own mortality. In the end, her happiness depended on her willingness to take the plunge into the fathomless sea of potential meanings of life, and to act in spite of the emotional strain of her unrealistic demands.

A Sexual Midlife Crisis: Desiring Younger Women

Vicki's life crisis resembled a midlife crisis in at least one respect. In a midlife crisis, the fact of your own mortality figures as a premise in your reasoning. Let me tell you about Dale, a forty-five-year-old jewelry salesman who came to me with a midlife crisis. His biological clock was ticking away and he knew it, and this fact became an all-pervasive feature of his conscious existence. On the one hand, he knew that there was nothing he could do to stop the clock. On the other, he didn't emotionally accept the fact that he was no longer a young man. The thought of growing old felt painful to his psyche. Married for eighteen years, with three teenage children, daily living seemed humdrum, and sexual encounters with his wife were unsatisfying. While Dale was trim with a full head of (dyed) light brown hair, his wife, somewhat overweight, had allowed her hair to turn gray. Busying herself with her children, part-time work as a receptionist, and donating her free time to helping out at church functions, she did not seem to mind her matronly appearance, but Dale did, and he often felt ashamed when he went out with her. He would often gaze at much younger women, and later, while masturbating, fantasize about intercourse with them. In fact, the desire to be with other, more youthful women continued to intensify, and he began to think seriously about having an affair with a twenty-two-year-old woman he met at work. After some flirtatious exchanges between the two, the woman gave him her phone number and asked him to call her. He kept her phone number hidden in a secret compartment of his wallet, took it out every so often, looked at it, and put it back.

"I would rather be dead than be an old man," he candidly told me.

"What is it about being old that you dislike most?" I asked.

"You look like shit. And the only women who find you attractive are women past menopause with sagging, wrinkled breasts."

Dale's characterization of being old (including his harsh stereotype of older women) made it clear to me why he was experiencing so much anxiety over getting older.

"It sounds to me that what you dislike the most about growing old is that you think you'll lose your sex appeal with younger women. Is this correct?"

"You also feel like shit when you get old," he answered. "I have aches and pains that I never had before, and I can't hold an erection nearly as long as I used to; but you're right; losing your sex appeal, that's probably the worst part of it."

It seemed to me that Dale had made his personal worth as a human being a function of the perceptions of mainstream society. Dale's outlook on aging was a product of a society biased in favor of the young. It's not hard to notice that, in the Western world, fashions, TV, movies, and advertisements are geared toward the young. In fact, I would go so far as to say that old age tends to be viewed as a disease rather than as a stage of maturation in life.

In this vein, I recall what a physician once told me about an elderly patient whom I had inquired about at the request of the family. The woman was ninety-eight years old and had developed pneumonia. When she was admitted to the hospital, she walked in on her two feet. Once admitted, the doctor ordered that she be taken off of her heart medicine (which didn't seem to have anything to do with her pneumonia). After a few days in the hospital, she became too weak to walk or get out of bed, and soon she began to lose consciousness. When I asked the doc about her condition, he responded, "What do you expect; she's ninety-eight years old!" I was asking about her disease and he told me her age, as though they were the same thing!

The treatment of age as though it were a terminal disease is not unusual in the medical world. In general, if you are under sixty-five, you can expect to get better care in a hospital than if you are older than sixty-five. Why? Well, because young folks are perceived as being worth more. Why invest in an old person who is soon to expire? Why spend money on a defunct piece of equipment when you can spend it on one that has more life in it? Like worn-out shoes, we tend to put our elderly away in a dark corner of our closet or simply discard them. So it's not surprising that Dale devalued aging and glorified youth. So does society!

Here's my take on Dale's reasoning:

Rule: If young women find me sexually desirable, then I'm a worthy person; otherwise I'm better off dead.
Report: If I'm old, then young women won't find me sexually desirable.
Emotion: Anxiety about getting old (with a sinking sense of the futility of living into old age).

It seemed clear to me that it was this line of reasoning that inclined Dale to think seriously about beginning a sexual relationship with the young woman whose phone number he secretly kept in his wallet. This was a vital secret for him. Like a badge of honor, he coveted that number. Possessing it, he felt a sense of purpose and value. So long as she found him sexually attractive, he was vindicated as a person. But the clock was ticking and his rule of Damnation of Self sealed his fate. Sooner or later, he would be reduced to a worthless pile of wrinkled flesh. To him, growing old was a disease that would, sooner or later, devour him.

But the real disease was his Damnation of Self, so I worked with him on the refutation of his virulent strain.

"That seems like a very fragile basis for living or dying," I said. "You are worth something when the young women want to get in your pants; and, as soon as they look the other way, you are ready for the junk pile. Anyway," I added, "whatever gave you the idea that all great men were popular with the young women? What about Abe Lincoln? He was not exactly a lady's man, but he was an extraordinary person."

Dale chuckled. He seemed to see the absurdity of his own rule.

What he needed was a more stable philosophical basis for accepting himself as a worthy person. We talked at length about what makes human beings valuable as a species, and Dale seemed to like Aristotle's definition of a human being as a rational animal. For Dale, the fact that he was *capable* of rational thinking, seemed like a good reason to have self-respect. Other animals, even insects (the love bug comes to mind!), are abundantly capable of sexual activity. But human beings have a value and dignity that sets them apart from love bugs: *They can reason!* This seemed to satisfy Dale.

The more we talked, the more evident it became to him that the bond he had forged with his wife over the years, a bond of human solidarity that only two rational beings could have, was worth far more than a roll in the hay with a beautiful young woman. This realization also seemed to enhance his sexual appreciation for his wife. The last time I spoke to Dale, he told me that his sexual relationship with his wife had significantly improved.

So far as I know, Dale never fully transcended his anxiety about growing old. His head still turned when a beautiful young woman walked by, and he still had the old sinking doubts about whether his age was showing, and whether the young women still found him attractive. A smile or nonchalant glance still left him wondering what she was really thinking. Emotionally, he still sought vindication for his existence in a young woman's look, but he was not tormented by his doubts as he was before.

The Woman Who Threw Out the Knives: A Case of Obsessive-Compulsiveness

As you can see, both Vicki and Dale experienced a sense of helplessness in confronting the inevitability of dying. Such a feeling of helplessness is, perhaps, no more apparent than in cases of obsessive-compulsive experience. In these cases, a sense of helplessness combines with that of utter desperation to make these emotional encounters a nightmarish hell. But here, the perceived enemy is not some objective, external fact like the inevitability of death. Instead, your perceived enemy is *you*. Let me tell you about the hellish encounters of one such desperate soul, Valerie.

Valerie was a thirty-five-year-old married mother of two children (ages eight and twelve), and a part-time bookkeeper. A rather quiet, serious woman, she was troubled by recurrent "horrific" thoughts that seemed to "pop" into her mind on their own and take over her consciousness. When this happened, she felt helpless. The more distressed she became over their presence, the more firmly they took control.

While these thoughts were diverse, she often had thoughts that she was going to murder her husband with a knife. The thoughts felt compelling and she could feel the urge to open the knife drawer, take out a knife, and stab her husband through the heart. So she removed all the knives from the drawer and threw them out. When her husband asked where the knives were, she responded that they were no good anymore and she threw them out. Frustrated by her action, her husband demanded that they buy new knives. Valerie became angry, and said that they really didn't need such sharp utensils hanging around the house, and that the children might get a hold of them and hurt themselves. So, the household was bereft of any knives.

Valerie would also have thoughts that she was going to put poison into her children's food. The thoughts, which were backed up by images of her slipping rat poison into their plates and their choking and dying, felt very "real" and "compelling" to her. The more she struggled to get free of them, the more forceful and distressing they became. As a result of their recurrence, she began to refuse to prepare meals for her family and insisted that they make their own food. She also refused to keep any insecticides or other household poisons in the house; and she would ritualistically ask her children how they were feeling. Sometimes, she would wake them up in the middle of the night to see if they were still alive, and she would stay up checking on them throughout the night.

"What are you telling yourself when you get these thoughts?" I asked.

"Sometimes, even when I'm at work, horrible thoughts come into my mind, like I picture myself stabbing my husband to death and smiling while I'm doing it, and then I start to think what kind of monster could even have such thoughts! And I start to think that I'm really an evil person and that I don't even deserve to be alive.

"Sometimes I have these thoughts when my husband or children are talking to me or in the next room, and I feel like I'm actually going to do it. Sometimes I'm so afraid that I might have done it without realizing it, and I try to find out by testing to see if they're OK. I once called my husband at work to see if he wasn't really dead. I can't talk about this to my husband because he just doesn't understand what I'm saying. I tried, but he just laughs and thinks it's funny. He doesn't really know what it's like."

"Did you ever actually do any of these things?" I asked.

"No. Oh God, no!"

"But you often thought and felt as though you were."

"Yes."

"But you still didn't, even though you thought and felt as though you were. There you were, the knife right there at your disposal, your husband standing next to you, and still you didn't do anything."

"Yes."

"So you may have thoughts and feelings of doing these things but that's all they are. You're afraid that you will actually do these things, but that's not even a realistic prediction. Your problem is not that you are actually going to do these things but rather that you are having *thoughts* and *feelings* that you might. Do you agree?"

"Yes," she said, nodding her head contemplatively.

"This is how I think you're reasoning," I continued. "First you picture yourself stabbing your husband and even feel like you're inclined to do it; then you tell yourself how awful, horrible, and terrible it would be if you actually did do it and how you couldn't stand it if you did. This is what I call the Slippery Slope Syndrome.[5] You exaggerate the probabilities of something bad happening and then you tell yourself how awful it would be and how you couldn't stand it."

"But it seems so real, like I'm going to do it!" she said in a troubled tone.

I saw a definite need for philosophical enlightenment here. The word "real" is such a weasel of a word!

"The feelings and thoughts are real," I said, "only in the sense that you are having them. But they're not real in the sense that they correspond to any actual or future events in the world. It's like dreaming that you are about to mount and ride a horse. When you are dreaming it, it feels quite real. But you are in fact in your bed, asleep, and not about to mount a horse. The thoughts and feelings you are having about your husband and children are real in a similar way in which a dream is real. It's a bad dream, but it's time to wake up. You need to be realistic. That's really the best antidote."

The Slippery Slope Syndrome

Here is my take on the syndrome that fueled Valerie's intense anxiety:

- *Slippery Slope*: As I have thoughts and feelings of stabbing my husband to death, I will actually go for a knife, lift it, and plunge it into him.
- *Awfulizing*: As I will do this, I will do something awful.
- *I-Can't-Stand-It-Itis*: As I will do something awful, I can't stand it.

Emotion: Anxiety about the prospect of stabbing my husband (with painful thoughts and images of plunging a knife into his chest).

As you can see, it's the Slippery Slope report in the first premise—she's going to stab her husband to death—that permits the slide to Awfulizing and then to I-Can't-Stand-It-Itis. Once you let the slide go through, you end up at the bottom of the slope in a heap of anxiety. Being realistic here means exposing this syndrome for the bogus bag of wind it really is. "There's that ridiculous thought again," you can say to yourself. "Oh well!"

Can you imagine murdering the people you love the most in the world? That would really be a bad scene. And that is precisely why Valerie conjured it up. In reality, Valerie loved her husband and children so much that it was utterly revolting for her to imagine actually killing them. The worse the thoughts, the more damaging they can be—if you let them! You empower them by fearing them. If you aren't afraid, you won't get hurt!

Damning Self-Doubts

Here's another unrealistic rule that infected Valerie's reasoning:

- If I have bad *thoughts*, then I am, myself, bad.

When Valerie told herself that she must be an evil person because she had the dreaded thoughts, she was applying this rule. A version of this Damnation of Self rule is behind many cases of obsessive thinking. This rule merely requires that you have bad *thoughts*, in order to be a bad person, not even that you actually *do* something bad. This is an anxiety producer because, so long as you accept this rule, you will be afraid of having bad thoughts. And, when you are afraid of having these thoughts, that's exactly when you give them power over you.

"Leave yourself alone!" was the antidote I conveyed to Valerie. As I explained, the fact that you have bad thoughts doesn't make you a bad person. If that were the case, all of us would be bad persons.

Will the person who is without any "sin in his heart" cast the first stone? I suspect that there will not be any honest stones cast, and that should be enough to show the absurdity of damning yourself if you have bad thoughts. Human beings have lots of different thoughts, some of which are "bad." So what! Stop playing hide and seek with your bad thoughts, trying to escape being human. It won't work!

As you can see, the bad thoughts that popped into Valerie's mind also led her to *do* certain irrational things in order to protect her loved ones. For example, she threw out all the knives in the house, she called her husband to see if he was still alive, she discarded insecticides and other household poisons, she refused to prepare and serve food, and she kept checking on her children throughout the night to make sure they weren't poisoned. This is what's known as *compulsive behavior*. So how could she deal with these compulsions that stemmed from her irrational thinking?

There is really only one realistic answer here. Valerie had to exercise her willpower in holding herself back. When she felt like checking on her children in the wee hours, she had to force herself to stay in bed. When she felt like calling her husband, she had to restrain herself. When she felt like stopping her husband from putting knives in the shopping cart, she had to hold herself back. And so on.

I am happy to say that Valerie has made excellent progress (without having to take medication). She now rarely engages in compulsive forms of behavior, and the bad thoughts only occasionally come into her mind, usually when she is under unusual stress. But she is able to counter them by saying, "There's that absurd thought again. Oh well!"

Afraid of the Dark: A Case of a Phobic Client

In obsessive-compulsive emotional encounters, the object of anxiety is usually *you*. Notice how Valerie feared what *she* might do to her husband and children, and how she did things, like throwing out knives and checking on her children, intended to protect them from herself.

In contrast, if you have a *phobia*, it is likely that you are intensely afraid of someone or something *other* than yourself. Let me tell you about Anita, a woman who had a phobia of the dark.

Anita was a thirty-year-old waitress. When I first met her, she had been married for six weeks. She and her husband had spent their honeymoon in Jamaica, and were having a fine time when the formidable thing happened. Asleep in their hotel room with a night-light on, there was suddenly a power outage, and the room became completely dark. Anita sprang from the bed and began to scream, "Help!" at the top of her lungs. Her husband was awakened from a deep slumber and became alarmed. "What's the matter!" he yelled to Anita, finding his way in the pitch black to her small frame that frantically contorted and trembled in a powerless frenzy. He grasped her and tried to comfort her, but she was incensed by the darkness and would not stop her chilling screams. In a few moments, the power returned and the night light came on. Instantly her screams ceased, and her panic subsided.

Anita explained to me that she had become afraid of the dark at the age of seven after having been trapped in a small laundry closet in an apartment complex while playing hide and seek with her friends. She explained how she thought that she was going to die and the sense of powerlessness she experienced as she sat huddled up on the floor for hours waiting for someone to find her. The young frightened girl was finally rescued by a passerby who heard her crying, but the trauma of the experience continued with her into her adulthood.

"What's going to happen," I asked, "if you are in a dark room with no lights?"

"I'm not going to be able to see. It's like I'm blind," she said, indignantly.

"OK," I said. "Well what would happen if you were blind, and not able to see?"

She looked disturbed. "I wouldn't be able to control anything; I would be completely helpless!" she said in a stressed tone.

"And what if that were the case? What if you really couldn't control anything and were completely helpless?"

Anita's expression grew even more disturbed. "That would be horrible; I would go insane!" she said, raising her voice.

"I see," I said in a reassuring tone.

Alas, the emotional syndrome that directed her fear of the dark was clear to me. Here was my take on it:

The Out-of-Control Panic Syndrome

- *Demanding Control* (A type of Demanding Perfection): As I must always be in (complete) control, I must never be rendered helpless and unable to control my situation.
- *Awfulizing*: As I *must never* be rendered helpless and unable to control my situation, and as my being in total darkness *has* so rendered me, it's awful.
- *I-Can't-Stand-It-Itis:* As it's awful, I can't stand it.

Emotion: Panic about being in the dark (with painful thoughts and images of helplessness and powerlessness).

As you can see, it was Anita's demand for control that was at the top of her hierarchy of irrational rules. This was the fundamental rule that drove her to experience feelings of helplessness and desperation when the lights went out in Jamaica. The blindness she experienced while in the pitch black was significant only as a report she had filed with herself, confirming that she was officially "out of control"! And this report along with her demand to be in control was what unleashed her panic.

This is what I mean by the Out-of-Control Panic syndrome: As I *must* always be in control (Demanding Control), it's *awful* that I'm not (Awfulizing), and, therefore, I can't stand it (I-Can't-Stand-It-Itis).

What to do?

A fruitful way to deal with this syndrome is to strike at its root, which is the Demand for Control. "If you always had to be in *complete* control," I told Anita, "then you couldn't drive a car, take an airplane, or even cross a busy street."

Anita had no fear of flying or of driving, so it wasn't difficult for her to see her own double standard. When you step into an airplane as a passenger, you have put your life in the hands of the crew and their equipment. You have little, if any, control left when that plane lifts off the ground. But still it's reasonable to board if you have rational grounds for believing that you are in safe hands. So, the control that you should concern yourself with is *rational* control, that is, the control you exercise when you make rational decisions. Such was the antidote I had for Anita's Demand for Control:

- You should accept *rational* limits to the control you can exercise over a situation.

To apply this bit of common sense, I suggested that she build up her willpower by spending brief moments in a dark room, ultimately working up to being able to stay in the dark for prolonged amounts of time. While Anita made some significant progress toward this goal, she still used a night-light and slept with a flashlight next to her bed.

Do you, like Anita, have any phobias? Are you desperately trying to maintain absolute control over your life circumstances? If so, then you, like Anita, may be suffering from the Out-of-Control Panic syndrome.

If your phobia is something less intrusive like fear of snakes, and you don't happen to have much contact with these slithery creatures, then you may prefer to get by without tending to your phobia. On the other hand, if, like Anita, your phobia is substantially interfering with the way you live, then you may want to do something about it. This would include working behaviorally to overcome the inertia of your emotional attachment to unrealistic rules, especially the demand for absolute control. This is likely to take considerable effort on your part, and, in the end, you may not entirely overcome those old phobic feelings. But, by putting in the work, you have a good chance of considerably improving the quality of your life!

The Nervous Nurse: A Case of Job-Related Anxiety

In Anita's case, her anxiety stemmed from an irrational Demand for Control. In some cases of anxiety, the control issue may actually be a symptom of another underlying problem. This was true in the case of Martin.

Martin was a thirty-five-year-old psychiatric nurse who was going for a master's degree in mental health counseling. Very interested in philosophy, he came to see me because he was having intense anxiety related to his job, and he thought that a philosophical approach to his problem might benefit him. He also thought that learning such an approach might help him to help his own patients work through *their* emotional problems.

Martin was an extremely compassionate and caring person. He cared deeply about the welfare of his patients. Married with a two-year-old son, he was also a devoted husband and father. Unfortunately, the intensity of his devotion to others often made it difficult for him to do things for himself without suffering intense anxiety and guilt. While he enjoyed such activities as working on his boat on weekends and walking along the beach by himself, he rarely did them because his wife typically had other plans for him. Rarely did he buy anything for himself. One Christmas, he bought himself a book and justified it by saying that it was a Christmas present from his son.

He once wanted a tie that had a tropical scene printed on it. You know what I mean: palm trees, flamingos, and the deep blue sea. While shopping with his wife, he would eye such ties and fancy how they would look on him. But he could not bring himself to buy one for fear of what his coworkers might say.

Each evening, Martin would take a shower, and while in the shower, he would become overwhelmed by anxiety. One recurrent object of his anxiety was what might happen if he made a mistake with a patient. Another object was the anticipation of having run-ins with his supervisor over work-related matters. A further source of anxiety was the possibility of rejection by male patients. "We don't want a male nurse. We want a real nurse—a woman" they sometimes said. And occasionally, some of these patients would refuse care from him because they thought he was gay.

"I have an important job," he told me. "The lives of these patients depend on me. I worry that there might be something I'll do wrong and a patient might get hurt or even die."

"Do you think that you must never do anything wrong?" I asked.

"That's right; there's no room for mistakes. I can't make any mistakes," he insisted.

On the surface, it seemed very straightforward. Martin was simply Demanding Perfection about *being in control*. "I have to always be on top of things," he demanded, "so that I don't make any mistakes." So I proceeded to refute his absolutistic demand for control.

"That would mean that you would have to be perfect!" I exclaimed. "You would have to be all-knowing, like God. That's not even humanly possible!"

On further inquiry, however, it became apparent to me that there was still a more fundamental, absolutistic demand that he was foisting upon himself. The more I pressed him, the more he seemed to speak about how others would judge him if he messed up.

The Control-to-Get-Approval Syndrome

What seemed to propel his anxiety was a syndrome based on a rule that demanded the *approval of others*:

- *Demanding the Approval of Others*: As I must always have the approval of others (especially my peers), I must never make any mistakes at work.
- *Demanding Control*: As I must never make any mistakes at work, I must always be in complete control.
- *Awfulizing*: As I must always be in (complete) control, it would be awful if I couldn't control something.

- *I-Can't-Stand-It-Itis*: As this would be awful, I couldn't stand it.

Emotion: Anxiety about remaining in complete control (with painful thoughts and images about making a mistake at work and losing peer approval).

As you can see, in this Control-to-Get-Approval syndrome the demand for control is really a symptom of the demand for approval. To get approval, Martin couldn't make any mistakes, and, if he couldn't make any mistakes, then he always had to be in control. This formed a hierarchy of demands with the approval demand at the very top of the hierarchy. Realizing this, I concentrated on trying to help him overcome his demand for approval as a way to help him resolve his control issue.

As I already mentioned, Martin had a problem doing things to please himself, particularly when they were likely to meet with the disapproval of others. Whether it was spending time alone on the beach, working on his boat, buying a book, or wearing a flashy tie, he would stop and consider the approval rating of his act before he could justify it.

Well, was there an antidote for what ailed him? I answered:

- Change your absolutistic, unrealistic *approval must* to a preference.

"It might be *preferable* to get the approval of others," I advised, "but you really don't *have* to have the approval of others."

I also gave him some homework:

- Buy that flamboyant tie you like and wear it to work!
- Tell your wife that you are taking some personal time this weekend.

Well, it took several weeks before Martin actually bought that tie and wore it to work, but when he did, to his surprise, he received several compliments, even from his supervisor. Go figure! But, even if they had hated it, that wouldn't have mattered. If you're not stepping on anyone else's toes in doing your own thing, then do your own thing!

That weekend, Martin also succeeded in telling his wife that he was taking some private time, and he spent a few peaceful hours on Saturday walking alone on the beach collecting his thoughts—as well as some sea shells.

Interestingly, the more Martin stood up to his strong emotional tendency to have others' approval, the less he felt the need for control. My hypothesis really worked! If you feel like you "have to control everything," then you may be suffering from the *Control-to-Get-Approval syndrome*. Your attempt to control everything may be symptomatic of an absolutistic demand for approval. This can conjure up a heap of anxiety in your life. If so, then, like Martin, you may profit from tending to your demand for approval. Change this demand to a preference, and flex your willpower muscle to do your own thing.

The last I saw Martin, he told me how much he would miss me. It was one of those warm and cuddly moments. We both resonated with the feeling of having successfully completed our journey. We wished each other well.

NOTES

1. *Ethics,* book 3, ch. 5.

2. Jean-Paul Sartre, *Existentialism and Human Emotions* (New York: Philosophical Library, Inc., 1985), pp. 32–33.

3. Plato, *Symposium*, in *Plato: The Collected Dialogs*, ed. Edith Hamilton and Huntington Cairns (Princeton, N.J.: Princeton University Press, 1973), pp. 542–44.

4. Anyone familiar with the rock group Pink Floyd will recall their expression of this point in their classic hit "Time."

5. See chapter 8.

Chapter 14

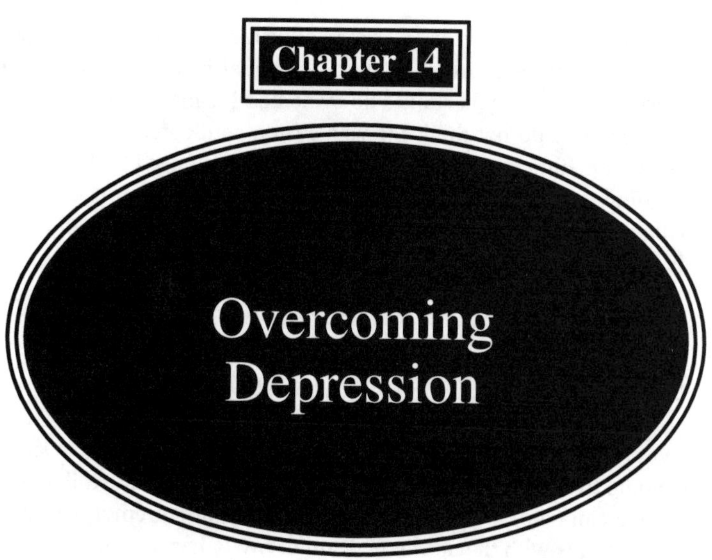

Overcoming Depression

Men say that one ought to love best one's best friend, and a man's best friend is one who wishes well to the object of his wish for his sake, even if no one is to know of it; and these attributes are found most of all in a man's attitude towards himself . . . he is his own best friend and therefore ought to love himself best.

—Aristotle[1]

Have you ever felt like not getting out of bed in the morning; like, if a truck ran you down, it wouldn't matter; like there was nothing left to look forward to in your future; like the world was a cold, barren sea and you were drowning in it; like you were a hopeless failure?

Most of us have felt like this at some point in the course of our lives. This common human emotion is called depression, and it is almost always due to irrational ways you are thinking about the things in your life. As I have mentioned earlier, overcoming depression sometimes requires medication like Prozac when it is due to a physiological abnormality in the brain that impairs your capacity for rational thinking. To find out if you require medication, you will need to be evaluated by a psychiatrist or physician. A mental health professional such as a psychologist, licensed clinical social worker, or mental health counselor can help you to determine whether you should be evaluated for medication.

Drugs, however, do not think for you. While antidepressants can eliminate physiological impediments to rational thinking, you still need to do the thinking. If you are going through a crisis such as a death in the family or a divorce, medication will not provide you with rational antidotes to get you through it. You will ultimately have to get *yourself* through it.

The Death of My Beloved Father: How I Grieved Eight Years Later

Getting yourself through the ordeals of life can be a challenge to any of us, including yours truly. Allow me to bare my soul. I know well the toll that the loss of a loved one can take on your life. It took eight years of emotional limbo for me to come to terms with the untimely death of my father, which occurred under most unusual circumstances. In this day of high-tech advances, we readily take for granted the accessibility of a simple telephone. We pick up the phone, hear the familiar dial tone, and we phone out. Like many other folks these days, I carry a cell phone and I expect instant service any time, any place.

Well, it has been over two decades now since the death of my father. Back then, the phone was generally to be found on a wall or table and not in your pocket, but the expectation of service was then as it is today. When you picked it up, you expected a dial tone. Unfortunately, when my mother lifted the receiver to call 911 the moment my father suffered a massive heart attack, the familiar tone did not sound. Instead, there was a cold silence. It took several minutes for my mother to run next door to get out the call, and by the time the paramedics arrived, my father was dead.

It was a brute fact. My father had died. He was a man of great talent and fortitude. He was so very much alive, but he was dead. The telephone had stood between the life and death of this man to whom I owed my life and my honor. A cable was down, I learned from the phone company, due to an automobile hitting a pole. How contingent this world really is. The effects of some unseen event, connected to your life only by a wire, could change your life forever. It changed mine. From the moment I learned of my father's untimely death at the age of sixty, I entered a dark tunnel of emotional stagnation.

You see, my father had suffered a first heart attack ten years earlier, and there was substantial cardiac damage. So, for ten years, I lived with the fear of having to confront the inevitable moment of his demise, not knowing when it would happen again. Now that the time had arrived, I never had to endure it again. It was all over. At first, I felt a sullen sense of relief, as though, in this tragedy, a tremendous weight had been lifted off my shoulders, and I told myself that I could go on with my life. Just like that, no questions asked. But in retrospect, I now see that this was only the beginning of a long and emotionally barren period in my life.

I did not take time out to mourn the death of my father. I had just received a small grant from the University of Florida to develop materials on the values dimensions of practical decision-making for the department of behavioral studies. In addition, I had also been in the midst of working on an article for a philosophy journal. I plunged headfirst into my work, and never looked back.

Through these hard times, I still managed to be productive in a scholarly sense, but inside I was flat and dead. I was not the compassionate person with a boyish sense of humor that I had previously been. I was a hollow man. The man that my wife loved had vanished from her life, and only the shell of that man remained. This was a difficult eight years for our relationship. Fortunately, the dark ages ended with a renaissance. The man who had retreated into a shell began to emerge like a perennial flower in the spring after an extraordinarily cold, barren winter.

I emerged from this emotional purgatory because I finally gave myself permission to mourn the death of my father. I got angry at the phone, at life, and at the world. I felt stressed, and intensely painful feelings began to swell up inside me. I proclaimed how things could-a/would-a/should-a been had that damn phone worked! It was just not fair; things so awful, horrible, and terrible should never happen to me. I was screwed by fate. I couldn't stand to live with this anymore. I was a pillar of irrationality. But this was the first sign of emotional life in me since the tragic day my beloved father died.

This is what it means to work through the death of a loved one. It means getting all the emotional rules and reports out on the table, inspecting them, and countering them with antidotes. It took me eight unhappy years to work through my grief because I never even gave myself the opportunity to howl at the moon. I did very little crying; I never caught myself Awfulizing or Could-a/Would-/Should-a-ing. I never said, "There I go again, demanding that the world be perfect and that shit never happen." Instead, I inhaled the fumes of these irrational rules and held them deep down inside. I never exhaled. I never let them out. And I never took an antidote. How could I? I never even knew which one to take!

The process of working through your grief begins with irrationality and ends with reason. I thought that I could get to the end of the process without going through the irrational stage. But it's not like that. You need to give yourself the opportunity to express your anger and grief. You need to do this not as an end in itself, but as a means to getting a grip on yourself. If you don't, then these irrational ideas will continue to work insidiously, consuming your happiness. There is really no shortcut to grieving. Let yourself howl at the moon. You can eventually begin to listen to your own howling, refute it, and find antidotes. This is what I did after eight long, depressed years of going through the motions of being alive.

My irrational, expressive stage lasted a few months. In this time, I was in an emotional tizzy. I cried, and I kicked, but the more I did, the more I began to see the light at the end of my dark tunnel. I began to see how irrational some of the ideas I expressed were. I began to see that it was unrealistic to expect that shit never happen to me, and that even as bad as this tragedy was, I had a wife and two healthy children whom I loved, and I had a future with prospects for happiness. I began to consider how my father still lived through me and through my children, and how the world wasn't necessarily a bad place because such a tragic event happened. I realized that the phone's failure to operate at the time of my father's heart attack was not some calculated plan by the cosmos to undermine my happiness. These were ideas that, philosophically, I well knew to be irrational, but to confront them *in me*, as they *emotionally* dictated the terms of my life, was a different matter.

They seemed beneath my dignity, like an affront to my status as a rational being and as a philosopher. By insisting that such irrationality was beneath me, I had demanded perfection of myself. In retrospect, I see that this was probably behind my refusal to work through my irrational ideas in the first place. I thought that, by admitting that I was troubled by such irrational ideas (ones that I told myself I *must* not have), I would have proven my own unworthiness as a philosopher, and, indeed, as a person. So, instead of confronting these ideas, I buried them *alive* in the depths of my psyche.

Perhaps I was also afraid that, in taking the time to deal with my personal issues, I might have detained myself from my life's work, bogged myself down, sidetracked myself, and further established my unworthiness. And perhaps, I conceived the reality of my father's death and the circumstances surrounding it to be just too terrible, horrible, and awful to acknowledge and dredge up, so I kept them buried in their psychological coffins, still alive. In the end, I only managed to prolong my depression.

I now see that such attempts to rescue myself from myself could only have been self-defeating, and that to have confronted and wrestled with these ideas in me could only have made me stronger, and, indeed, a better philosopher. Here are two general antidotes that I came away with after eight years of living as a dead man:

- Don't think that you are too rational to be irrational. Do not demand perfection as a rational being.
- Instead of trying to fool yourself by denying or burying your irrational ideas, work through them—acknowledge, express, confront, identify, refute, and find antidotes to them—even if this is a painful process.

If you don't heed these words, then you are likely to defeat your own purposes. I know this, personally.

Recognizing irrational ideas that you are trying to keep hidden from yourself can be difficult precisely because you *are* trying to hide them from yourself. It's like pulling yourself up by your own bootstraps. You need something to get hold of and you need a stable framework upon which to stand. A telltale sign that you are trying to deny your own irrationality is when the very suggestion that you are being irrational, say, Demanding Perfection, "hits a nerve." This is when you get angry and self-defensive at the very suggestion that you are thinking or acting irrationally. If you catch yourself doing this, then you can use it as a handle for getting hold of your own irrationality. You need then to muster up the willpower to savor what feels so very unsavory, namely your own irrationality.

This is much easier if you start with the premise that you, like all other human beings, are not beyond irrationality. Once you garner the strength to look upon your own fallibility, you can learn a good deal. You can uncover your emotional rules and the reports you have filed under them, from which you deduce your own distress. This is what I did in confronting the tragic death of my father, albeit eight years later.

The pain of such loss does not evaporate with a good antidote. Working through a loss does not mean that you will no longer feel those hollow feelings at the thought of your loss, and that you won't, even many years later, still weep on the birthday of the beloved deceased, or occasionally, in the silence of night, lying awake in your bed, feeling those same blunt feelings of powerlessness over the finality of the beloved's demise. It does not mean that you will ever forget.

But, there is a difference between the irrational kind of desperation that destroys your ability to function and go on with your life, and the solemnity that comes with antidotal relief. It is rational to weep on occasion and to miss a loved one, but it is not rational to tell yourself that you cannot go on, that your life is over, that the world is a horrible place, that shit must never happen, and so on. These are dysfunctional ideas because they undermine the possibility of your happiness, and that of significant others who may love you as much as you have loved the deceased. I still mourn the death of my father, but I am much stronger now because I no longer irrationally try to hide my own irrationality from myself. I am open to my own fallibility as you should be to yours.

The Dutiful Mourner

In bereaving the death of a loved one, you may find yourself feeling as though giving up your irrational ideas would be a kind of betrayal of the deceased. You may feel that it would be an abandonment of your love to let yourself be happy. In my case, I tried to deny and bury my irrational thoughts. In this case, you dutifully refuse to stop thinking about them. As Aristotle would remind you, both extremes are to be avoided. Here is a version of this Dutiful Mourner rule, which can keep you in a continued state of grief:

- If I have suffered a loss of someone I truly loved, then I have a moral duty to prove my continued love for the deceased by continuing to upset myself over my loss; and, if I don't continue to upset myself over my loss, then I am a horrible person who never truly loved this person.[2]

According to this rule, no matter what you do, you have reason to be upset. If you comply with your duty to upset yourself, then you must remain in a state of grief. On the other hand, if you stop being upset, then you are a horrible person who never loved the deceased. So either way, you end up making yourself miserable.

In reality, you do not have a moral duty to deprive yourself or others of future happiness as a consequence of your loss. While religious traditions typically stipulate parameters of mourning, they do not, and should not, expect you to give up your prospects for future happiness. This would involve a double standard since, if you truly love others, such as your own children, you would not want them to give up their prospects for happiness as a consequence of your death. This is why parents usually bequeath their worldly possessions to their children and list them as beneficiaries to life insurance policies, in the hope that these measures will ensure their children's future happiness.

A useful antidote against the Dutiful Mourner rule is to give yourself permission and affirm your moral right to be happy; and to exert your willpower to go on with your life by doing things that will bring you happiness. This is not a denial of your love for the deceased, and it does not make you a horrible person! It is a consistent application of the standards of care that any loving person would apply to those whom they love.

I still profoundly love my dad, and I know that he would have wanted me to be happy. Would the loved ones whom you mourn have wanted you to destroy your life over their death? You can stop tormenting yourself out of respect for them, but you should also do it for yourself. Take care of yourself!

A Suicidal, Sexually Abused Woman

If you have ever felt like "ending it all," then you can join the club called humanity. It is not unusual for people to feel fed up, disenchanted with life, or apathetic toward living or dying. These thoughts and feelings may arise in the context of a perceived major life crisis such as a divorce, fight with significant other, loss of a job or money, death of a loved one, failure, and rejection by others. Almost always, the reasoning underlying this suicidal ideation has fallacies in it. Often, the strain of a challenging situation coupled with a tendency toward self-downing thinking can lead you to such self-destructive states of mind. So, if you catch yourself having these dangerous thoughts and feelings, before you allow yourself to be carried off by them, stop and look carefully at your thinking.

Let me show you how doing this helped to improve the life of Ester, a thirty-year-old sexual abuse survivor and mother of three. This young woman was born into poverty and was raised by her mother. She never knew her father. The strongest male presence in her life was her Uncle Sig, who sexually molested her from the age of four until she left home at eighteen.

Ester ran off with a young man whom she married one year later. She had two daughters with this man, but their marriage ended in divorce after nine years. Alone and seeking the guidance of a man in her life and a father for her two children, she married Stan, a college-educated, unemployed alcoholic, with whom she had a third daughter.

While Ester never finished high school, she had a steady, full-time job in a factory, and managed to make enough money to support the family. Ester paid the bills, shopped, made the meals, and was the primary caretaker for their three children. Stan rarely worked and invariably managed to get himself fired when he was fortunate enough to get hired. On the other hand, Ester often relied upon Stan's "educated perspective" on problems of child rearing and other domestic matters. He was, from Ester's perspective, "the brains" of the family.

One evening, when she was passing by the upstairs bathroom, Ester peered into a partially ajar bathroom door, and saw her oldest daughter performing oral sex on Stan. She stood there in astonishment for a moment, and then quietly went downstairs and stood motionlessly at the mouth of the staircase. Soon her husband descended the stairs and stood before her, gazing back at her defiantly. "Why are you standing there like that," he said angrily.

Ester confronted him with what she had seen and Stan chastised her for having a "dirty mind." He angrily denied her allegations and he told her that she was insane and that she was hallucinating. Amid this hostile, emphatic rebuttal, Ester began to question her own perception. "I thought that's what I saw," she declared, "but I must have been mistaken."

One evening, three years later, Ester was watching a TV talk show on the topic of sexual abuse. After the show, she asked her daughter if Stan ever touched her. The daughter, now fourteen, affirmed that oral sex had escalated to sexual intercourse. She also said that Stan would sometimes rape her and beat her if she tried to refuse his advances. Frantically, Ester sought out her second daughter, now thirteen, only to hear similar tales of sexual abuse.

With tears in her eyes, she confronted Stan once again. He had been drinking and immediately flew into a rage. Forcing Ester and her three daughters into the family car, he went speeding down the highway threatening to kill all of them. The police began to follow the car, and a high-speed chase occurred. The police finally stopped the car and Stan was arrested. Eventually, he was also charged and convicted for the sexual abuse of his two stepdaughters.

It was at this time that Ester sought counseling. Alone again, without a man, she doubted her ability to do an adequate job raising her three children on her own. Overwhelmed by the heavy burden she perceived, tormented by her own feelings of insecurity, she wondered if her children were better off without her. She began to think about "ending it all."

"What good am I anyway," she proclaimed. "I'm stupid and my husband was smart."

She blamed herself for the abuse of her two children: "If I had done something sooner, this never would have gotten so far out of hand."

She doubted her own womanliness: "Maybe if I had been better in bed, he never would have done this to my babies."

It was evident to me that she was attempting to build an argument for suicide. I asked her if she had any plan to kill herself and she said that she didn't. Nor was she herself convinced that her argument was sound. What I suspect she really wanted was a good refutation. This woman loved her children dearly, and it was not her intention to do anything capricious that would cause further harm to them. So we set out on an examination of her premises.

"Why do you think that you're stupid," I asked.

"My husband graduated from college. He was an English major and knows about literature. What do I know about these things? I never even graduated high school!"

Her reasoning seemed quite straightforward:

Rule: If you graduate from college, then you're smart.
Report: I didn't even graduate from high school.
Emotion: Shame about not "even" graduating from high school.

This is like arguing that, since all apples are fruit, and since an orange is not an apple, it must not be a fruit. Obviously, there are more types of fruit than apples. Likewise, there are more types of intelligence than that acquired through a formal education.

Also assumed in her thinking was the related bogus line of reasoning:

Rule: Either I'm smart or I'm stupid.
Report: I'm not smart (because I didn't graduate from high school, let alone college)
Emotion: Depression (with self-damning thoughts of being stupid or inept).

The above rule contains Black-or-White Thinking, the pigeonholing of reality into two mutually exclusive slots. Not being smart does not imply being *stupid*. You can be "average"!

Notice also how black-or-white words, like "smart" and "stupid," as applied to *entire persons* dangerously oversimplify reality. You can be smart in some things, average in others, and bad in still others. You can excel in fixing things, read at an average rate, and stink at drawing. In calling herself stupid, Ester globally damned herself without due consideration for her individual abilities.

If you are feeling depressed, watch out for such Black-or-White Thinking. It's extremely prevalent in depression. "Either I have you or I have nobody"; "Either I succeed or I'm a worthless failure"; "Either everything goes my way or nothing can ever be right"; "Either the world is perfect or everything is shitty." Can you see how such Black-or-White Thinking can lead to a bleak outlook about the world, yourself, and your future prospects? The world's not perfect, but that doesn't make it totally bad!

These were distinctions I conveyed to Ester. The more we talked, the more it became clear to her that she had certain abilities such as her work-related, housekeeping, cooking, and record-keeping abilities. She was empathetic, compassionate, and affectionate. She even had a talent for singing, while her husband had a "tin ear."

Still, she insisted that she was to blame for the abuse of her two children, and that she really didn't deserve to live. "I should have done something to stop him, but instead I let him."

The Guilt Trip Syndrome

Ester's Could-a/Would-a/Should-a Thinking supported *intense guilt*. A mother, after all, has a moral obligation to protect her young. Her children depended upon her for their welfare and she had let them down. This idea of a moral violation played upon her conscience and she would not let herself alone. In her mind, this went to the heart of her motherhood. What kind of mother could do this to her own children? Her answer was "a no-good worthless one." So she damned *herself as a person*. Her self-elected punishment was to play and replay her own perceived moral violation in her mind, over and over again, torturing herself with the thought of her heinous misdeed. She was sending herself on a Guilt Trip. Here's my take on the irrational rules that comprise this syndrome:

- *Could-a/Would-a/Should-a Thinking*: As I could have, and should have, prevented my husband from abusing my children but instead did nothing to stop him, I am guilty of the most despicable thing imaginable.
- *Damnation of Self*: As I am guilty of such heinous conduct, I am a horrible person who deserves to burn in hell.
- *Thou Shalt Upset Yourself*: As I am a horrible person who deserves to burn in hell for my unconscionable behavior, I have a moral duty to continually torture myself and never let myself off the hook for it.

Emotion: Depression about not having prevented the abuse of her children (along with suicidal ideation).

According to this syndrome, when Ester sent herself on this Guilt Trip, she told herself that she *could-a/should-a* done something to prevent the abuse; that, therefore, she was *guilty* of the most despicable thing imaginable; that, therefore, she was a *horrible person*; and that, therefore, she *must*, as an absolute and unconditional moral duty, continually torture herself with the thought of what she had done. The result was an agonizing existence from which, by her design, there is no escape. This was the sorry state of this poor woman!

"This Could-a/Would-a/Should-a Thinking gets you nowhere," I said. "The important thing is that you are doing something about it *now*. You are there for your children now regardless of whatever misjudgments you might have made in the past. Even if you made a mistake," I explained, "this does not make you a bad person. You are human, after all. Humans make mistakes!"

She constantly stressed how terrible her mistake was, and that she couldn't just let it go. I pointed out that her *couldn't* was really a *wouldn't*, that she was *choosing* to ruminate about it. I stressed that a duty to torture herself was self-defeating since this would prevent her from doing what she could do *now* to rectify the situation. I emphasized how it would take willpower to fight off the guilty feelings that kept her in a state of inertia. I also pointed out that, by calling herself a horrible person, she was further preventing constructive actions for her children's future welfare.

I challenged her to rethink her Damnation of Self: "If you were truly a horrible person, then how could you even care about helping your children?"

As for her doubts about her womanliness, I explained to her that her husband had a mental illness called pedophilia, and that this had nothing to do with her sexual prowess. There was simply no *evidence* that had she been better in bed, her husband would have kept his hands off of her daughters. I emphasized that such *could-a/would-a/should-a-ing* was both groundless and pointless.

As you recall, Ester was herself a survivor of sexual abuse. It is remarkable how victims of abuse so often manage to find other predators with whom to share their lives. In Ester's case, as in many other cases of victimization, this was a consequence of her rule of Damnation of Self, which dictated the terms of her life:

> *Rule*: If I'm damaged goods, I must be treated accordingly (disregarded, abused, disrespected, and so forth).
>
> *Report*: I'm damaged goods.
>
> *Action*: I put myself in situations in which I'm treated like damaged goods.

Under the direction of this line of reasoning, it is easy to see how suicide might have appeared as a viable option for Ester. This was just another manner of treating damaged goods: disposing of them!

I suspect that Ester's tendency toward could-a/would-a/should-a-ing played a significant role in shaping her negative self-concept. Victims of sexual abuse often tell themselves how they must have done something to deserve their abuse;

that had they been better behaved, gotten into less trouble, or been more helpful, they wouldn't have been treated so badly. This allows them to shift the blame from the perpetrator to themselves. They think that they deserved just what they got. This variety of Guilt Trip also supports their victim mentality by making it more likely that they will choose an abusive partner who will continue the reign of abuse. Like a magnet, they are drawn to others who treat them like dirt.

Are you attracted to people who treat you disrespectfully or abusively? If this rings a bell with you, then you too should look at your premises. There's a good chance that you are adopting a rule of Damnation of Self something like the one formulated above. This is easy to refute. Human beings are not objects that should be "thrown out" like an old shoe. Recall the advice of philosopher Immanuel Kant: Treat yourself as a rational, self-determining person and not as an object manipulated![3]

If you were sexually abused as a child and have carried the guilt for what the perpetrator has done to hurt you, then you should give yourself permission to get angry. Your personhood was violated and you have the right! When you let go of your guilt, you may find yourself feeling the rage swell up inside you. You may tell yourself how horrible it was that you were treated like this; what a terrible person the perpetrator was; and you may feel like getting back at this person. Letting these thoughts out into the open so that you can once and for all deal with them is healthy. You can then come to see their inherent irrationality.

The guilt you have carried might have been a defense against having to deal with these beliefs. It might have been easier for you to blame yourself than to condemn the perpetrator, especially if that person happened to have been a very close relation such as your father. How many children want to tell themselves that their fathers are horrible monsters? The reality is, all fathers are human beings, not monsters, and some have very serious problems. By seeing your irrational ideas in such light of reason, and by exposing and refuting these fallacies that have invisibly haunted your psyche for many years, you can get beyond the guilt and the rage.

You would also do well to recall the antidotes I listed earlier for Damnation.[4] First, you should stick to rating your actions and not yourself. Leave yourself alone! Accept yourself unconditionally, not according to your successes, failures, or the approval or disapproval of others.

Further, choose a philosophical basis for your self-worth with which you are comfortable (child of God; human being; rational being; autonomous, free, self-determining being; being with inalienable rights to life, liberty, and the pursuit of happiness; conscious, experiencing, self-aware being). No matter how you cut the mustard, you are a valuable being, and this value does not depend upon whether or not you screw up. Learn from your mistakes. Resolve to do better in the future. But leave yourself alone!

These were the antidotes I recommended to Ester. Although the emotional baggage she carried was heavy, she managed to muster up the willpower to get back into the saddle. She took her children to counseling to work through their abuse, and she joined a group for survivors of sexual abuse to help work through her own issues. She began to date men having an eye for ones who treated her respectfully and were not abusive alcoholics. These actions reflected a sense of self-worth and self-respect. Again, in Kant's terms, she was treating herself as a rational, self-determining person, not like an old shoe; not like a victim. The last I heard, she was alive and feeling better!

A Suicidal Woman with Lou Gehrig's Disease

As you have seen, Ester's reasons for considering suicide as a solution to her problems of life were degrading and irrational. So, are there ever any cases where suicide is a *rational* option, where you are not treating yourself like an old shoe but rather seeking to preserve your dignity as a human being through a final act of freely determining how you die?

I once had a thirty-five-year-old student, Kerry, who was suffering from Lou Gehrig's Disease, a crippling, fatal, neuromuscular disease. Kerry was a student in my counseling ethics class. During one of my classes in which I was discussing the ethics of counseling suicidal clients, she disclosed to me and to the rest of the class that she was contemplating ending her life.

Kerry was married and had two children. She was quite intelligent and was doing excellent work in my class. The ravages of her disease were becoming apparent, however. Her voice was slurred, she was unable to control her hands in order to write, she had leg braces and crutches, and could barely walk on her own. She knew that her disease was progressive and that she would eventually completely lose control over her body, including her ability to breathe on her own.

Kerry was a very brave and noble person. She was not being cowardly in considering suicide as an option. She was concerned with ending her life to preserve her dignity. Unlike Ester, she did not perceive herself as damaged goods, but rather as an autonomous, self-determining person who wanted to use such powers to control her death style. I had compassion and empathy for her plight. Nevertheless, I encouraged her to live. So did the rest of the class.

Kant also said that you would be contradicting yourself if you killed yourself out of self-love. This, he said, would amount to trying to improve your life by destroying it.[5] I am inclined to think that this argument against suicide out of self-love or self-respect can be a potent one. I proposed it to Kerry, and she seemed to think so also.

But there were other reasons why Kerry had good reason to live. She had a husband and children who loved her and whom she loved. There was still potential to love and be loved; there was meaningful life and relating still ahead.

In the end, Kerry decided against suicide. A few years after our discussion,

I met her at a shopping mall. She was in a wheelchair and was accompanied by her children. Although her condition had substantially deteriorated, she was still in a relationship of mutual love and caring.

Kerry's case underscores the importance of rational thinking when life hangs in the balance. Because human life is so precious, it should not be sacrificed on false premises. Kerry had an inaccurate estimate of the extent of meaningful life she had left to live. She was shortsighted in her view of the significance of her life to others who loved her. She failed to see how such a decision would have been inconsistent with her own values of children and family. A decision to end life based on such inaccuracies and oversights would have been wrong. Fortunately, Kerry realized this in time. The question, however, remains. Could there *ever* be a sound decision in favor of suicide? What if, contrary to fact, Kerry's reasoning in favor of suicide was flawless?

The issue of whether there is such a thing as *rational* suicide is a very controversial and complex one. Some folks, like Kant, think that suicide can *never* be rational. Nevertheless, whether it can be rational is not the same question as whether you agree with it. Most religious faiths absolutely condemn it, but that does not mean that you are being irrational if you don't. The rationality of suicide refers to your logic, not to your values or religious faith. There is room for disagreement on values, and I am not going to tell you what values you should have. That's your bag!

By definition, a rational decision to commit suicide would have to be one based on sound reasoning. This means that you could not commit any fallacies in coming to your conclusion. It means that you would have to have thoroughly inspected your premises and confirmed that they were complete, accurate, and realistic. A rational decision would not be the result of pressure or intimidation exerted on you by others; and it would not go against your own wishes, personal values, and goals. Kerry's reasoning was not based on premises that were complete, accurate, and realistic. Nor was it consistent with her personal values of children and family. So it flunked the test.[6]

Now read this carefully: You should *not* attempt to determine the rationality of suicide on your own. This would be like walking a tightrope without a net. If you screw up, there is no way to undo your mistake. Without a net of verification and confirmation, you are already doing something irrational. If you are suffering from an incurable disease such as Lou Gehrig's, multiple sclerosis, advanced cancer, or AIDS, and you are thinking about ending your life, you should consult a competent psychologist, clinical social worker, mental health counselor, or philosophical counselor. Don't play fast and easy with your life. Get help!

More Than One Fish in the Sea: A Woman Going through Divorce

Do you know how it feels to be "riding high in April, shot down in May"? You know the feeling, right? Finding your fiancée in bed with your best friend can feel like you have been struck by lightening. Hearing the words, "I'm leaving you," uttered by the one person with whom you vowed to spend the rest of your life can feel like you have been shot in the heart. But in June you can be back in the saddle, and "riding high" once again. Fortunes do change, but you can exert considerable control over your life by how you perceive these changes and what you do in response to them. Let me tell you about Diane, who learned this lesson well.

Diane, twenty-seven, was married for two years when her thirty-two-year-old husband, Monty, announced that he was leaving her for another woman. He had been having an affair with a woman he had met at work. The affair had been going on for two months unbeknownst to Diane. So confident in her husband's loyalty, she was dumbfounded at her husband's confession. He told her that she was not the woman that she was before they were married. He said that, while they used to have sex almost "anywhere and any time," she was "hardly ever in the mood now." He said that they used to talk about things and that she was interested in his work, and now she just changes the subject when he brings it up. These words penetrated her like knives tearing through her flesh.

"Without him, my whole life is over," she told me, as she wept.

"Your *whole* life?" I asked.

"Yes, nothing matters anymore. I might as well be dead."

"*Nothing* matters?" I asked.

"Yes, nothing," she affirmed.

As you can see, Diane depressed herself with overgeneralizations about the prospects of life without Monty. Indeed, Monty was *part* of Diane's life, but not her *whole* life. Among other things, she had friends, a mother who loved her, and she was attending community college with the career goal of becoming a registered nurse.

Sure, she knew that there was more than Monty to her life, but on an emotional level, nothing else *felt* important anymore. This loss was so colossal to her that everything else seemed like small decaying fish in a polluted stream. There was nothing that could compensate for this tremendous loss, in her mind.

"What about your plan to become a nurse?" I asked. "Is that not worth looking forward to?"

"My heart is just not in it now," she solemnly disclosed. "I thought we were building a life together and this was part of it. Was I mistaken!"

"Then why don't you just find someone else!" I exclaimed.

"You don't understand," she said as tears streamed down her cheeks. "I still love him. We were so good together. I'm never going to find someone like him again. And I really don't feel like going out with anyone else."

The halo was cast about Monty's head. He was transformed in her mind from the man who cheated on her to an irreplaceable, priceless gem. He was so terrific that losing him was such a terrible thing. Terrificizing yielded to Awfulizing, and things once desired and held in high esteem now faded into oblivion. Where there was light, there was now darkness; where there was hope there was now an overwhelming sense of the futility of life.

It was as though she had, by some fluke, survived the ravages of a nuclear winter that left the earth barren and the atmosphere polluted and gray. When asked if she wanted to start over and build another life amid the rubble and debris of things that once flourished with life, her answer was clearly, "No." And how could you blame her, from her bleak perspective? The slide down the slippery slope to oblivion was so utterly complete that nothing *could* matter anymore. It all was consumed in the flames when her husband walked out on her. This was how she felt, but what was the reality?

The Halo Syndrome

Diane appeared to suffer from a version of a common loss syndrome I call the Halo Syndrome. Here's my take on the rules that drove her syndrome:

- *Terrificizing/Awfulizing*: As my husband was so terrific and I've lost him, my whole life is over and nothing else will ever matter again.
- *I Can't-Stand-It-Itis*: As something so terrible as this has happened to me, I can't stand to go on living anymore.

Emotion: Depression about having lost her husband (with thoughts about the futility of trying to live without him).

If you have the Halo syndrome, first you Terrificize what you have lost. Then you Awfulize about having lost it. Then you tell yourself how you just can't go on living without it.

This syndrome trades on the assumption that the more valuable the thing lost is, the worse it is to have lost it, so that the loss of something perfect is equivalent to the worst thing imaginable. The bug here is in applying this to human beings.

"If Monty were perfect, he wouldn't have cheated on you in the first place," I asserted. "The truth is, human beings are never perfect, and that goes for Monty too."

Diane was silent for a moment as she searched for a rebuttal. Finally she spoke. "I know he's not perfect, but we were really good together."

"What did you like about him that makes you still want him back?" I asked.

Again she paused. "I really don't know," she confessed. "To tell you the truth, I can't think of anything now," she added. And then she smiled.

Diane finally came up with the belief that he was handsome and that he was intelligent. But she also admitted that she knew other men whom she believed to be just as handsome and intelligent as her husband.

I suggested to Diane that, instead of idealizing people, she should view them as having both desirable and undesirable features. Monty, she admitted, tended to drink too much, and he also snored and kept her awake at night. He had a "quick temper" but he was also very willing to help out his friends and neighbors when they were in trouble.

It had been a month since Diane's husband had left her. She had withdrawn from her nursing classes. While she still kept in contact with a few of her close friends, she usually refused their invitations to have lunch and their attempts to "set her up" with other men.

I encouraged Diane to get out more and to re-enroll in classes the next semester. I encouraged her to have lunch with her friends, and to accept some dates. This advice was viewed with dissention at first. Going out with other men still *felt* wrong, even though she admitted that there was really nothing morally wrong with it since her husband had, in fact, already filed for a divorce.

Monty was, after all, the only man she had been with for years, and the thought of dating other men felt like betrayal, even though this was unrealistic. Such feelings that support old ways can be powerful detriments to change, but you can do it with the right amount of willpower! Fighting back to gain control over your life can feel like you are swimming upstream, but, if you have reason on your side, it can be worth the effort in the long run. Diane did eventually get up enough willpower to put her life back together. She re-enrolled in classes and she began to date. As a result, she met another man, Joe, with whom she became intimate.

When Monty heard about Joe, he called Diane and asked her to lunch. Meeting her at an outdoor café, the two sat across from one another, dining on a small round table. Monty told Diane how much he had missed her, that he still loved her, and that he wanted to try again to make it work. Diane looked Monty in the eyes, smiled, and sweetly spoke, "Now I know why I was so attracted to you. You have always had such beautiful eyes."

Monty smiled at her and grasped her hand. Then Diane spoke again. "I'm seeing someone else now, and I don't think that would be a good idea."

Monty quickly removed his hand from Diane's and snarled, "OK, if that's the way you want to be about it!" Then he got up from the table abruptly and hurried off, leaving Diane with the tab. Mr. Terrific also left without his halo!

NOTES

1. *Ethics*, book 9, ch. 7.

2. You may recognize this rule as a version of *Thou Shalt Upset Yourself,* which I discussed in chapter 5.

3. Immanuel Kant, *Groundwork of the Metaphysics of Morals* (New York: Harper & Row, 1964), p. 96.

4. See in chapter 10.

5. Kant, *Groundwork of the Metaphysics of Morals*, p. 89.

6. I do believe, however, that there are some cases of irremediable pain and suffering due to serious physical illnesses that could, under very strict conditions, make suicide a rational option. See my articles, "Permitted Suicide: Model Rules for Mental Health Counseling," *Journal of Mental Health Counseling* 23, no. 4 (2001); "Permitting Suicide in Philosophical Counseling," *International Journal of Philosophical Practice* 1, no. 1, (2001), available on-line at: www.ijpp.net; "Permitting Suicide of Competent Clients in Counseling: Legal and Moral Considerations," *International Journal of Applied Philosophy* 14, no. 2 (2000).

Chapter 15

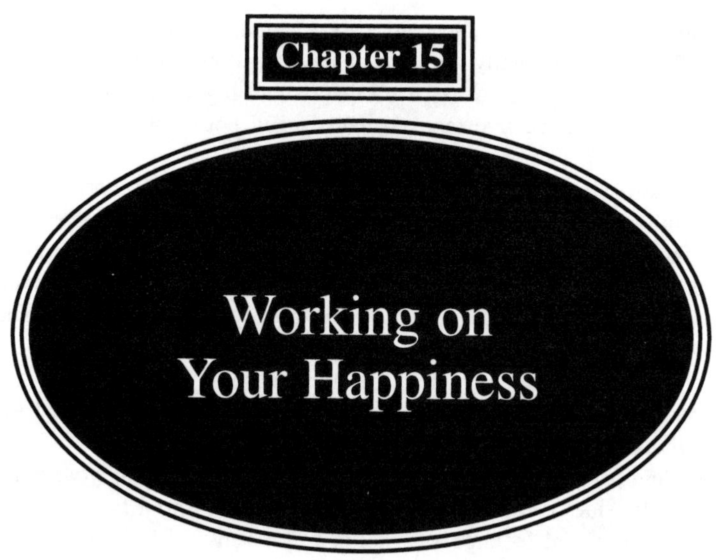

Working on Your Happiness

[O]ne swallow does not make a summer, nor does one day; and so too one day or a short time, does not make a man blessed and happy.

—Aristotle[1]

I hope that you now see how your own native power of reason can help you to cope with the common confusions of everyday life. The five steps I have discussed in this book should become second nature to you with practice. You can get quite "professional" at addressing fallacies in your thinking. Keep working at it!

Beware Faulty Thinking

If you find yourself often distressed about everyday life issues, then chances are you have some persistent irrational premises—rules and reports—in your reasoning from which you are deducing your distress. You can treat yourself to greater happiness by putting your native power of reason to work in your life.

Irrational thoughts can undermine your happiness without your even realizing it. You can irrationally think you have something to be worried or upset about, while it is really the worry itself that is your biggest problem. You can be fraught with self-destructive mental anguish, and not even recognize the irrational thinking that drives your agony. So beware!

Little things can be catapulted in your mind, taking on enormous proportions. Stubborn adherence to a moral duty to upset yourself can leave you and significant others in a fruitless state of torment. Irrational rules dictating that you get back at or blackmail your loved ones can defeat the very affections that you seek to preserve. As you have seen, there are myriad ways in which human beings screw themselves and the ones they love.

You are not alone in this fight against these virulent strains of faulty thinking that obstruct the pathway to happiness. This is a *human* struggle. Let the first person without fallacy "cast the first stone"!

Fighting back means putting yourself in control by flexing your willpower muscle on the side of reason to keep from exploding into a rage; going into a deep dark depression; feeling overwhelmed by a sense of futility of life; living with a debilitating sense of guilt. Fighting back means committing yourself on the side of Aristotle, riding in his chariot of reason.

This ancient antidote to human unhappiness is much like the crude that can be excavated from the earth and harnessed. It can lie dormant in your soul, untapped. But it can also provide an immeasurable wealth of power. The prescription to live according to reason is of the utmost value for a happy life, but these are hollow words if you don't know how to harness your power.

Recognizing the fallacies that thwart your happiness is an important step in putting your reason to work. Refuting your fallacies and finding antidotes to them are other important steps. Through refutation, you can expose inflated and exaggerated generalizations; reveal your Could-a/Would-a/Should-a thinking for what it is, empty speculation; reveal the double standard in your The-World-Revolves-Around-Me thinking; and defrock syndromes of fallacies that have collectively whittled away your happiness. Through antidotal reasoning, you can direct yourself to judge people on their own merit; attain greater tolerance for other people's preferences; get along instead of Getting Even; accept yourself as a rational, self-determining person instead of sending yourself on a self-deprecating Guilt Trip. You can stop Demanding Perfection and give yourself permission to be a fallible human being. You can do these things and many more to improve your happiness.

Of course, it's easier to sit back and go with the flow of your irrational tendencies. But to what avail?

Aristotle said that there are many ways you can go wrong and relatively very few in which you can go right—"to miss the mark easy, to hit it difficult."[2] Think of all the ways you can miss! If you are aiming with your eyes shut, you will almost invariably aim badly. Opening your eyes is the best way to improve your aim. Reason is an eye-opener. Open your eyes!

Rational self-talk has no harmful side effects, and it is free! In this day and age of managed care and high costs of health insurance, this is a good deal. What is more, by expending the *willpower*, this internal medicine is at your disposal twenty-four seven. Just ask yourself, “What would Aristotle do?”

Aristotle’s Antidote

Here’s a little poem to keep handy or, even better, memorize. It tells you how to attain self-control through the power of reason. Speak it to yourself whenever you could use a reality shot:

If you are wrought with frustration
Identify your vexation
File your *report*, and find your *rule*
On them, try a *refutation*
Whatever premise you refute
Of its flaw, take careful note
And treat it with an *antidote*
Flex your *willpower* hard and free
And make yourself act rationally.

This is what Aristotle would do!

Notes

1. *Ethics*, book 1, ch. 7.
2. *Ethics*, book 2, ch. 6.

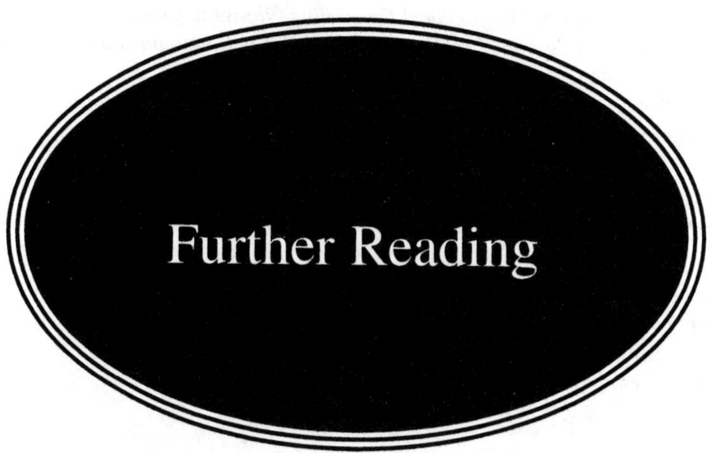

Further Reading

Aristotle. *Nichomachean Ethics*. Translated by W. D. Ross. New York: Oxford University Press, 1998.

Beck, Aaron T. *Cognitive Therapy and the Emotional Disorders*. New York: Meridian, 1979.

Berne, Eric. *Games People Play*. New York: Ballantine, 1964.

Cohen, Elliot D. *Caution: Faulty Thinking Can Be Harmful to Your Happiness*. Self-Help Ed. Ft. Pierce, Fla.: Trace-Wilco, Inc, 1994.

———, ed. *Philosophers at Work: Issues and Practice of Philosophy*, 2d ed. Fort Worth, Tex.: Harcourt College Publishers, 2000.

Damasio, Antonio R. *Descartes' Error: Emotion, Reason, and the Human Brain*. New York: Avon Books, 1994.

De Botton, Alain. *The Consolations of Philosophy*. New York: Random House, 2000.

Ellis, Albert. *Feeling Better, Getting Better, Staying Better: Profound Self-Help Therapy for Your Emotions*. Atascadero, Calif.: Impact Publishers, 2001.

———. *Overcoming Destructive Beliefs, Feelings, and Behavior*. Amherst, N.Y.: Prometheus Books, 2001.

Frankl, Viktor. *Man's Search for Meaning*. New York: Simon & Schuster, 1985.

Gilligan, Carol. *In a Different Voice: Psychological Theory and Women's Development*. Cambridge: Harvard University Press, 1993.

Goleman, Daniel. *Emotional Intelligence*. New York: Bantam Books, 1997.

Lahav, Ran, and Maria Da Venza Tillmanns, eds. *Essays on Philosophical Counseling*. New York: University Press of America, 1995.

Le Bon, Tim. *Wise Therapy*. London: Continuum, 2001.
Mill, John Stuart. "The Subjection of Women." In *Philosophers at Work*, ed. Elliot D. Cohen. Belmont, Calif.: Wadsworth, 1999.
Raabe, Peter B. *Issues in Philosophical Counseling*. Westport, Conn.: Praeger, 2000.
Schuster, Shlomit. *Philosophy Practice: An Alternative to Counseling and Psychotherapy*. Westport, Conn.: Praeger, 1999.
Solomon, Robert. *The Passions: The Myth and Nature of Human Emotion*. New York: Anchor Books, 1977.

JOURNALS

International Journal of Applied Philosophy
http://www.pdcnet.org/ijap.html
International Journal of Philosophical Practice
http://www.ijpp.net

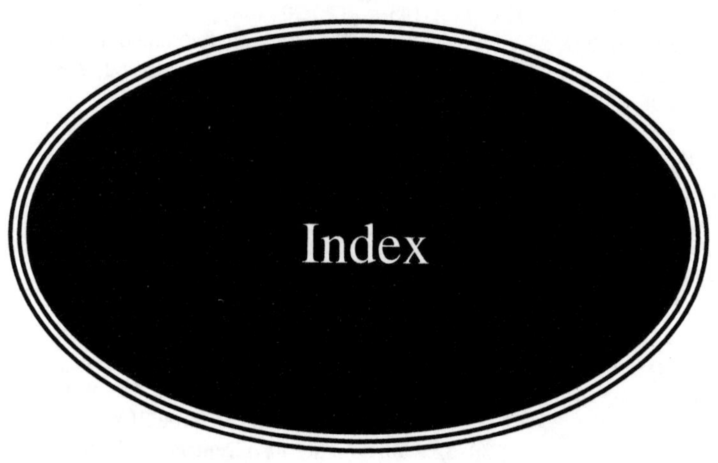

Index

About the Author

Elliot D. Cohen, Ph. D., Brown University, is director of the Institute of Critical Thinking, Port St. Lucie, Florida, where he conducts clinical research on using philosophy and critical thinking to solve problems of living. One of the principle founders of philosophical counseling in the United States, he is cofounder and co-executive director of the Society for Philosophy, Counseling, and Psychotherapy, and editor in chief and founder of two distinguished periodicals, *International Journal of Applied Philosophy* and *International Journal of Philosophical Practice.* The author of ten books and numerous articles, his books include *Caution: Faulty Thinking Can Be Harmful to Your Happiness* (Trace-Wilco, 1994); *Philosophers at Work: Issues and Practice of Philosophy* (Harcourt, 2000); and *The Virtuous Therapist: Ethical Practice of Counseling and Psychotherapy* (Wadwsorth, 1999). Dr. Cohen teaches applied philosophy, ethics, and critical thinking to a diverse population of students at Indian River Community College located on Florida's Treasure Coast and also serves as an ethics consultant for several local health care organizations, including hospice. His pioneering work in philosophical counseling and applied philosophy has earned him worldwide acclaim.